BBC

DOCTOR WHO

THE THIRD DOCTOR

VOL 1: HERALDS OF DESTRUCTION

D1232408

"Cornell's handle on character and the tone of the old serials makes The Third Doctor #1 a richly entertaining classic Who experience."
NEWSARAMA

"This one managed to pull me in quickly, and kept me engaged the entire way."
MULTIVERSITY COMICS

"Neatly capturing the likenesses of Pertwee's Doctor along with Roger Delgado's Master and the UNIT team, Jones makes a perfect foil for Cornell, who here produces some of his finest work in the Whoniverse."
SFX

"A very welcome blast from the past."
PASTRAMI NATION

"If you haven't ever read a Doctor Who comic before, this is the one to start with."
KABOOOOOM

"A book that's fun, exciting and perfect for longtime fans."
WE THE NERDY

"It manages to honour classic Doctor Who while making it feel fresh for the contemporary fans."
THAT'S NOT CURRENT

"This is classic Who with a modern perspective."
NERDIST

"Jolly, yet meaningful interactions that leave you feeling like you just watched a classic episode... Personally, it sent me into fits of squeals of delights."
COMICOSITY

TITAN COMICS

EDITOR
John Freeman

SENIOR COMICS EDITOR
Andrew James

ASSISTANT EDITORS
Jessica Burton, Amoona Saohin,
Lauren McPhee, Lauren Bowes

COLLECTION DESIGNER
Andrew Leung

TITAN COMICS EDITORIAL
Tom Williams, Jonathan
Stevenson

PRODUCTION SUPERVISOR
Maria Pearson

PRODUCTION CONTROLLER
Peter James

**SENIOR PRODUCTION
CONTROLLER**
Jackie Flook

ART DIRECTOR
Oz Browne

SENIOR SALES MANAGER
Steve Tothill

PRESS OFFICER
Will O'Mullane

COMICS BRAND MANAGER
Chris Thompson

ADS & MARKETING ASSISTANT
Tom Miller

**DIRECT SALES & MARKETING
MANAGER** Ricky Claydon

COMMERCIAL MANAGER
Michelle Fairlamb

HEAD OF RIGHTS
Jenny Boyce

PUBLISHING MANAGER
Darryl Tothill

PUBLISHING DIRECTOR
Chris Teather

OPERATIONS DIRECTOR
Leigh Baulch

EXECUTIVE DIRECTOR
Vivian Cheung

PUBLISHER
Nick Landau

FOR RIGHTS INFORMATION CONTACT jenny.boyce@titanemail.com

Special thanks to Steven Moffat, Brian Minchin, Mandy
Thwaites, Matt Nicholls, James Dudley, Edward Russell,
Derek Ritchie, Scott Handcock, Kirsty Mullan, Kate Bush, Julia
Nocciolino, and Ed Casey, for their invaluable assistance.

BBC WORLDWIDE

DIRECTOR OF EDITORIAL GOVERNANCE
Nicolas Brett

**DIRECTOR OF CONSUMER
PRODUCTS AND PUBLISHING**
Andrew Moultrie

HEAD OF UK PUBLISHING
Chris Kerwin

PUBLISHER
Mandy Thwaites

PUBLISHING CO-ORDINATOR
Eva Abramik

DOCTOR WHO: THE THIRD DOCTOR
VOL 1: HERALDS OF DESTRUCTION
HB ISBN: 9781785857317 SB ISBN: 9781785857331
Published by Titan Comics, a division of Titan Publishing Group, Ltd.
144 Southwark Street, London, SE1 0UP.

A CIP catalogue record for this title is available from the British Library.
First edition: XXXXX 2017.

10 9 8 7 6 5 4 3 2 1

Printed in China.

Titan Comics does not read or accept unsolicited DOCTOR WHO submissions of ideas, stories or artwork.

ALISTAIR LETHBRIDGE-STEWART APPEARS COURTESY OF **CANDY JAR** BOOKS,
WITH THANKS TO HANNAH HAISMAN, HENRY LINCOLN, AND ANDY FRANKHAM-
ALLEN. VISIT *WWW.LETHBRIDGESTEWART.CO.UK* FOR MORE!

BBC

DOCTOR WHO

THE THIRD DOCTOR

VOL 1: HERALDS OF DESTRUCTION

WRITER: PAUL CORNELL

ARTIST: CHRISTOPHER JONES

COLORIST: HI FI

LETTERS: RICHARD STARKINGS AND COMICRAFT'S JIMMY BETANCOURT

ALISTAIR LETHBRIDGE-STEWART CREATED BY MERVYN HAISMAN AND HENRY LINCOLN

Titan COMICS   BBC

BBC

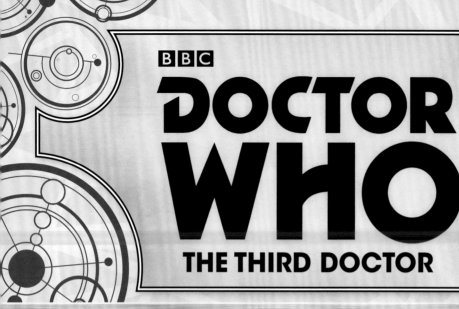

DOCTOR WHO

THE THIRD DOCTOR

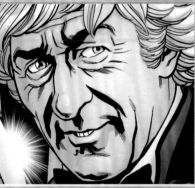

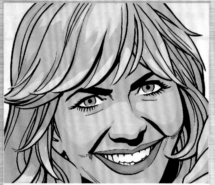

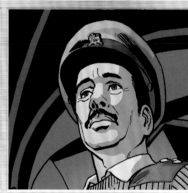

THE DOCTOR

Recently freed of his exile from his home planet of Gallifrey, the Doctor still watches over the people of Earth: a Time Lord who works among them. As UNIT's scientific advisor, he is on hand to battle any foe, even if he doesn't approve of human military authority...

JO GRANT

Jo has proven her worth as a UNIT civilian employee with a flair for science, and her daring attitude makes her the perfect companion. With the TARDIS once more functional, Jo's next stop is the entire universe... if an invasion of Earth doesn't stop her first!

THE BRIGADIER

Brigadier Alistair Gordon Lethbridge-Stewart is the founder and UK commander of UNIT. While he and the Doctor may not always see eye to eye, the two have become fast friends, protecting the Earth from alien infiltration together!

PREVIOUSLY...

After enlisting the help of his former selves to defeat the insane Time Lord Omega, the Third Doctor was rewarded by the Time Lords for his victory with a new dematerialization circuit for the TARDIS, and by returning the knowlege of time and space travel to him. His Earth-bound exile was lifted, and his beloved TARDIS is now ready to set off on all manner of adventures!

But can it be long before his adopted planet needs him again...?

When you've finished reading the collection, please email your thoughts to doctorwhocomic@titanemail.com

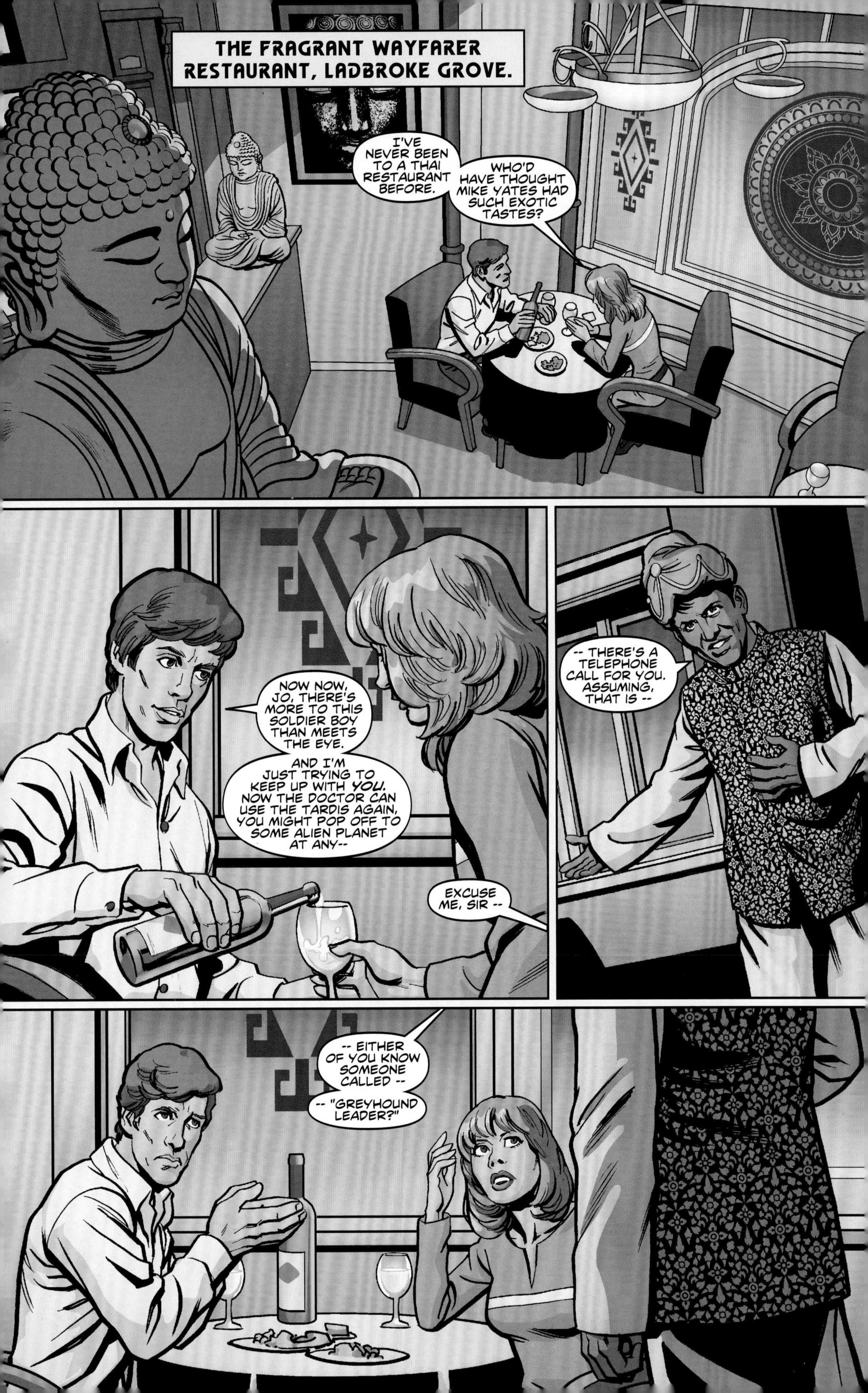
THE FRAGRANT WAYFARER RESTAURANT, LADBROKE GROVE.
I'VE NEVER BEEN TO A THAI RESTAURANT BEFORE.
WHO'D HAVE THOUGHT MIKE YATES HAD SUCH EXOTIC TASTES?
NOW NOW, JO, THERE'S MORE TO THIS SOLDIER BOY THAN MEETS THE EYE.
AND I'M JUST TRYING TO KEEP UP WITH YOU. NOW THE DOCTOR CAN USE THE TARDIS AGAIN, YOU MIGHT POP OFF TO SOME ALIEN PLANET AT ANY--
EXCUSE ME, SIR --
-- THERE'S A TELEPHONE CALL FOR YOU. ASSUMING, THAT IS --
-- EITHER OF YOU KNOW SOMEONE CALLED --
-- "GREYHOUND LEADER?"

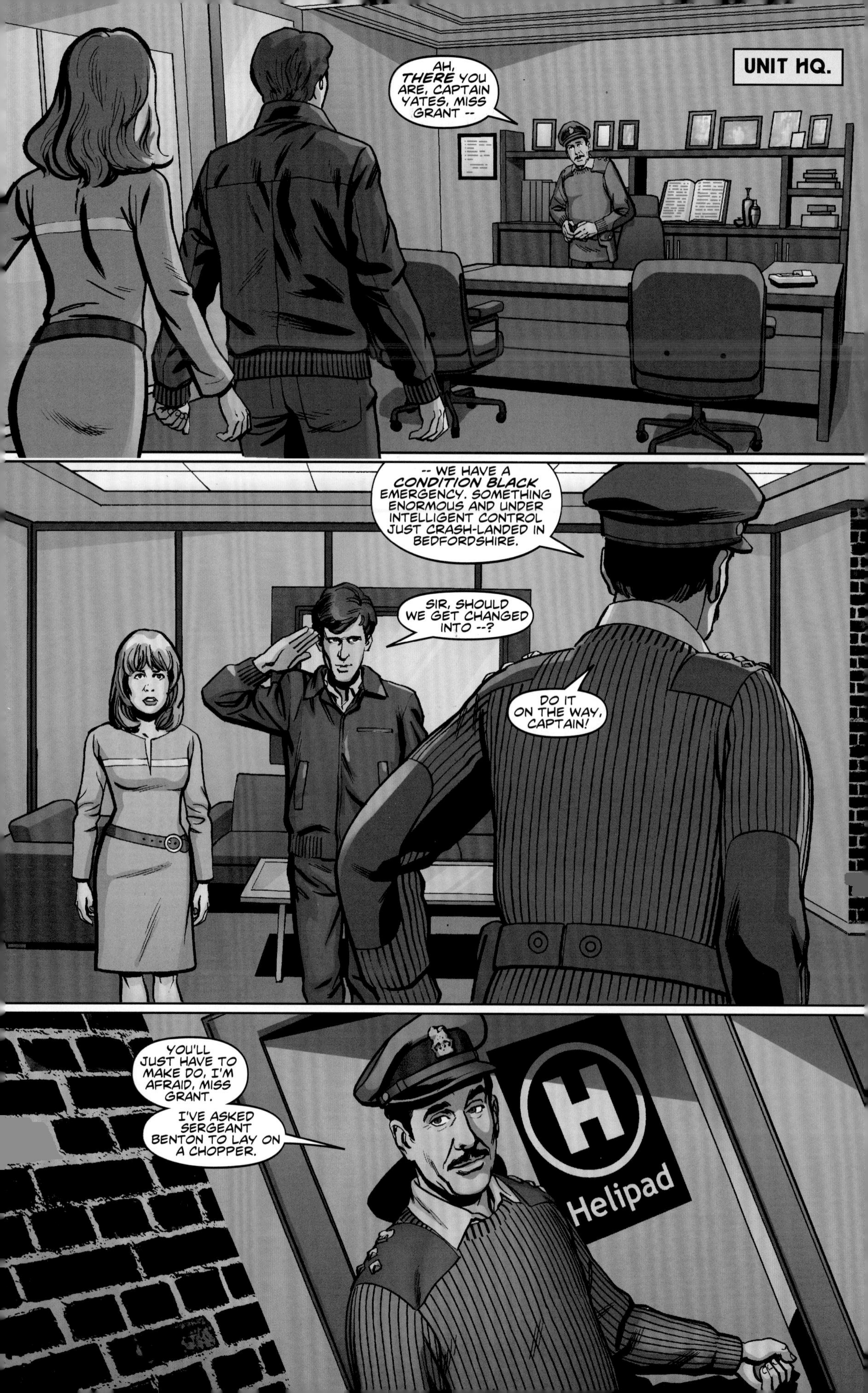
UNIT HQ.
AH, THERE YOU ARE, CAPTAIN YATES, MISS GRANT --
-- WE HAVE A CONDITION BLACK EMERGENCY. SOMETHING ENORMOUS AND UNDER INTELLIGENT CONTROL JUST CRASH-LANDED IN BEDFORDSHIRE.
SIR, SHOULD WE GET CHANGED INTO --?
DO IT ON THE WAY, CAPTAIN!
YOU'LL JUST HAVE TO MAKE DO, I'M AFRAID, MISS GRANT.
I'VE ASKED SERGEANT BENTON TO LAY ON A CHOPPER.
H
Helipad

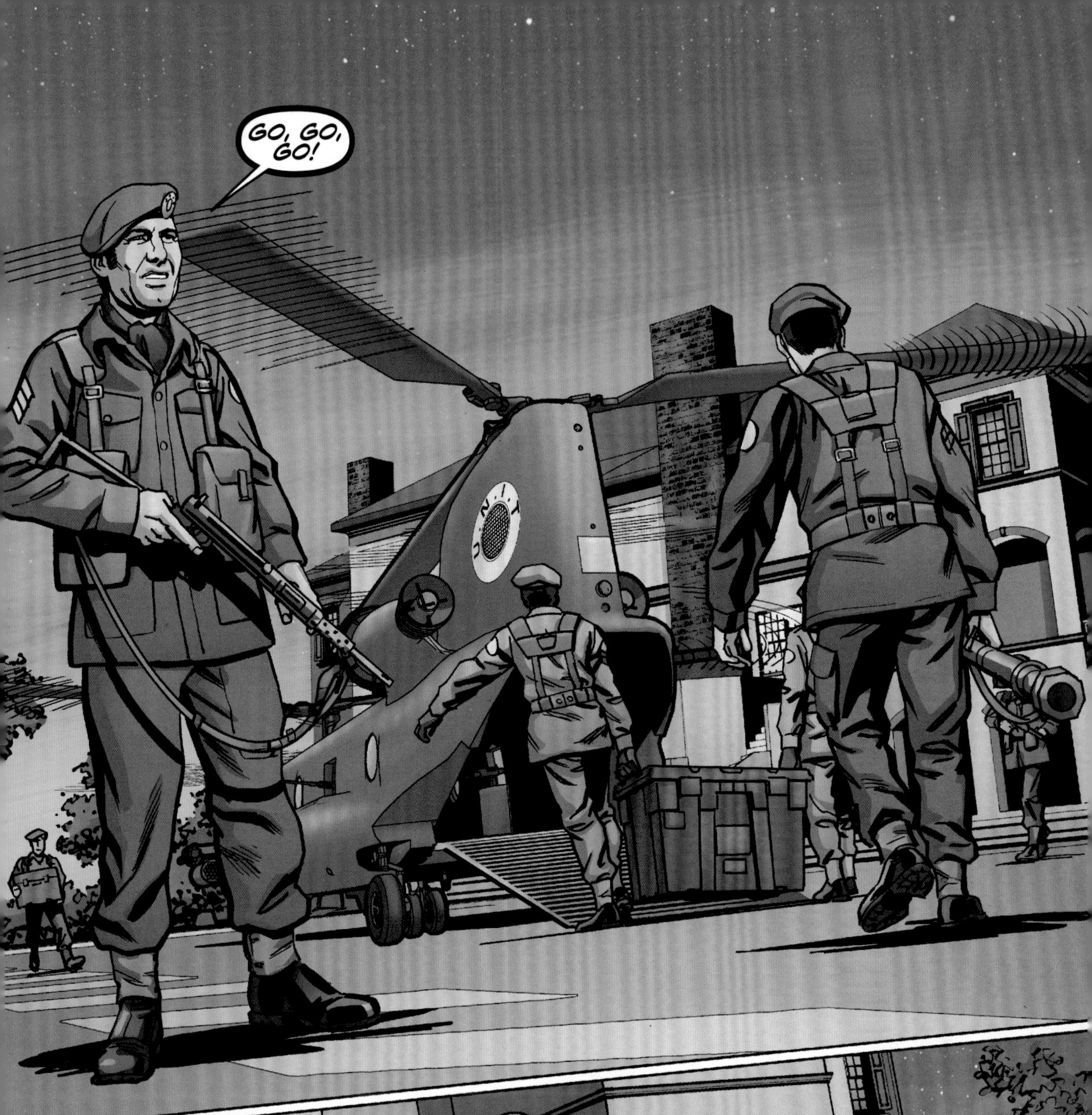
GO, GO, GO!

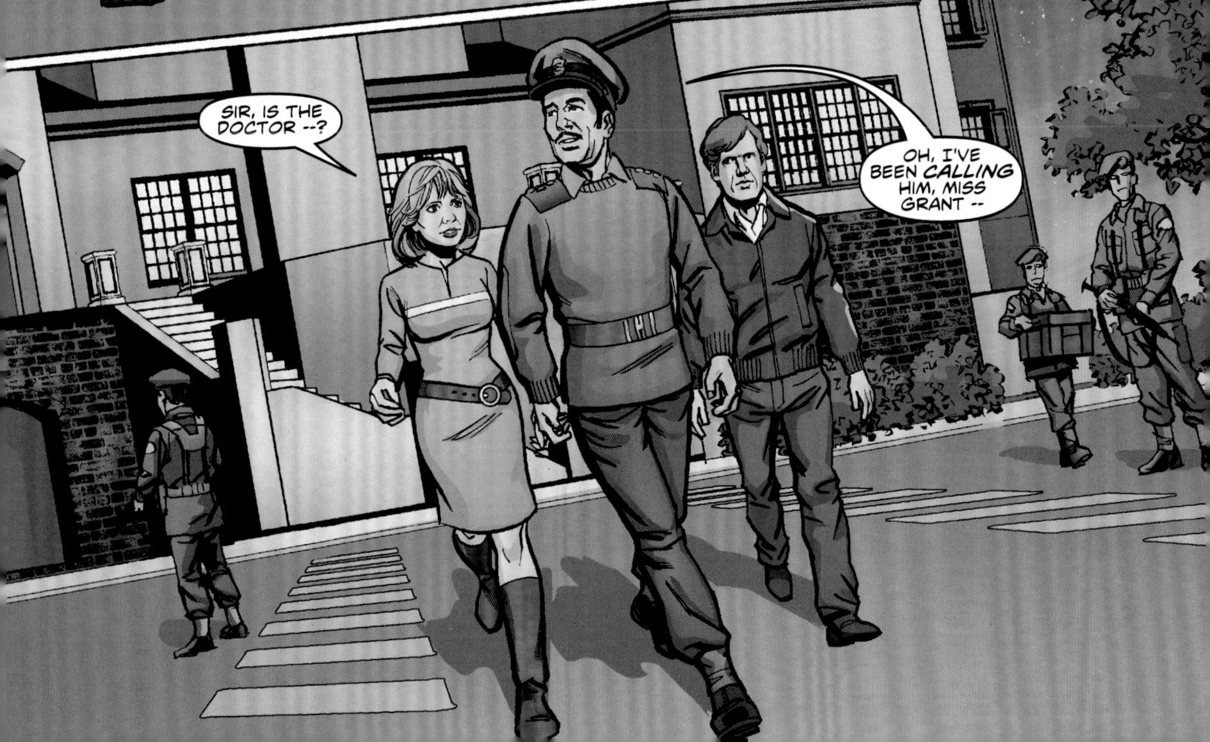
SIR, IS THE DOCTOR --?
OH, I'VE BEEN CALLING HIM, MISS GRANT --

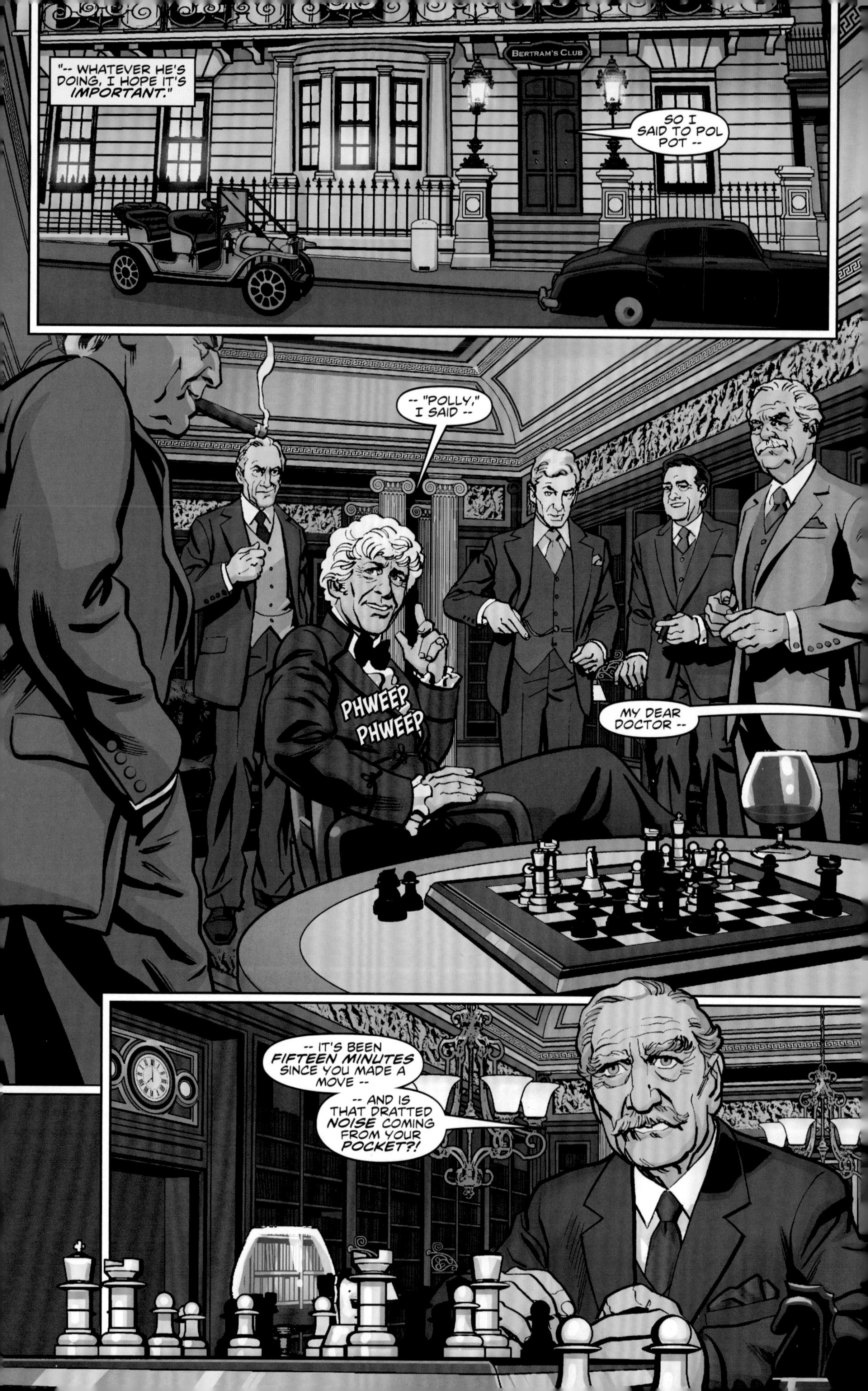
"-- WHATEVER HE'S DOING, I HOPE IT'S *IMPORTANT.*"
BERTRAM'S CLUB
SO I SAID TO POL POT --
-- "POLLY," I SAID --
PHWEEP PHWEEP
MY DEAR DOCTOR --
-- IT'S BEEN *FIFTEEN MINUTES* SINCE YOU MADE A MOVE --
-- AND IS THAT DRATTED *NOISE* COMING FROM YOUR *POCKET?!*

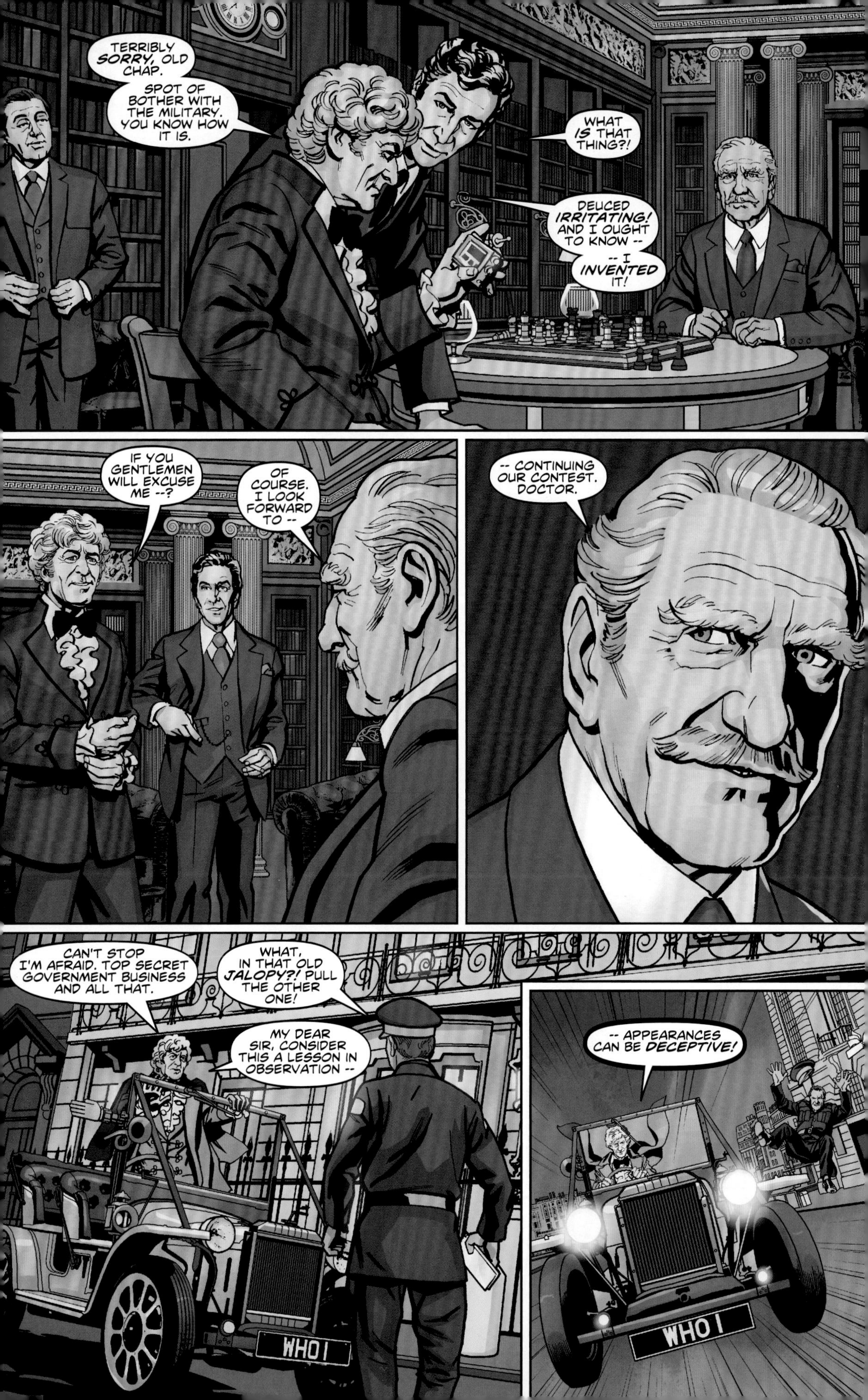
TERRIBLY SORRY, OLD CHAP.
SPOT OF BOTHER WITH THE MILITARY. YOU KNOW HOW IT IS.
WHAT IS THAT THING?!
DEUCED IRRITATING! AND I OUGHT TO KNOW --
-- I INVENTED IT!
IF YOU GENTLEMEN WILL EXCUSE ME --?
OF COURSE. I LOOK FORWARD TO --
-- CONTINUING OUR CONTEST. DOCTOR.
CAN'T STOP I'M AFRAID. TOP SECRET GOVERNMENT BUSINESS AND ALL THAT.
WHAT, IN THAT OLD JALOPY?! PULL THE OTHER ONE!
MY DEAR SIR, CONSIDER THIS A LESSON IN OBSERVATION --
WHO 1
-- APPEARANCES CAN BE DECEPTIVE!
WHO 1

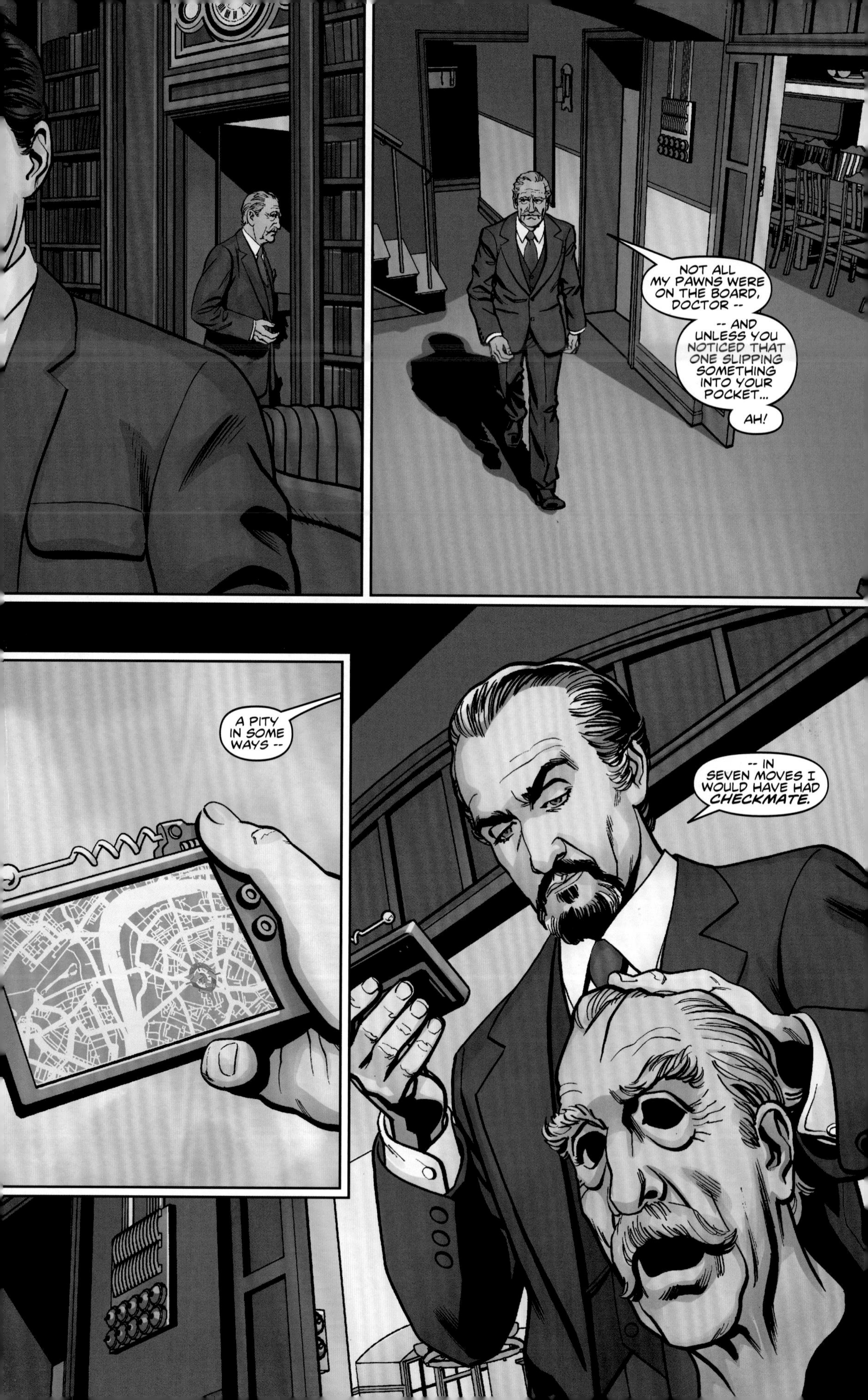
NOT ALL MY PAWNS WERE ON THE BOARD, DOCTOR --
-- AND UNLESS YOU NOTICED THAT ONE SLIPPING SOMETHING INTO YOUR POCKET...
AH!
A PITY IN SOME WAYS --
-- IN SEVEN MOVES I WOULD HAVE HAD CHECKMATE.

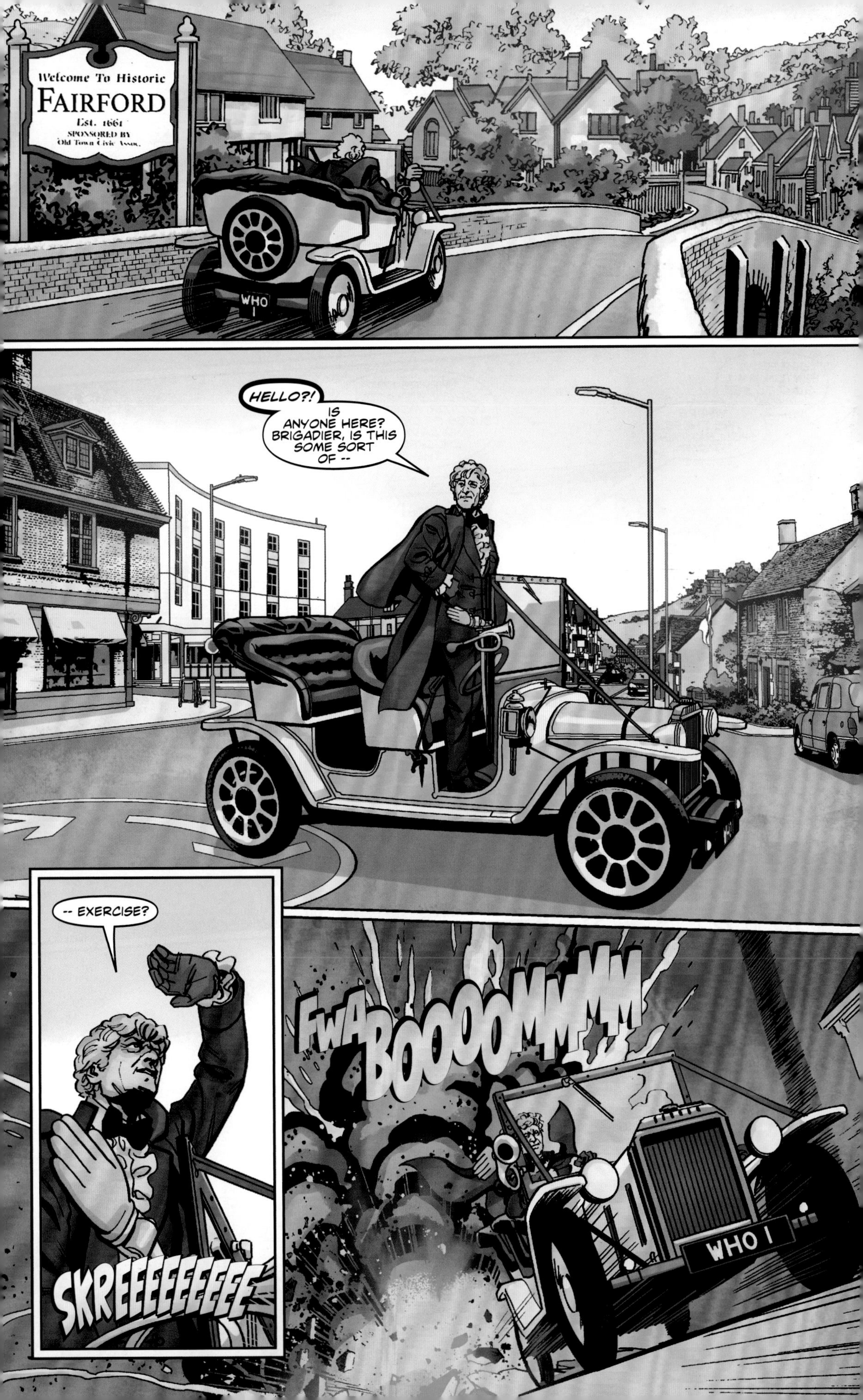
Welcome To Historic
FAIRFORD
Est. 1661
SPONSORED BY
Old Town Civic Assoc.
WHO 1
HELLO?!
IS ANYONE HERE? BRIGADIER, IS THIS SOME SORT OF --
-- EXERCISE?
SKREEEEEEEEEE
FWABOOOOMMMM
WHO 1

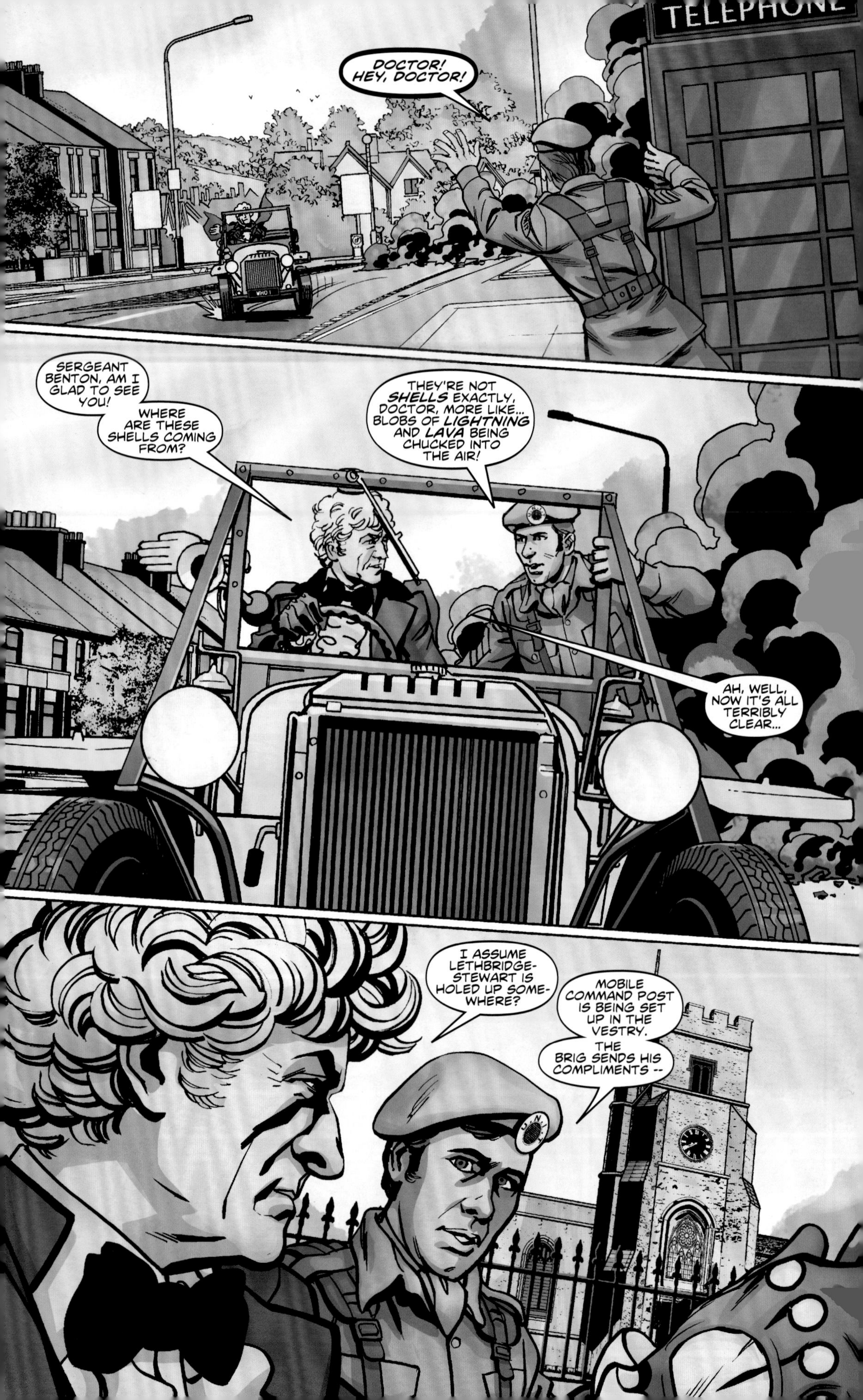
TELEPHONE
DOCTOR! HEY, DOCTOR!
WHO 1
SERGEANT BENTON, AM I GLAD TO SEE YOU!
WHERE ARE THESE SHELLS COMING FROM?
THEY'RE NOT SHELLS EXACTLY, DOCTOR, MORE LIKE... BLOBS OF LIGHTNING AND LAVA BEING CHUCKED INTO THE AIR!
AH, WELL, NOW IT'S ALL TERRIBLY CLEAR...
I ASSUME LETHBRIDGE-STEWART IS HOLED UP SOME-WHERE?
MOBILE COMMAND POST IS BEING SET UP IN THE VESTRY.
THE BRIG SENDS HIS COMPLIMENTS --

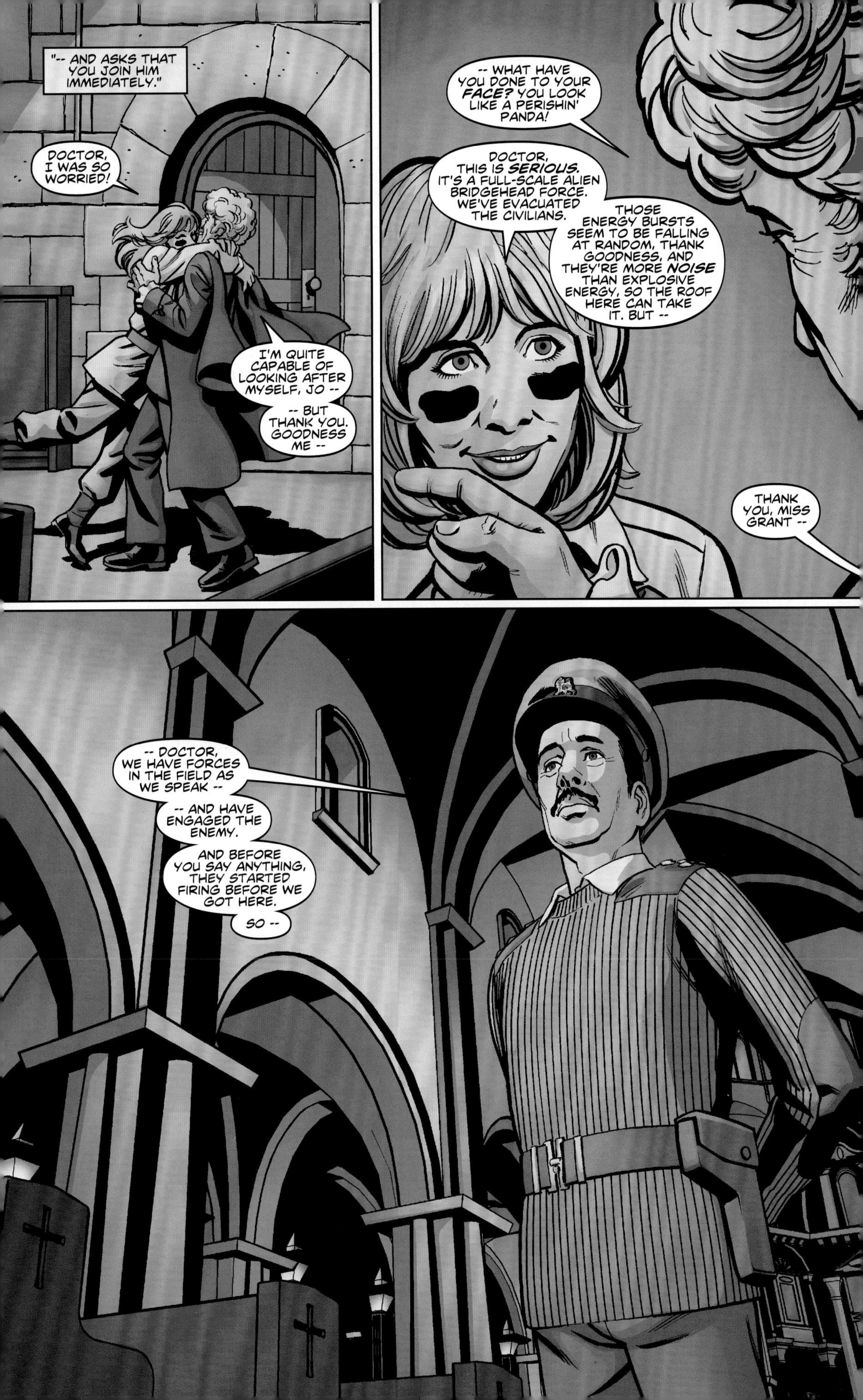
"-- AND ASKS THAT YOU JOIN HIM IMMEDIATELY."
DOCTOR, I WAS SO WORRIED!
I'M QUITE CAPABLE OF LOOKING AFTER MYSELF, JO --
-- BUT THANK YOU. GOODNESS ME --
-- WHAT HAVE YOU DONE TO YOUR FACE? YOU LOOK LIKE A PERISHIN' PANDA!
DOCTOR, THIS IS SERIOUS. IT'S A FULL-SCALE ALIEN BRIDGEHEAD FORCE. WE'VE EVACUATED THE CIVILIANS.
THOSE ENERGY BURSTS SEEM TO BE FALLING AT RANDOM, THANK GOODNESS, AND THEY'RE MORE NOISE THAN EXPLOSIVE ENERGY, SO THE ROOF HERE CAN TAKE IT. BUT --
THANK YOU, MISS GRANT --
-- DOCTOR, WE HAVE FORCES IN THE FIELD AS WE SPEAK --
-- AND HAVE ENGAGED THE ENEMY.
AND BEFORE YOU SAY ANYTHING, THEY STARTED FIRING BEFORE WE GOT HERE.
SO --

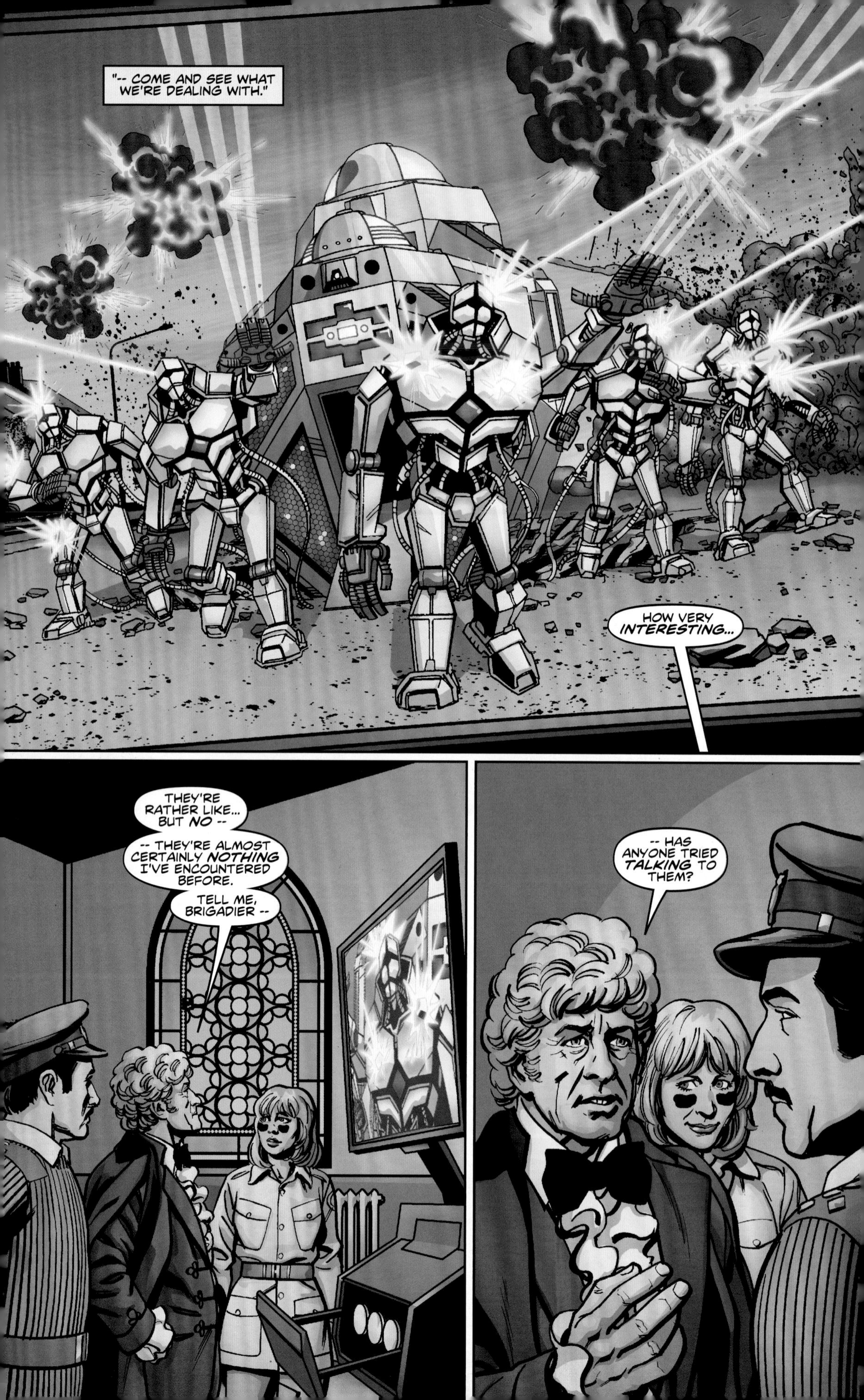
"-- COME AND SEE WHAT WE'RE DEALING WITH."
HOW VERY *INTERESTING*...
THEY'RE RATHER LIKE... BUT *NO* --
-- THEY'RE ALMOST CERTAINLY *NOTHING* I'VE ENCOUNTERED BEFORE.
TELL ME, BRIGADIER --
-- HAS ANYONE TRIED *TALKING* TO THEM?

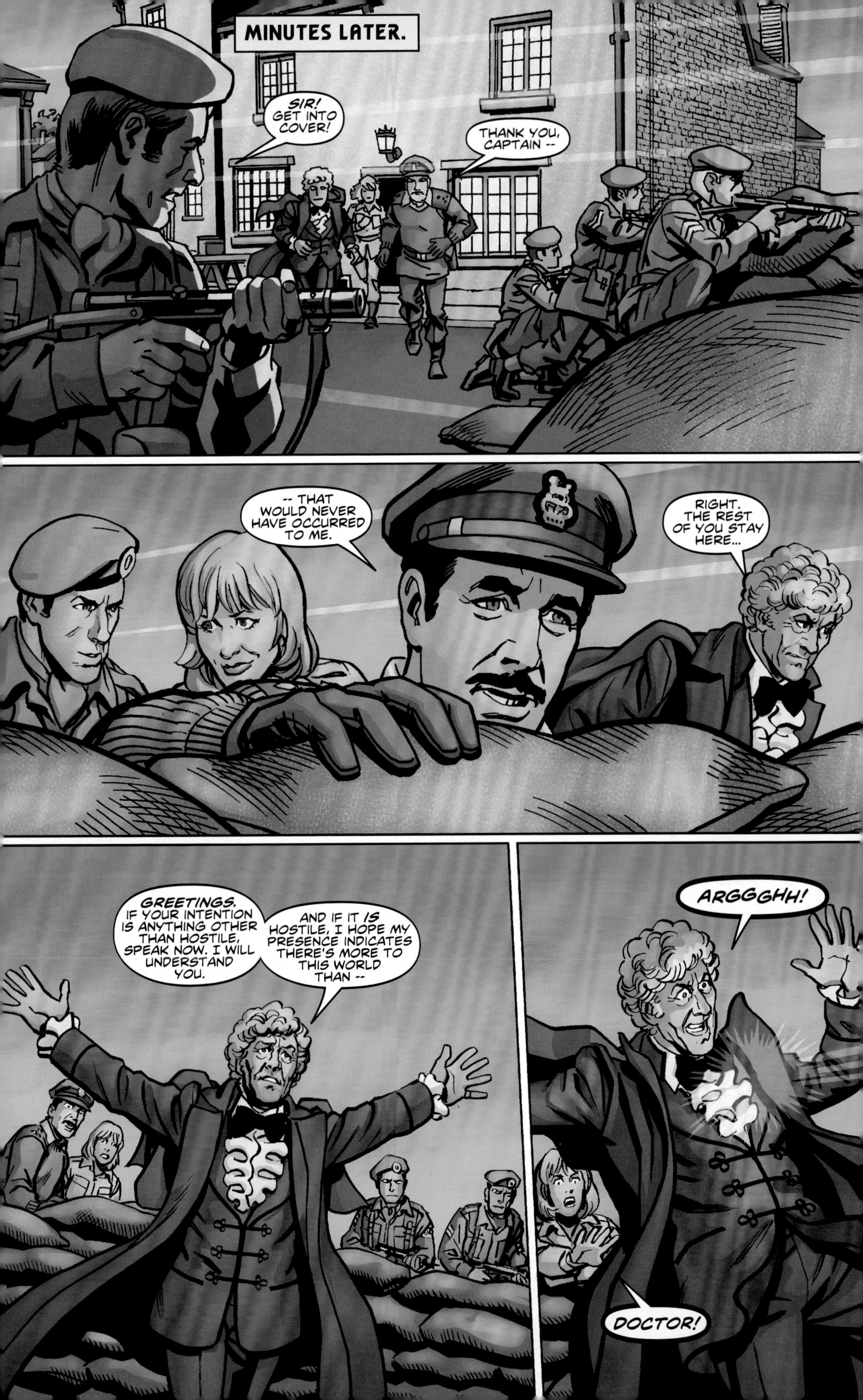
MINUTES LATER.
SIR! GET INTO COVER!
THANK YOU, CAPTAIN --
-- THAT WOULD NEVER HAVE OCCURRED TO ME.
RIGHT. THE REST OF YOU STAY HERE...
GREETINGS. IF YOUR INTENTION IS ANYTHING OTHER THAN HOSTILE, SPEAK NOW. I WILL UNDERSTAND YOU.
AND IF IT IS HOSTILE, I HOPE MY PRESENCE INDICATES THERE'S MORE TO THIS WORLD THAN --
ARGGGHH!
DOCTOR!

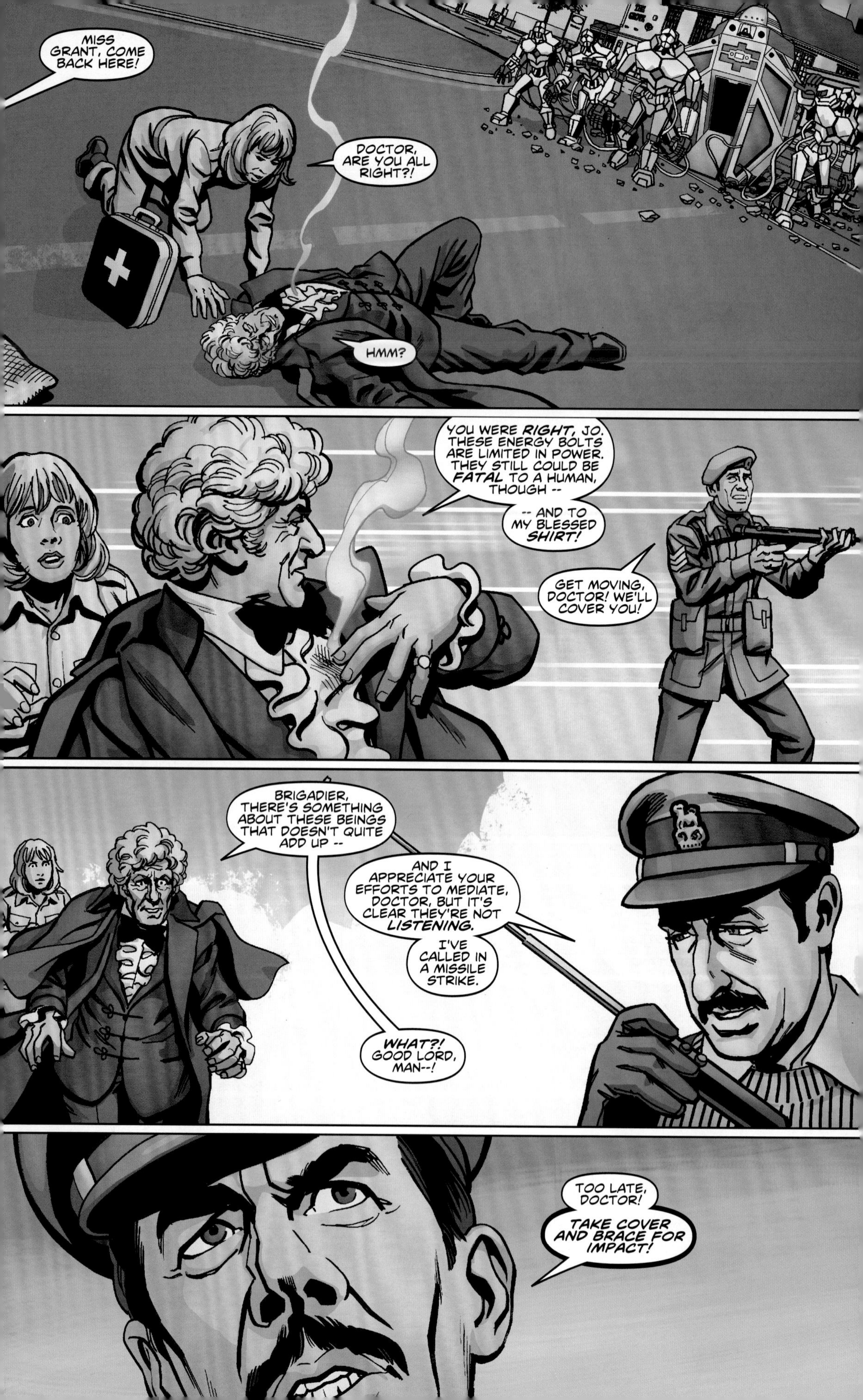
MISS GRANT, COME BACK HERE!
DOCTOR, ARE YOU ALL RIGHT?!
HMM?
YOU WERE RIGHT, JO. THESE ENERGY BOLTS ARE LIMITED IN POWER. THEY STILL COULD BE FATAL TO A HUMAN, THOUGH --
-- AND TO MY BLESSED SHIRT!
GET MOVING, DOCTOR! WE'LL COVER YOU!
BRIGADIER, THERE'S SOMETHING ABOUT THESE BEINGS THAT DOESN'T QUITE ADD UP --
AND I APPRECIATE YOUR EFFORTS TO MEDIATE, DOCTOR, BUT IT'S CLEAR THEY'RE NOT LISTENING.
I'VE CALLED IN A MISSILE STRIKE.
WHAT?! GOOD LORD, MAN--!
TOO LATE, DOCTOR!
TAKE COVER AND BRACE FOR IMPACT!

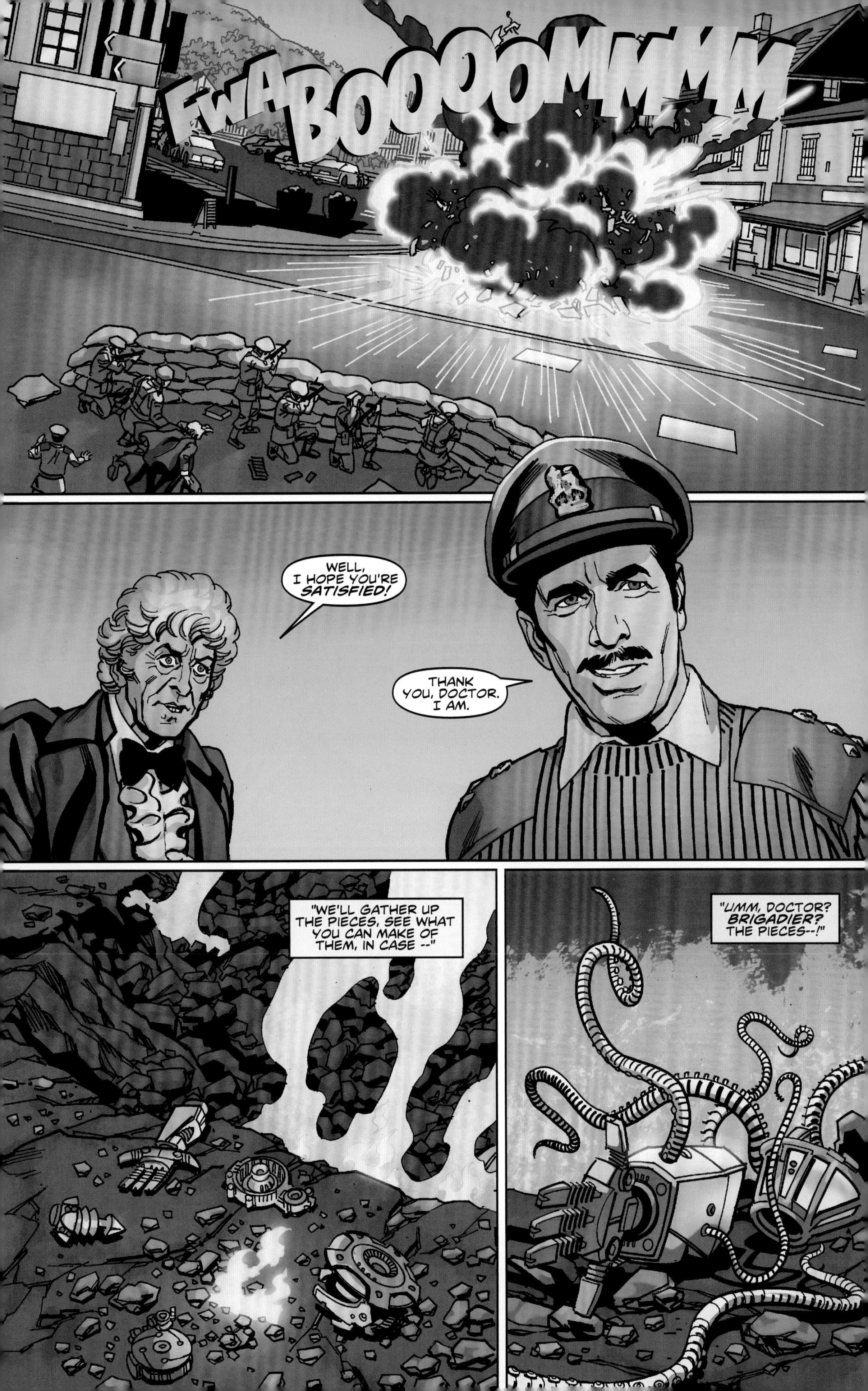
FWABOOOOOMMMM
WELL, I HOPE YOU'RE *SATISFIED!*
THANK YOU, DOCTOR. I AM.
"WE'LL GATHER UP THE PIECES, SEE WHAT YOU CAN MAKE OF THEM, IN CASE --"
"*UMM*, DOCTOR? *BRIGADIER?* THE PIECES--!"

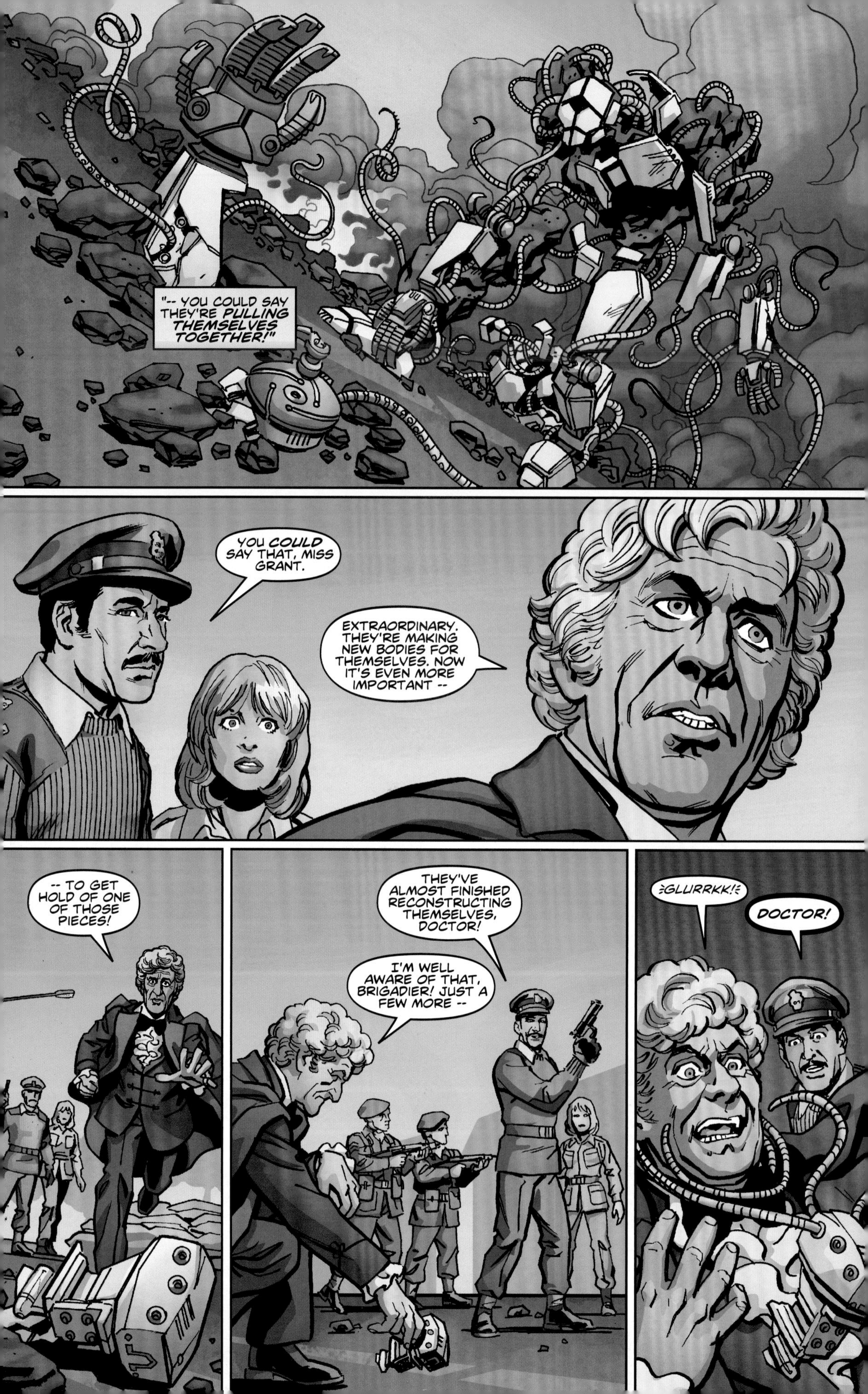
"-- YOU COULD SAY THEY'RE PULLING THEMSELVES TOGETHER!"
YOU COULD SAY THAT, MISS GRANT.
EXTRAORDINARY. THEY'RE MAKING NEW BODIES FOR THEMSELVES. NOW IT'S EVEN MORE IMPORTANT --
-- TO GET HOLD OF ONE OF THOSE PIECES!
THEY'VE ALMOST FINISHED RECONSTRUCTING THEMSELVES, DOCTOR!
I'M WELL AWARE OF THAT, BRIGADIER! JUST A FEW MORE --
GLURRKK!
DOCTOR!

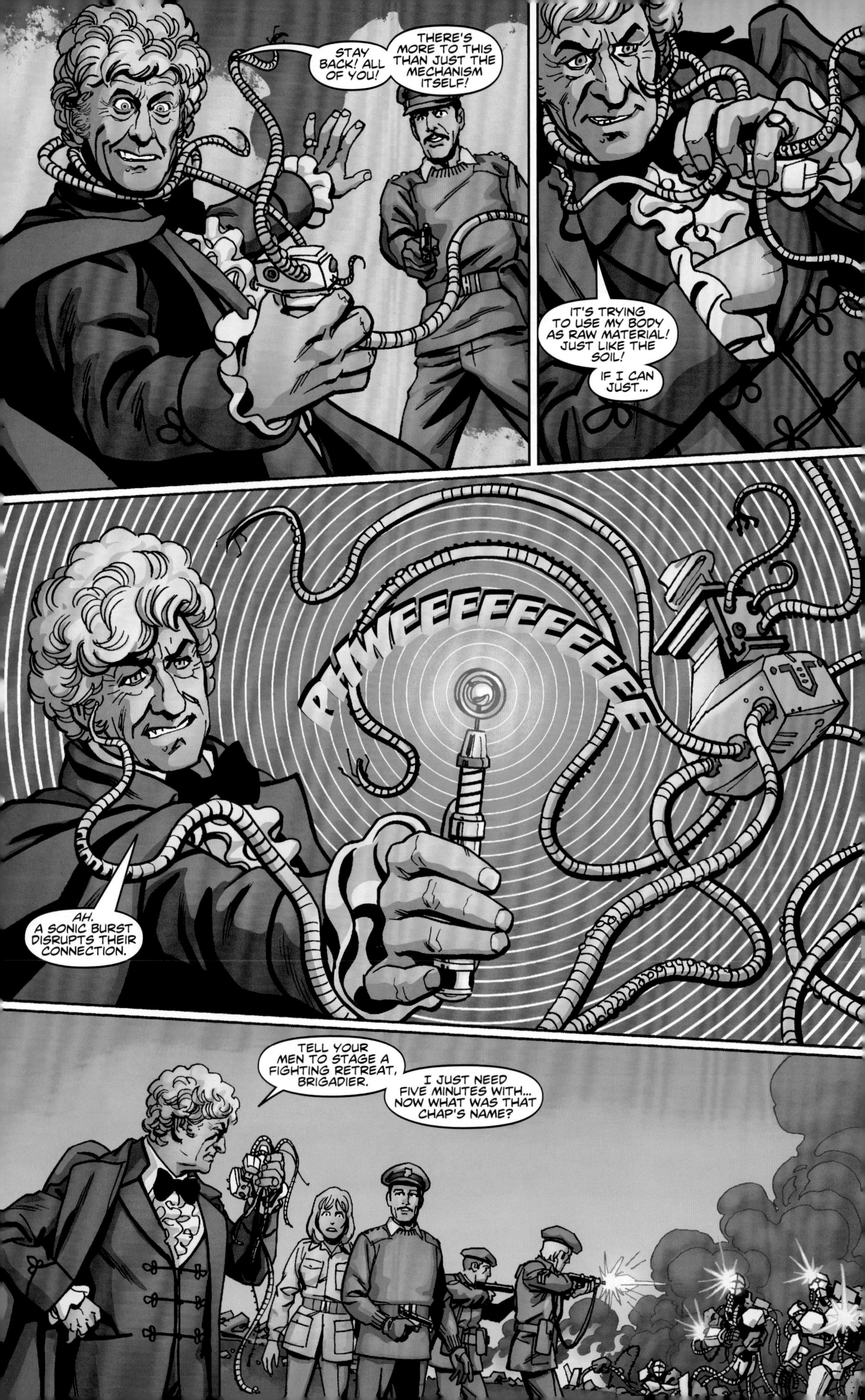

STAY BACK! ALL OF YOU!
THERE'S MORE TO THIS THAN JUST THE MECHANISM ITSELF!
IT'S TRYING TO USE MY BODY AS RAW MATERIAL! JUST LIKE THE SOIL!
IF I CAN JUST...
PHWEEEEEEEEEEEE
AH. A SONIC BURST DISRUPTS THEIR CONNECTION.
TELL YOUR MEN TO STAGE A FIGHTING RETREAT, BRIGADIER.
I JUST NEED FIVE MINUTES WITH... NOW WHAT WAS THAT CHAP'S NAME?

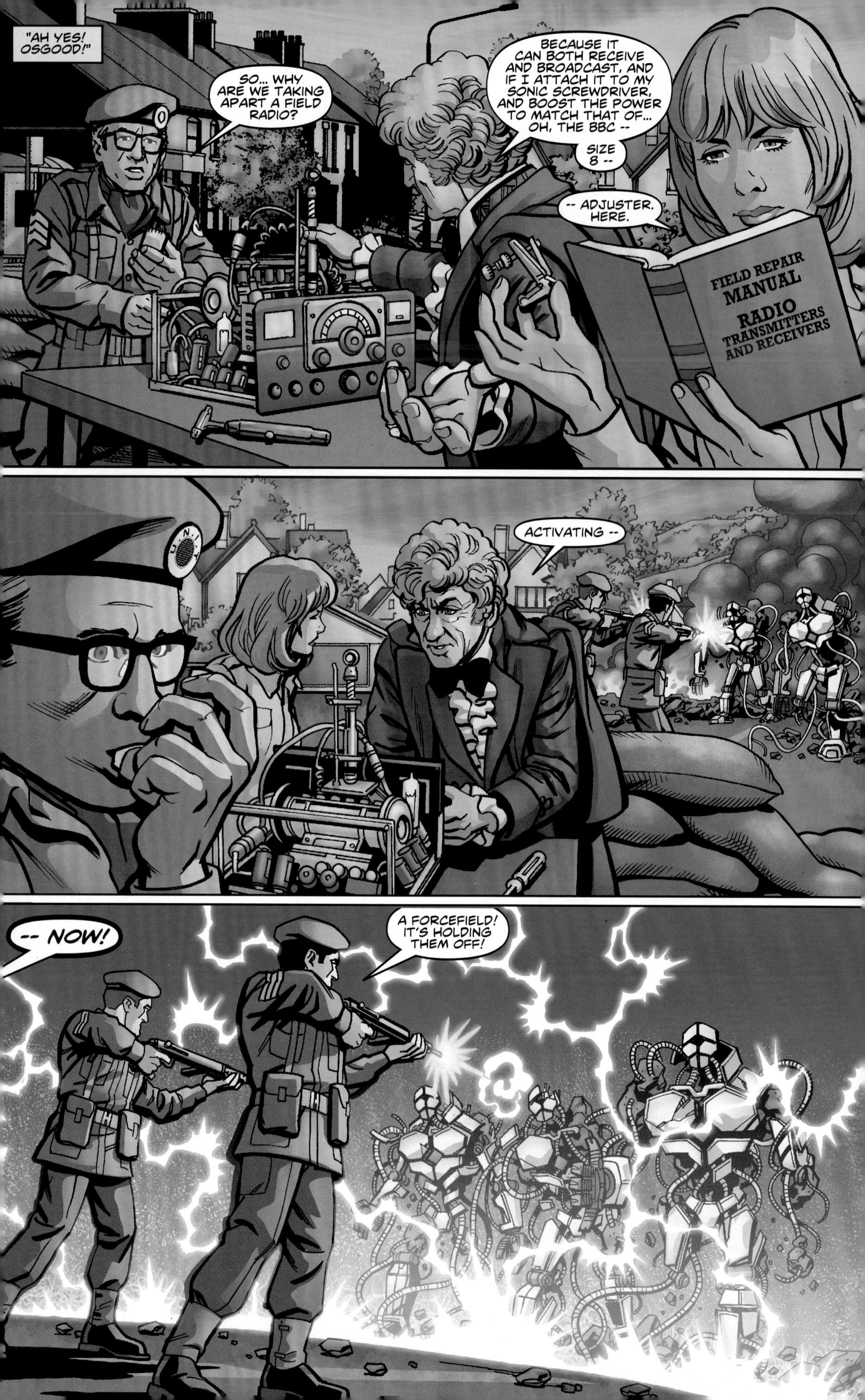
"AH YES! OSGOOD!"
SO... WHY ARE WE TAKING APART A FIELD RADIO?
BECAUSE IT CAN BOTH RECEIVE AND BROADCAST, AND IF I ATTACH IT TO MY SONIC SCREWDRIVER, AND BOOST THE POWER TO MATCH THAT OF... OH, THE BBC --
SIZE 8 --
-- ADJUSTER. HERE.
FIELD REPAIR MANUAL
RADIO TRANSMITTERS AND RECEIVERS
ACTIVATING --
-- NOW!
A FORCEFIELD! IT'S HOLDING THEM OFF!

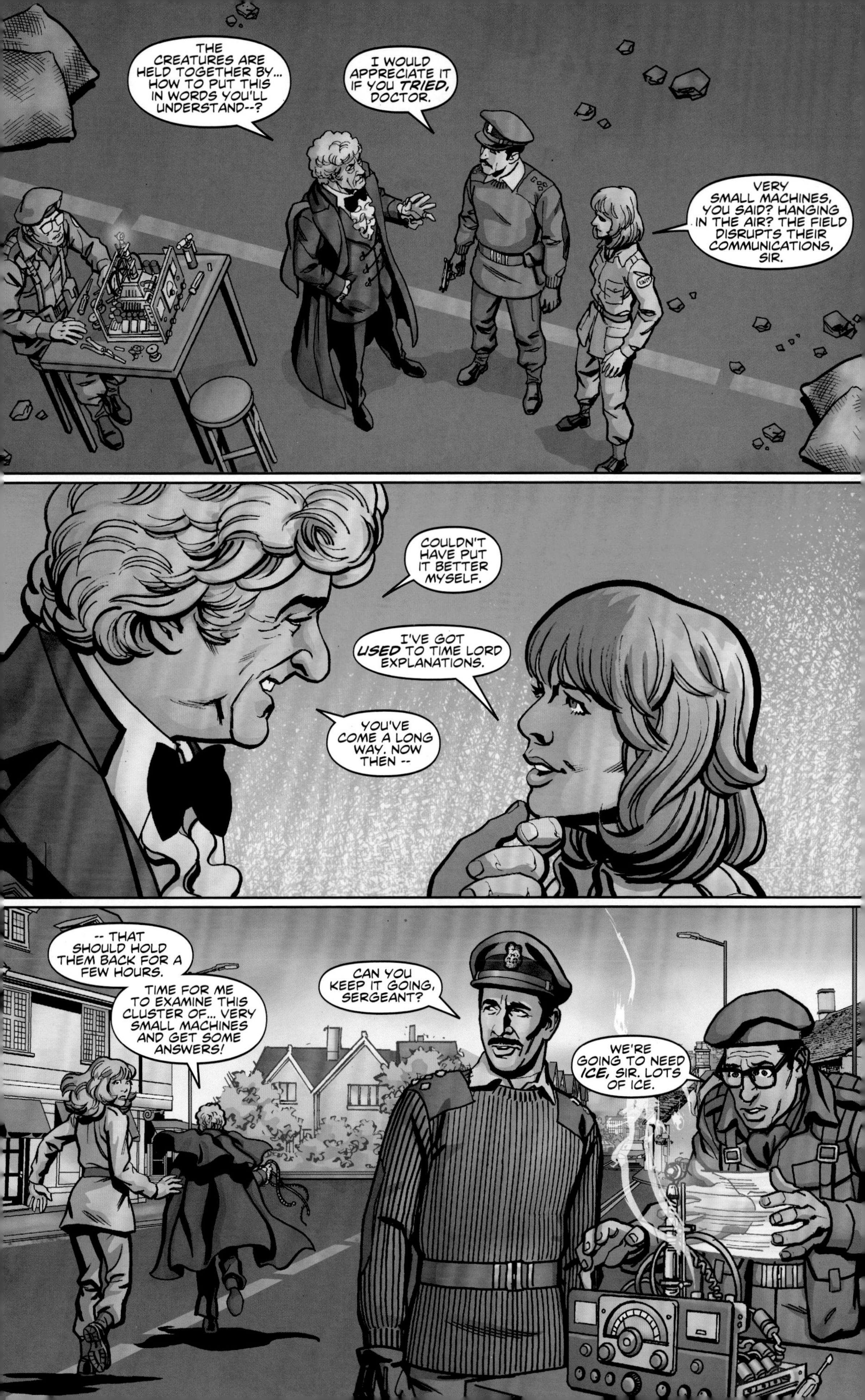

THE CREATURES ARE HELD TOGETHER BY... HOW TO PUT THIS IN WORDS YOU'LL UNDERSTAND--?
I WOULD APPRECIATE IT IF YOU TRIED, DOCTOR.
VERY SMALL MACHINES, YOU SAID? HANGING IN THE AIR? THE FIELD DISRUPTS THEIR COMMUNICATIONS, SIR.
COULDN'T HAVE PUT IT BETTER MYSELF.
I'VE GOT USED TO TIME LORD EXPLANATIONS.
YOU'VE COME A LONG WAY. NOW THEN --
-- THAT SHOULD HOLD THEM BACK FOR A FEW HOURS.
TIME FOR ME TO EXAMINE THIS CLUSTER OF... VERY SMALL MACHINES AND GET SOME ANSWERS!
CAN YOU KEEP IT GOING, SERGEANT?
WE'RE GOING TO NEED ICE, SIR. LOTS OF ICE.

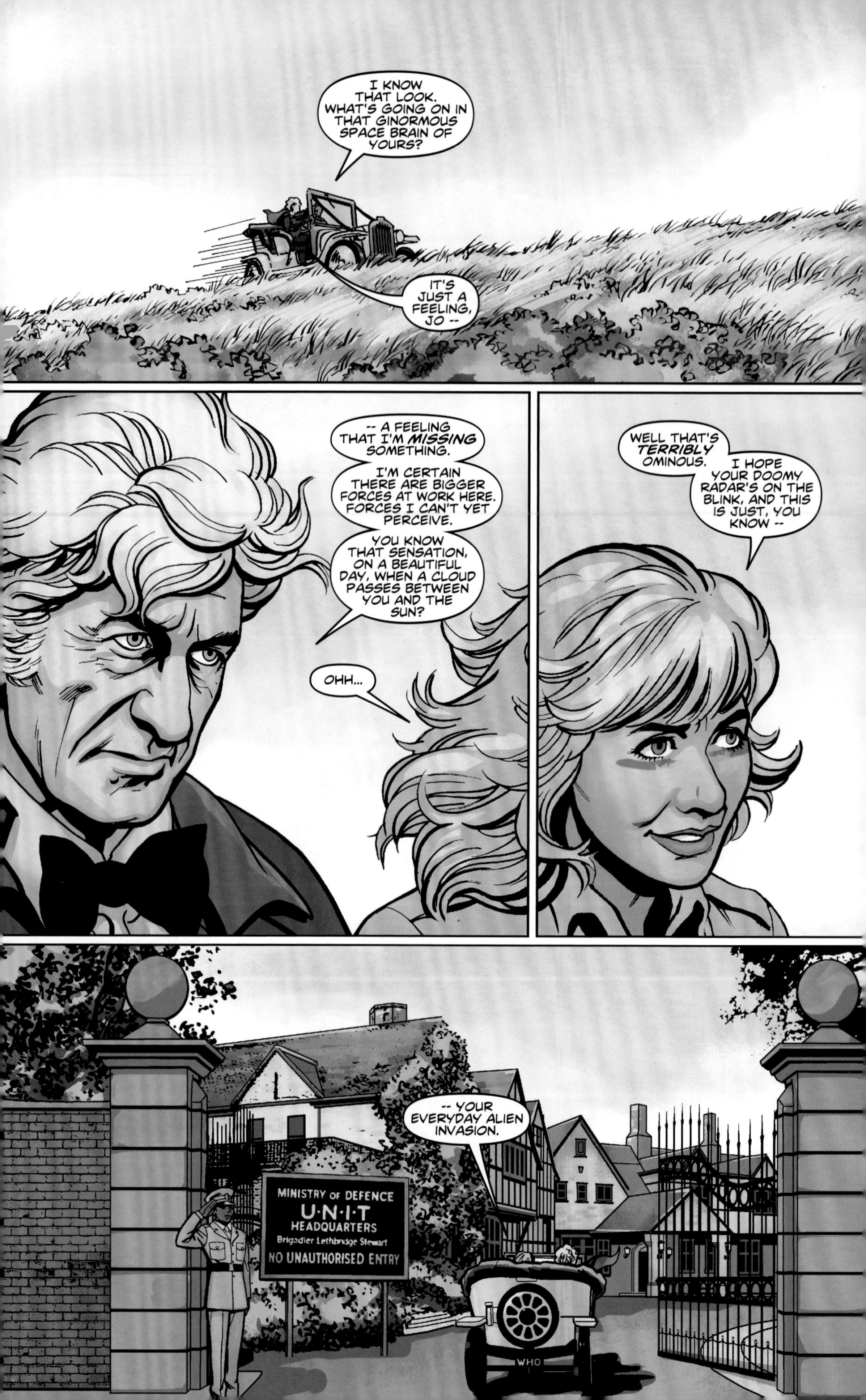
I KNOW THAT LOOK. WHAT'S GOING ON IN THAT GINORMOUS SPACE BRAIN OF YOURS?
IT'S JUST A FEELING, JO --
-- A FEELING THAT I'M MISSING SOMETHING.
I'M CERTAIN THERE ARE BIGGER FORCES AT WORK HERE. FORCES I CAN'T YET PERCEIVE.
YOU KNOW THAT SENSATION, ON A BEAUTIFUL DAY, WHEN A CLOUD PASSES BETWEEN YOU AND THE SUN?
OHH...
WELL THAT'S TERRIBLY OMINOUS.
I HOPE YOUR DOOMY RADAR'S ON THE BLINK, AND THIS IS JUST, YOU KNOW --
-- YOUR EVERYDAY ALIEN INVASION.
MINISTRY OF DEFENCE
U·N·I·T
HEADQUARTERS
Brigadier Lethbridge Stewart
NO UNAUTHORISED ENTRY
WHO

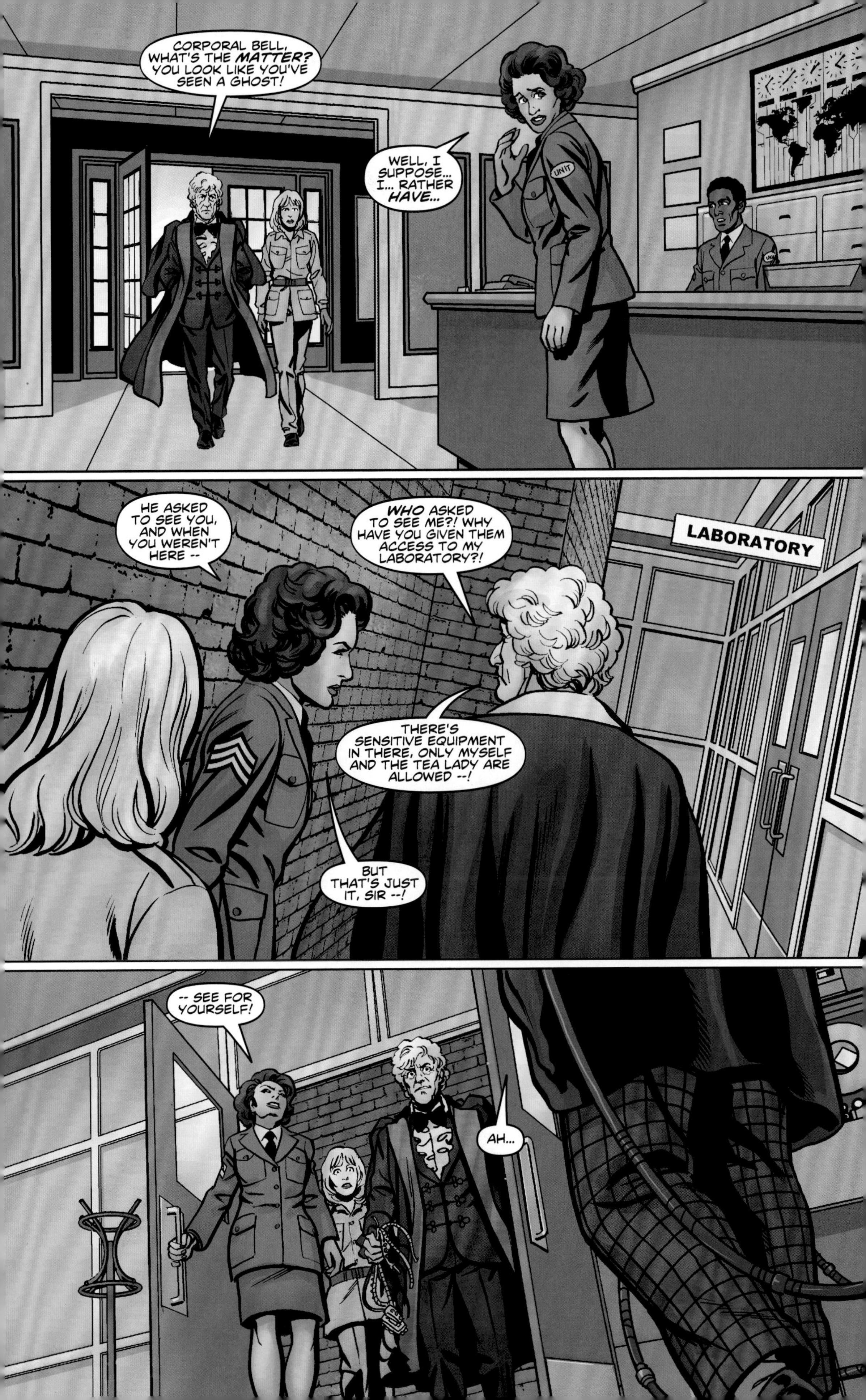
CORPORAL BELL, WHAT'S THE *MATTER?* YOU LOOK LIKE YOU'VE SEEN A GHOST!
WELL, I SUPPOSE... I... RATHER *HAVE...*
UNIT
LABORATORY
HE ASKED TO SEE YOU, AND WHEN YOU WEREN'T HERE --
WHO ASKED TO SEE ME?! WHY HAVE YOU GIVEN THEM ACCESS TO MY LABORATORY?!
THERE'S SENSITIVE EQUIPMENT IN THERE, ONLY MYSELF AND THE TEA LADY ARE ALLOWED --!
BUT THAT'S JUST IT, SIR --!
-- SEE FOR YOURSELF!
AH...

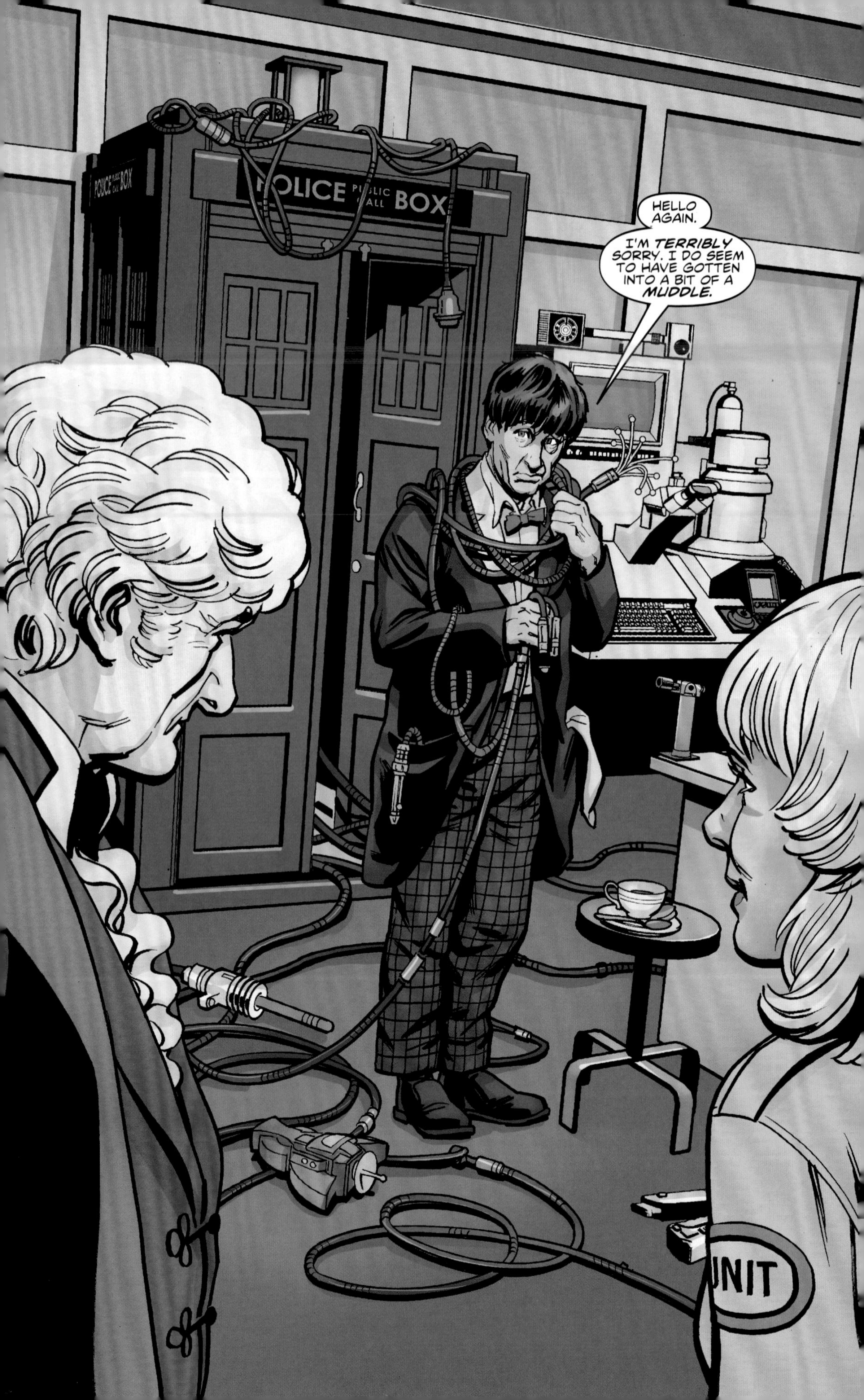
POLICE PUBLIC CALL BOX
HELLO AGAIN.
I'M *TERRIBLY* SORRY. I DO SEEM TO HAVE GOTTEN INTO A BIT OF A ***MUDDLE.***
UNIT

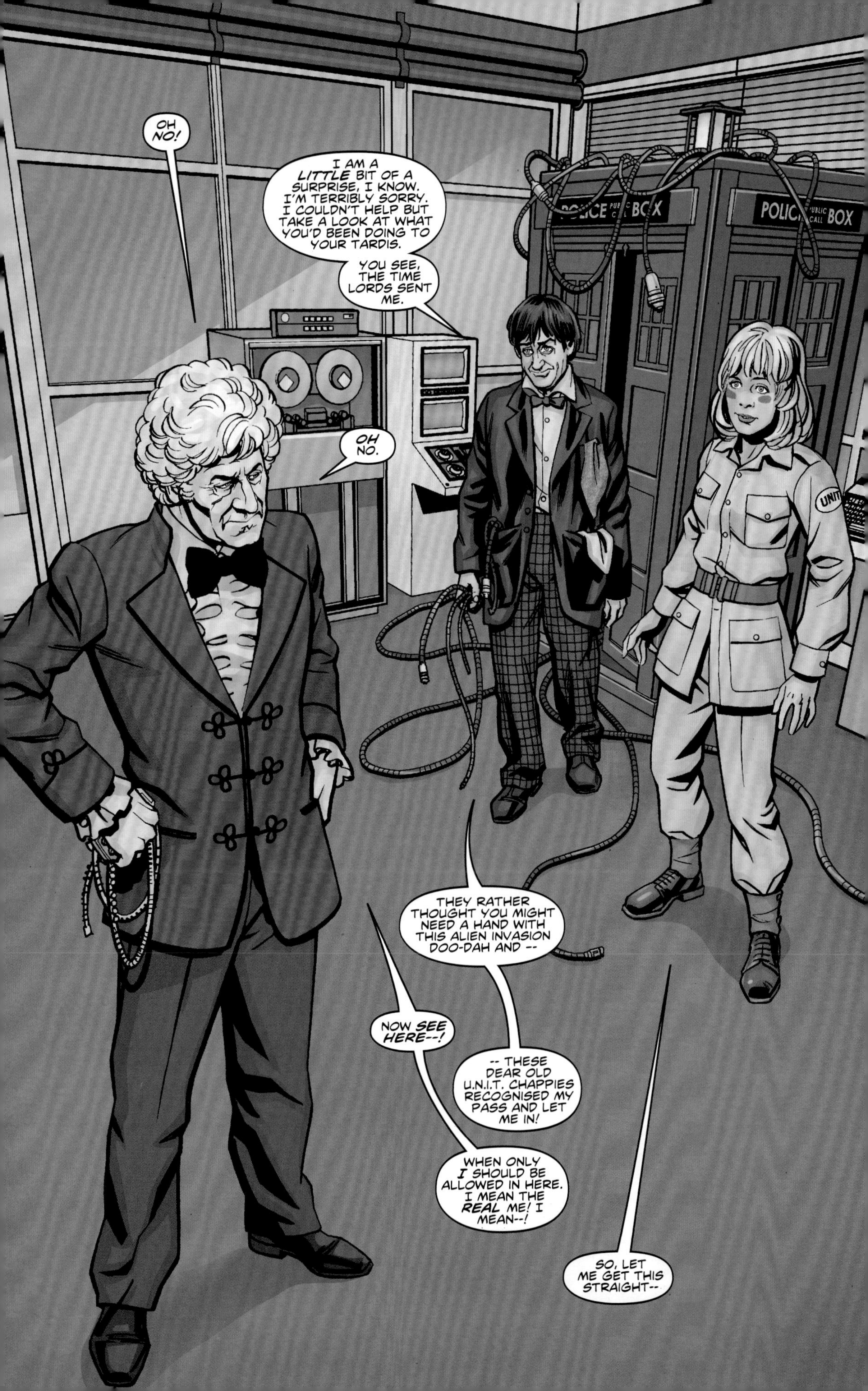
OH NO!
I AM A LITTLE BIT OF A SURPRISE, I KNOW. I'M TERRIBLY SORRY. I COULDN'T HELP BUT TAKE A LOOK AT WHAT YOU'D BEEN DOING TO YOUR TARDIS.
YOU SEE, THE TIME LORDS SENT ME.
POLICE PUBLIC CALL BOX
POLICE PUBLIC CALL BOX
OH NO.
UNIT
THEY RATHER THOUGHT YOU MIGHT NEED A HAND WITH THIS ALIEN INVASION DOO-DAH AND --
NOW SEE HERE--!
-- THESE DEAR OLD U.N.I.T. CHAPPIES RECOGNISED MY PASS AND LET ME IN!
WHEN ONLY I SHOULD BE ALLOWED IN HERE. I MEAN THE REAL ME! I MEAN--!
SO, LET ME GET THIS STRAIGHT--

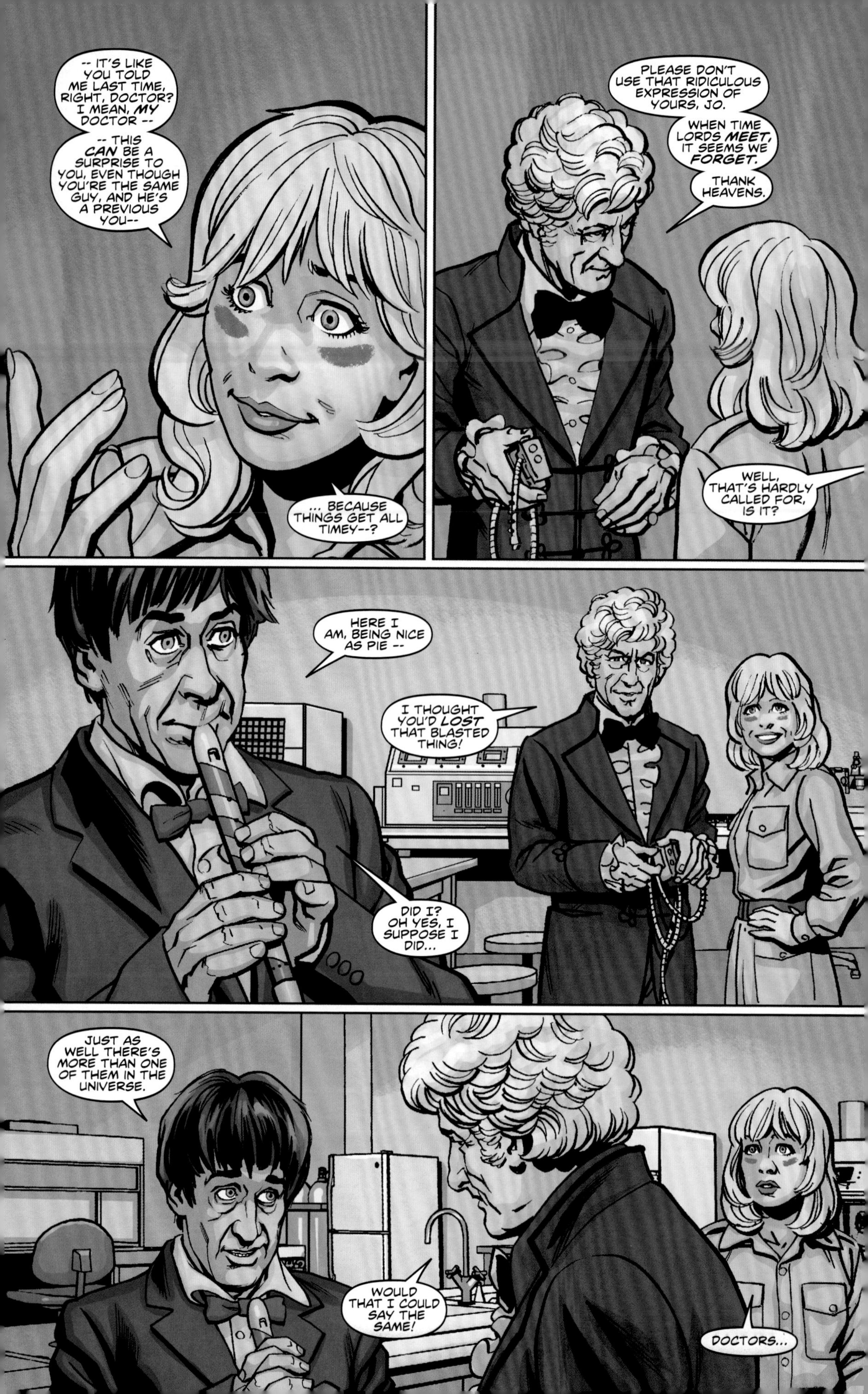
-- IT'S LIKE YOU TOLD ME LAST TIME, RIGHT, DOCTOR? I MEAN, MY DOCTOR --
-- THIS CAN BE A SURPRISE TO YOU, EVEN THOUGH YOU'RE THE SAME GUY, AND HE'S A PREVIOUS YOU--
... BECAUSE THINGS GET ALL TIMEY--?
PLEASE DON'T USE THAT RIDICULOUS EXPRESSION OF YOURS, JO.
WHEN TIME LORDS MEET, IT SEEMS WE FORGET.
THANK HEAVENS.
WELL, THAT'S HARDLY CALLED FOR, IS IT?
HERE I AM, BEING NICE AS PIE --
I THOUGHT YOU'D LOST THAT BLASTED THING!
DID I? OH YES, I SUPPOSE I DID...
JUST AS WELL THERE'S MORE THAN ONE OF THEM IN THE UNIVERSE.
WOULD THAT I COULD SAY THE SAME!
DOCTORS...

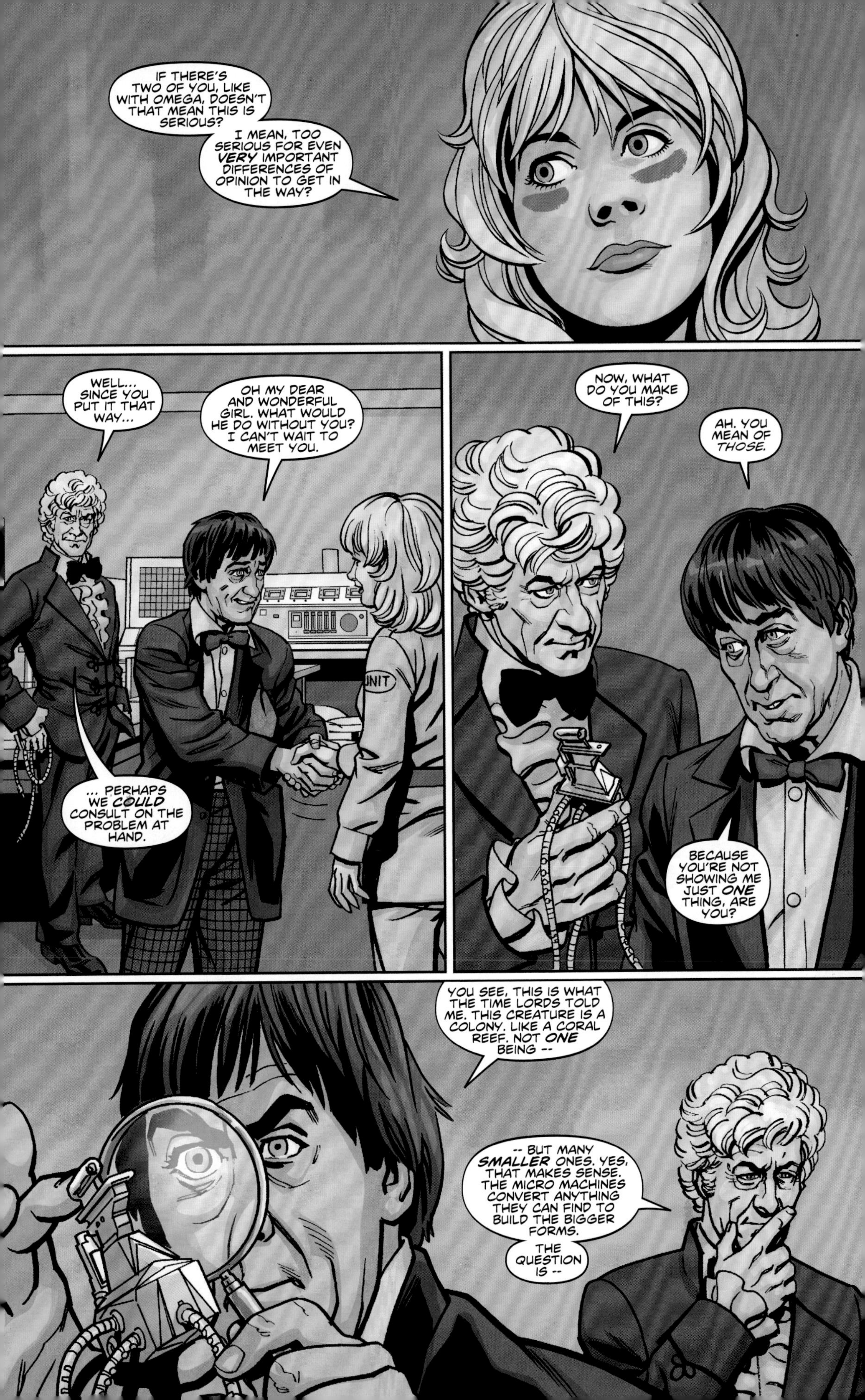
IF THERE'S TWO OF YOU, LIKE WITH OMEGA, DOESN'T THAT MEAN THIS IS SERIOUS?
I MEAN, TOO SERIOUS FOR EVEN VERY IMPORTANT DIFFERENCES OF OPINION TO GET IN THE WAY?
WELL... SINCE YOU PUT IT THAT WAY...
OH MY DEAR AND WONDERFUL GIRL. WHAT WOULD HE DO WITHOUT YOU? I CAN'T WAIT TO MEET YOU.
... PERHAPS WE COULD CONSULT ON THE PROBLEM AT HAND.
UNIT
NOW, WHAT DO YOU MAKE OF THIS?
AH. YOU MEAN OF THOSE.
BECAUSE YOU'RE NOT SHOWING ME JUST ONE THING, ARE YOU?
YOU SEE, THIS IS WHAT THE TIME LORDS TOLD ME. THIS CREATURE IS A COLONY. LIKE A CORAL REEF. NOT ONE BEING --
-- BUT MANY SMALLER ONES. YES, THAT MAKES SENSE. THE MICRO MACHINES CONVERT ANYTHING THEY CAN FIND TO BUILD THE BIGGER FORMS.
THE QUESTION IS --

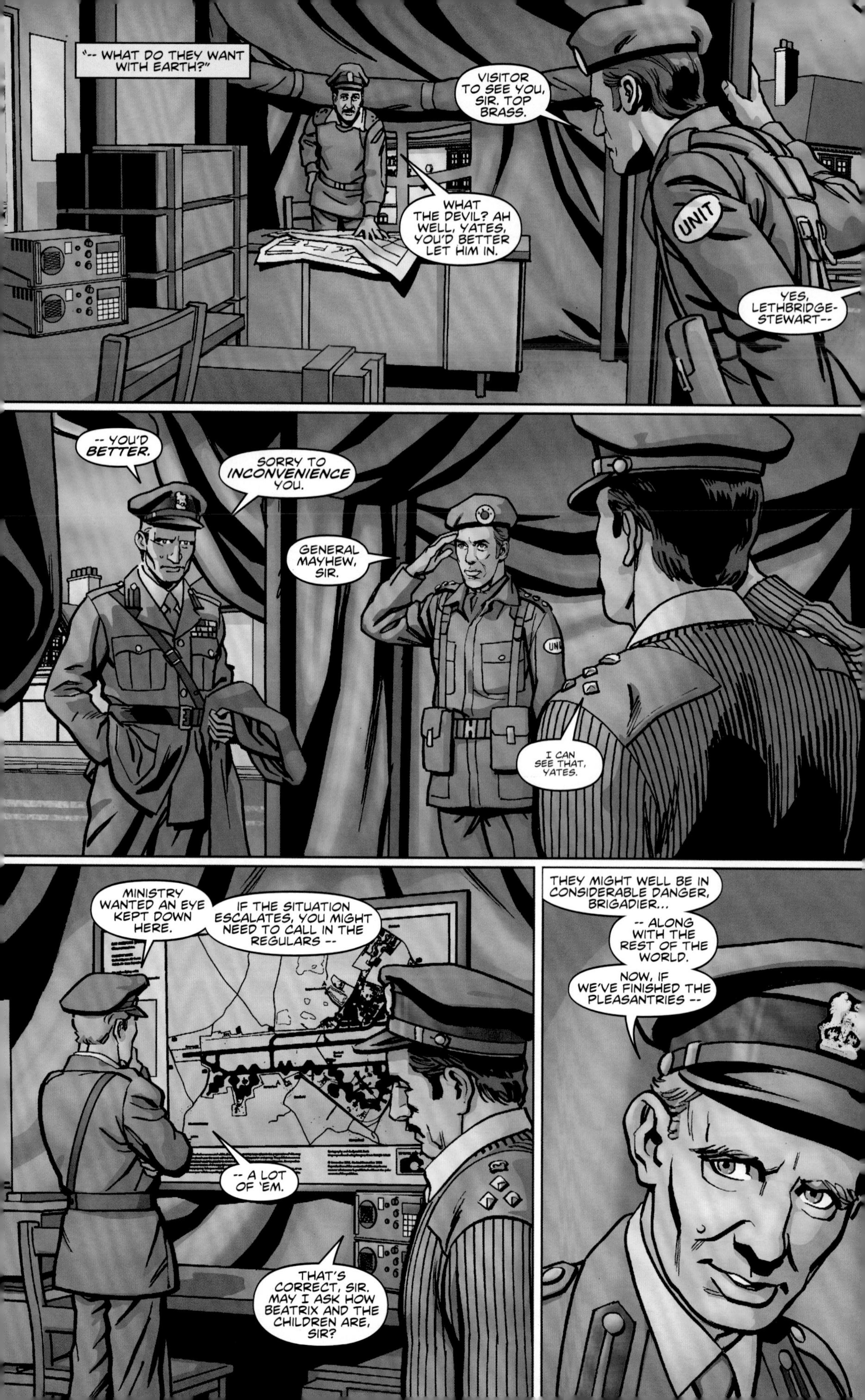
"-- WHAT DO THEY WANT WITH EARTH?"
VISITOR TO SEE YOU, SIR. TOP BRASS.
WHAT THE DEVIL? AH WELL, YATES, YOU'D BETTER LET HIM IN.
UNIT
YES, LETHBRIDGE-STEWART--
-- YOU'D *BETTER.*
SORRY TO *INCONVENIENCE* YOU.
GENERAL MAYHEW, SIR.
I CAN SEE THAT, YATES.
MINISTRY WANTED AN EYE KEPT DOWN HERE.
IF THE SITUATION ESCALATES, YOU MIGHT NEED TO CALL IN THE REGULARS --
-- A LOT OF 'EM.
THAT'S CORRECT, SIR. MAY I ASK HOW BEATRIX AND THE CHILDREN ARE, SIR?
THEY MIGHT WELL BE IN CONSIDERABLE DANGER, BRIGADIER...
-- ALONG WITH THE REST OF THE WORLD.
NOW, IF WE'VE FINISHED THE PLEASANTRIES --

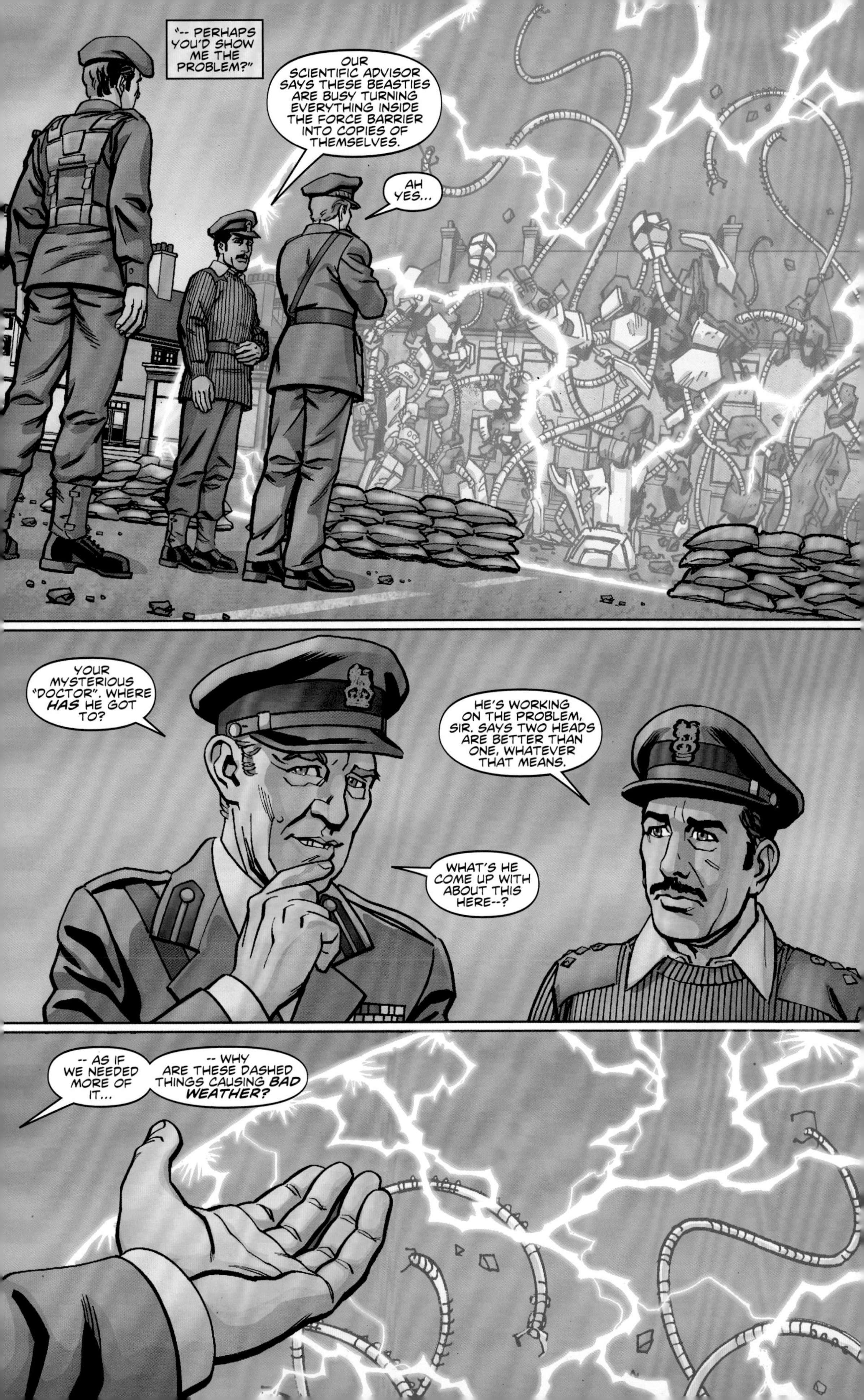
"-- PERHAPS YOU'D SHOW ME THE PROBLEM?"
OUR SCIENTIFIC ADVISOR SAYS THESE BEASTIES ARE BUSY TURNING EVERYTHING INSIDE THE FORCE BARRIER INTO COPIES OF THEMSELVES.
AH YES...
YOUR MYSTERIOUS "DOCTOR". WHERE *HAS* HE GOT TO?
HE'S WORKING ON THE PROBLEM, SIR. SAYS TWO HEADS ARE BETTER THAN ONE, WHATEVER THAT MEANS.
WHAT'S HE COME UP WITH ABOUT THIS HERE--?
-- WHY ARE THESE DASHED THINGS CAUSING *BAD WEATHER?*
-- AS IF WE NEEDED MORE OF IT...

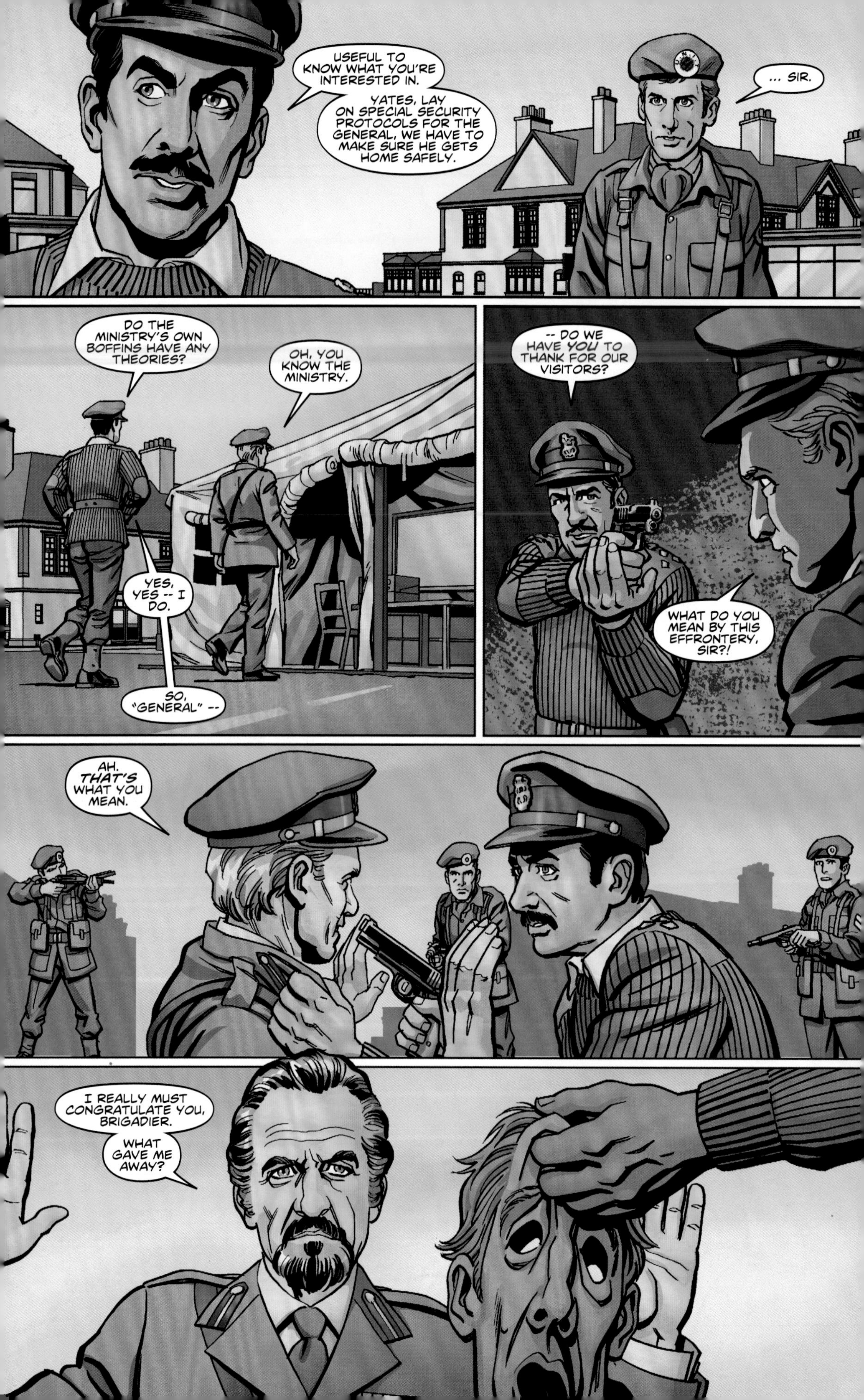
USEFUL TO KNOW WHAT YOU'RE INTERESTED IN.
YATES, LAY ON SPECIAL SECURITY PROTOCOLS FOR THE GENERAL, WE HAVE TO MAKE SURE HE GETS HOME SAFELY.
... SIR.
DO THE MINISTRY'S OWN BOFFINS HAVE ANY THEORIES?
OH, YOU KNOW THE MINISTRY.
YES, YES -- I DO.
SO, "GENERAL" --
-- DO WE HAVE *YOU* TO THANK FOR OUR VISITORS?
WHAT DO YOU MEAN BY THIS EFFRONTERY, SIR?!
AH. *THAT'S* WHAT YOU MEAN.
I REALLY MUST CONGRATULATE YOU, BRIGADIER.
WHAT GAVE ME AWAY?

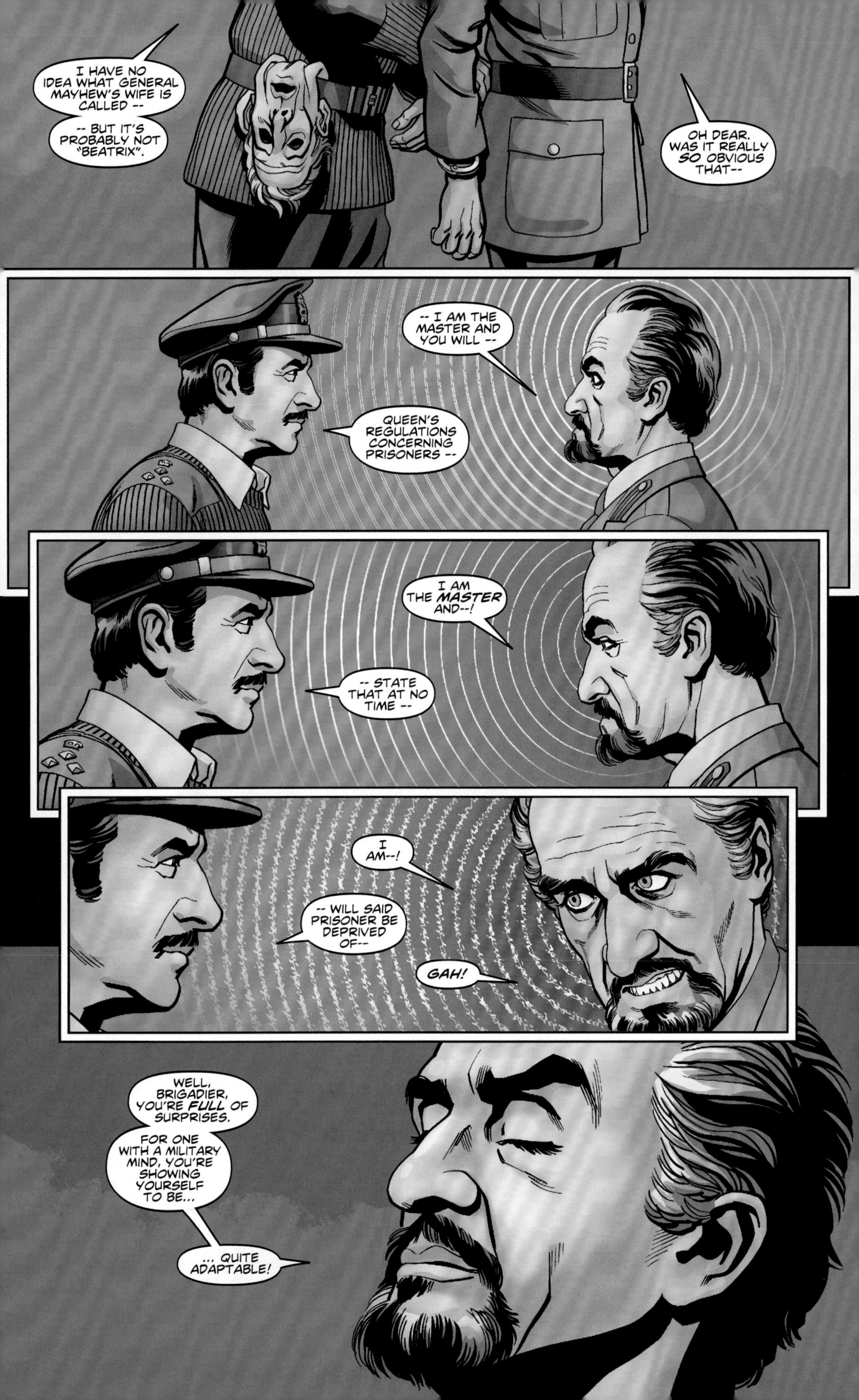
I HAVE NO IDEA WHAT GENERAL MAYHEW'S WIFE IS CALLED --
-- BUT IT'S PROBABLY NOT "BEATRIX".
OH DEAR. WAS IT REALLY SO OBVIOUS THAT--
-- I AM THE MASTER AND YOU WILL --
QUEEN'S REGULATIONS CONCERNING PRISONERS --
I AM THE MASTER AND--!
-- STATE THAT AT NO TIME --
I AM--!
-- WILL SAID PRISONER BE DEPRIVED OF--
GAH!
WELL, BRIGADIER, YOU'RE FULL OF SURPRISES.
FOR ONE WITH A MILITARY MIND, YOU'RE SHOWING YOURSELF TO BE...
... QUITE ADAPTABLE!

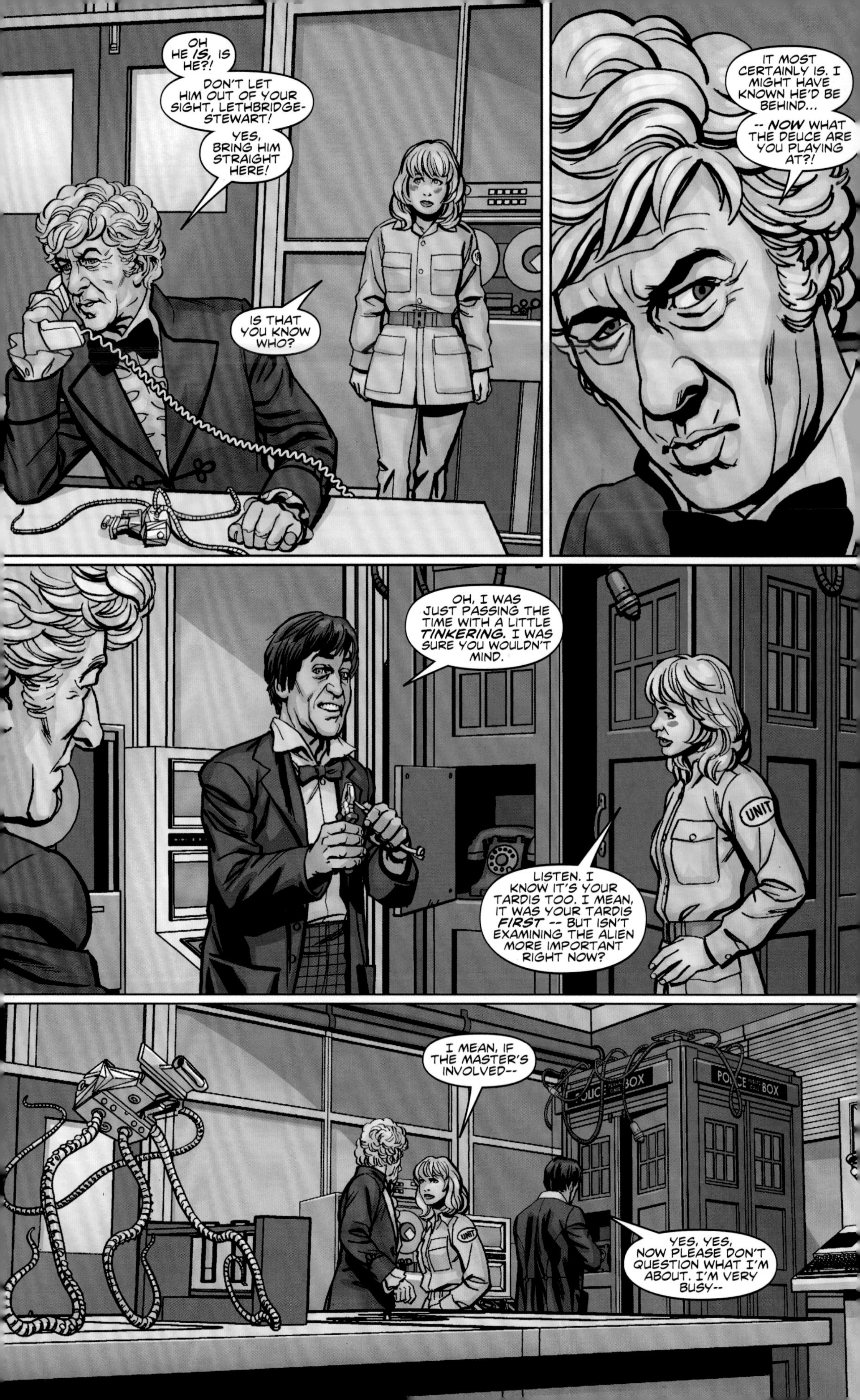
OH HE *IS*, IS HE?!
DON'T LET HIM OUT OF YOUR SIGHT, LETHBRIDGE-STEWART!
YES, BRING HIM STRAIGHT HERE!
IS THAT YOU KNOW WHO?
IT MOST CERTAINLY IS. I MIGHT HAVE KNOWN HE'D BE BEHIND...
-- ***NOW*** WHAT THE DEUCE ARE YOU PLAYING AT?!
OH, I WAS JUST PASSING THE TIME WITH A LITTLE ***TINKERING.*** I WAS SURE YOU WOULDN'T MIND.
LISTEN. I KNOW IT'S YOUR TARDIS TOO. I MEAN, IT WAS YOUR TARDIS ***FIRST*** -- BUT ISN'T EXAMINING THE ALIEN MORE IMPORTANT RIGHT NOW?
I MEAN, IF THE MASTER'S INVOLVED--
YES, YES, NOW PLEASE DON'T QUESTION WHAT I'M ABOUT. I'M VERY BUSY--

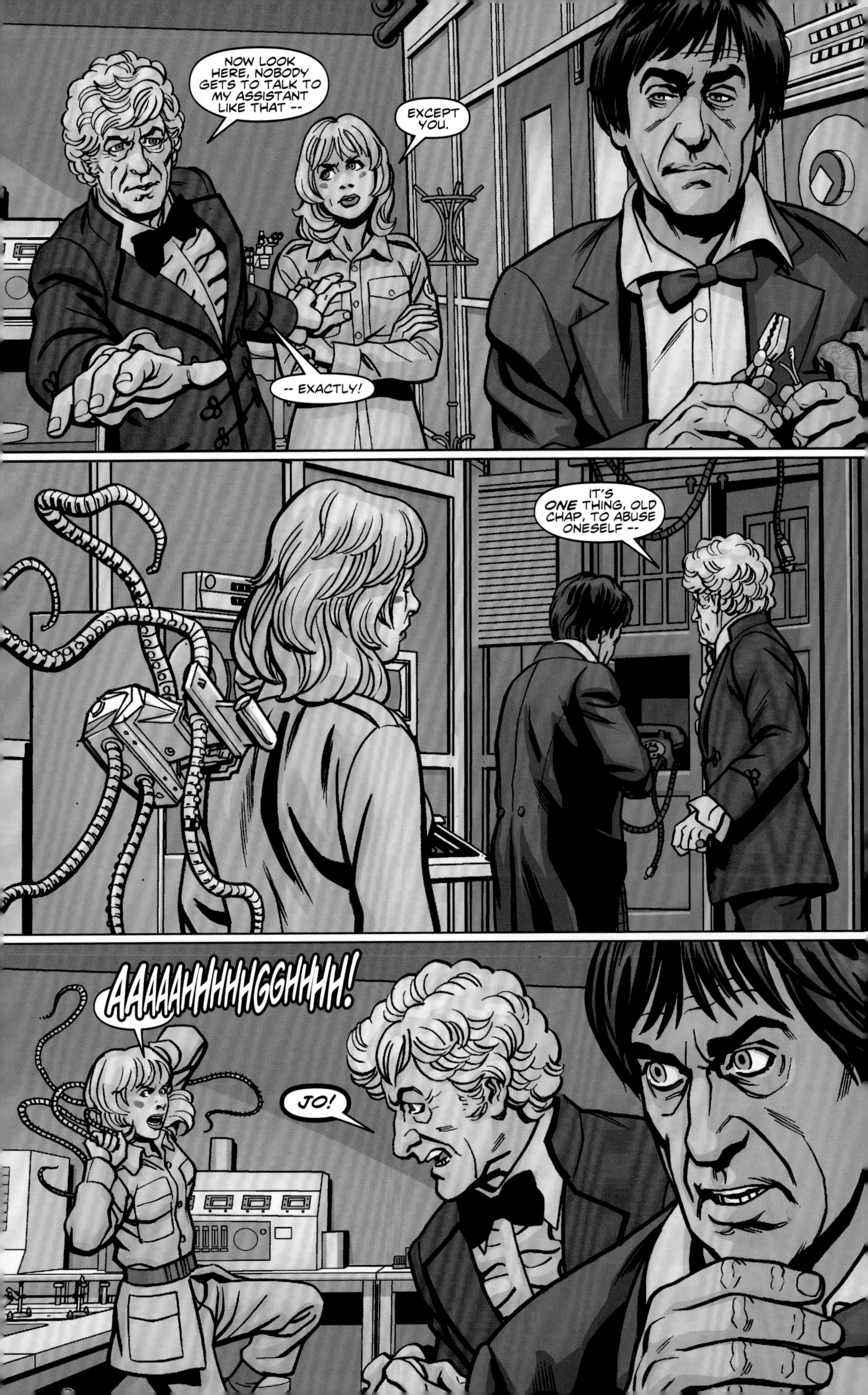
NOW LOOK HERE, NOBODY GETS TO TALK TO MY ASSISTANT LIKE THAT --
EXCEPT YOU.
-- EXACTLY!
IT'S ONE THING, OLD CHAP, TO ABUSE ONESELF --
AAAAAHHHHHGGHHHH!
JO!

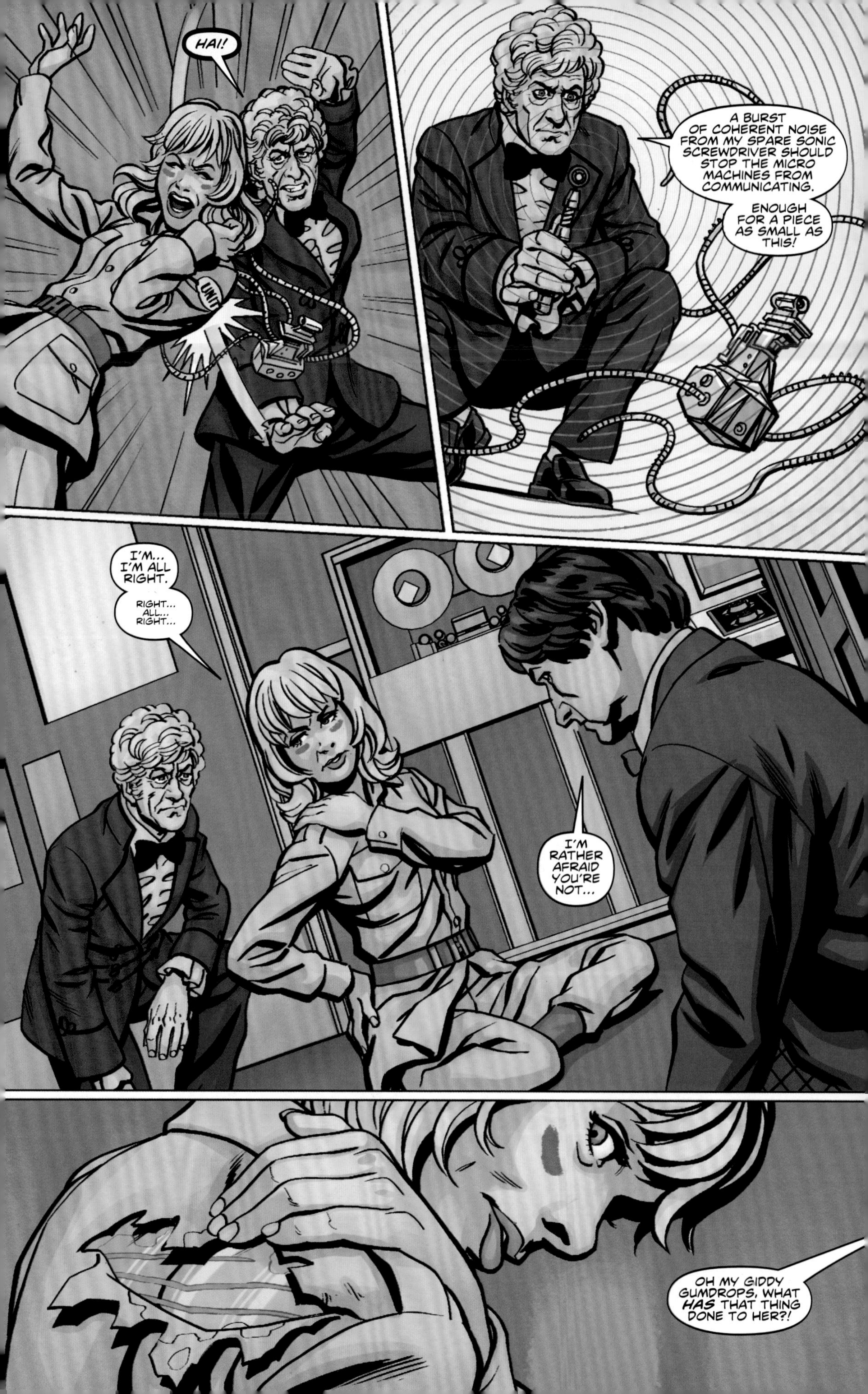
HAI!
A BURST OF COHERENT NOISE FROM MY SPARE SONIC SCREWDRIVER SHOULD STOP THE MICRO MACHINES FROM COMMUNICATING.
ENOUGH FOR A PIECE AS SMALL AS THIS!
I'M... I'M ALL RIGHT.
RIGHT... ALL... RIGHT...
I'M RATHER AFRAID YOU'RE NOT...
OH MY GIDDY GUMDROPS, WHAT *HAS* THAT THING DONE TO HER?!

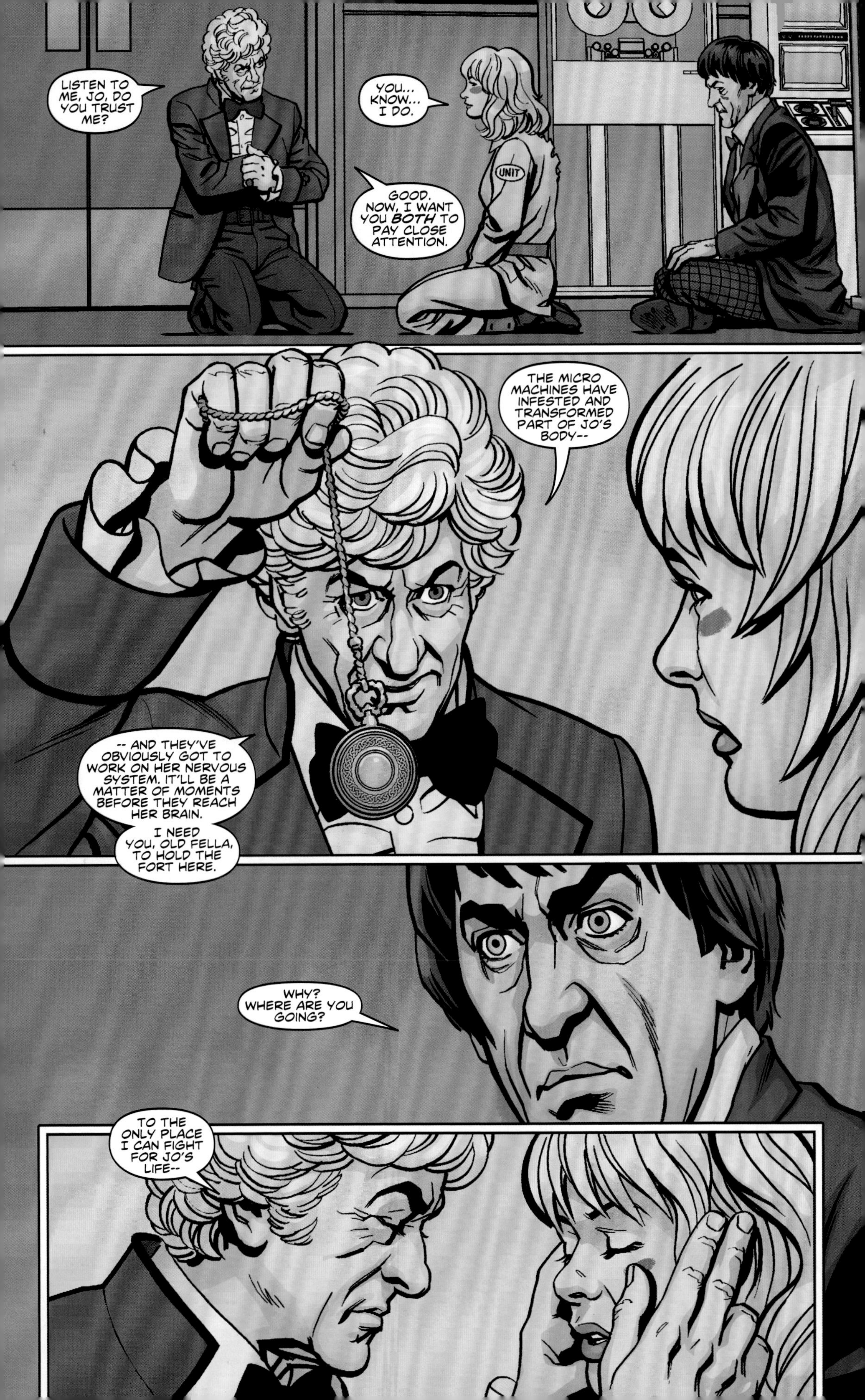
LISTEN TO ME, JO, DO YOU TRUST ME?
YOU... KNOW... I DO.
GOOD. NOW, I WANT YOU BOTH TO PAY CLOSE ATTENTION.
THE MICRO MACHINES HAVE INFESTED AND TRANSFORMED PART OF JO'S BODY--
-- AND THEY'VE OBVIOUSLY GOT TO WORK ON HER NERVOUS SYSTEM. IT'LL BE A MATTER OF MOMENTS BEFORE THEY REACH HER BRAIN.
I NEED YOU, OLD FELLA, TO HOLD THE FORT HERE.
WHY? WHERE ARE YOU GOING?
TO THE ONLY PLACE I CAN FIGHT FOR JO'S LIFE--

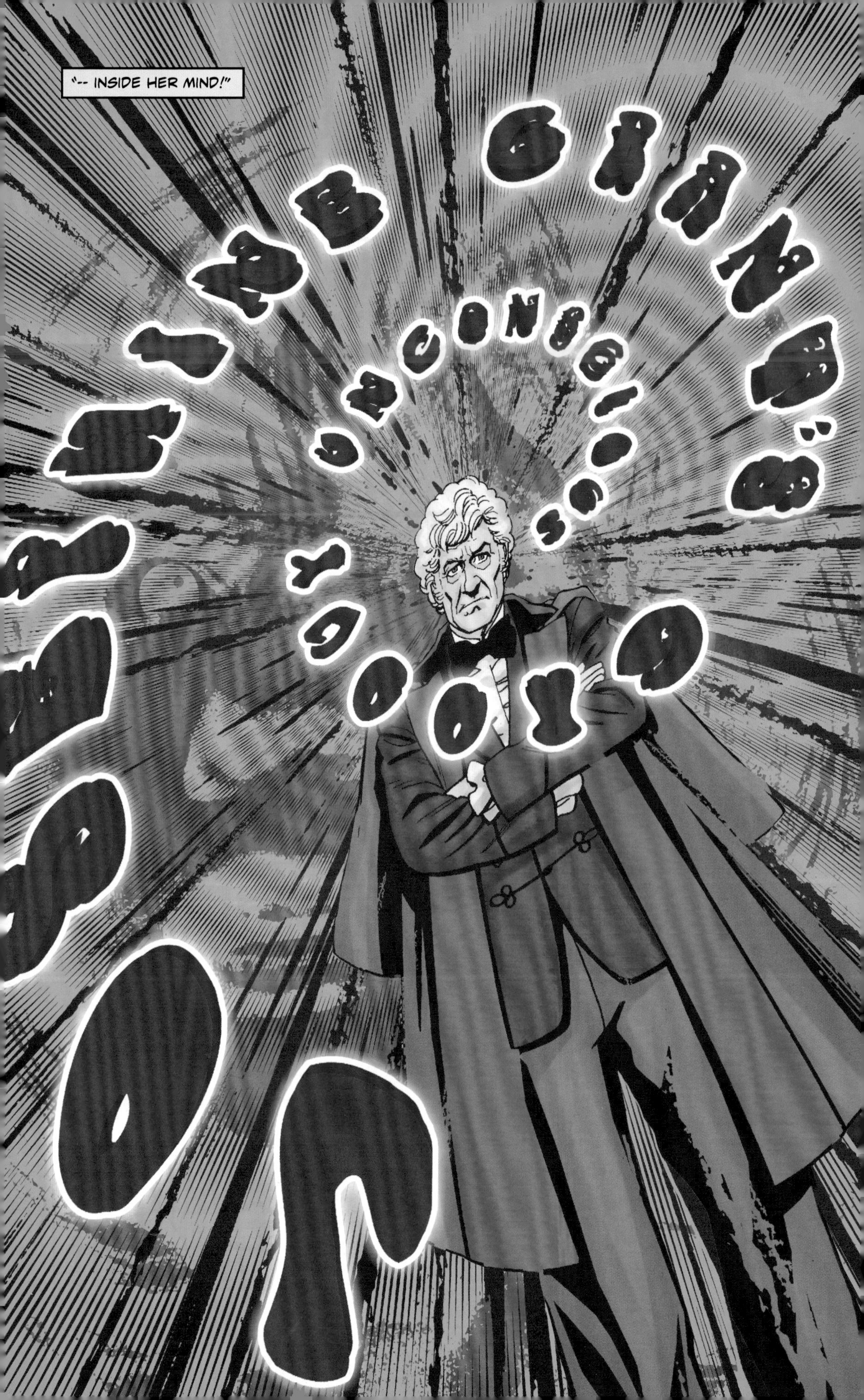
"-- INSIDE HER MIND!"

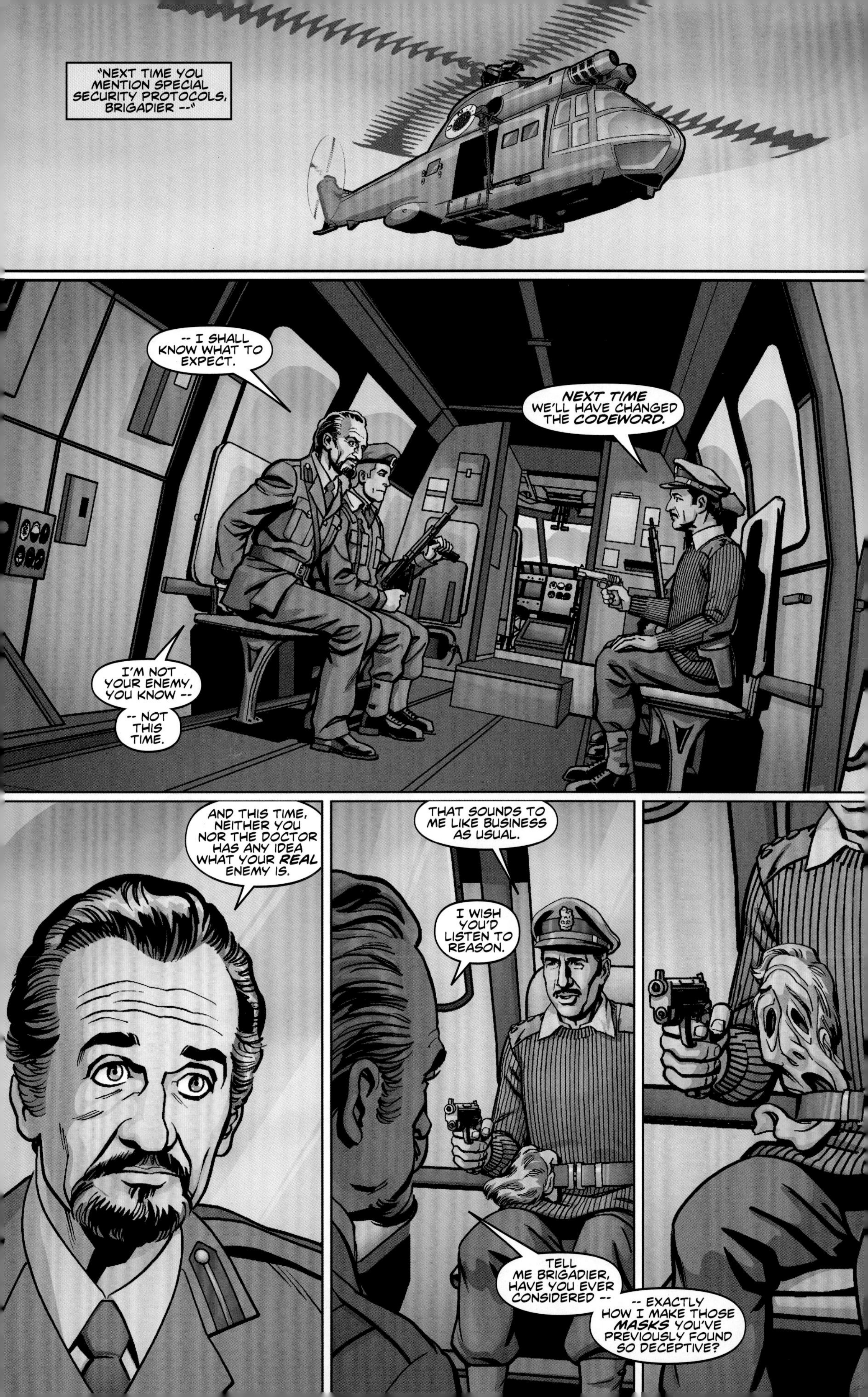
"NEXT TIME YOU MENTION SPECIAL SECURITY PROTOCOLS, BRIGADIER --"
-- I SHALL KNOW WHAT TO EXPECT.
NEXT TIME WE'LL HAVE CHANGED THE CODEWORD.
I'M NOT YOUR ENEMY, YOU KNOW --
-- NOT THIS TIME.
AND THIS TIME, NEITHER YOU NOR THE DOCTOR HAS ANY IDEA WHAT YOUR REAL ENEMY IS.
THAT SOUNDS TO ME LIKE BUSINESS AS USUAL.
I WISH YOU'D LISTEN TO REASON.
TELL ME BRIGADIER, HAVE YOU EVER CONSIDERED --
-- EXACTLY HOW I MAKE THOSE MASKS YOU'VE PREVIOUSLY FOUND SO DECEPTIVE?

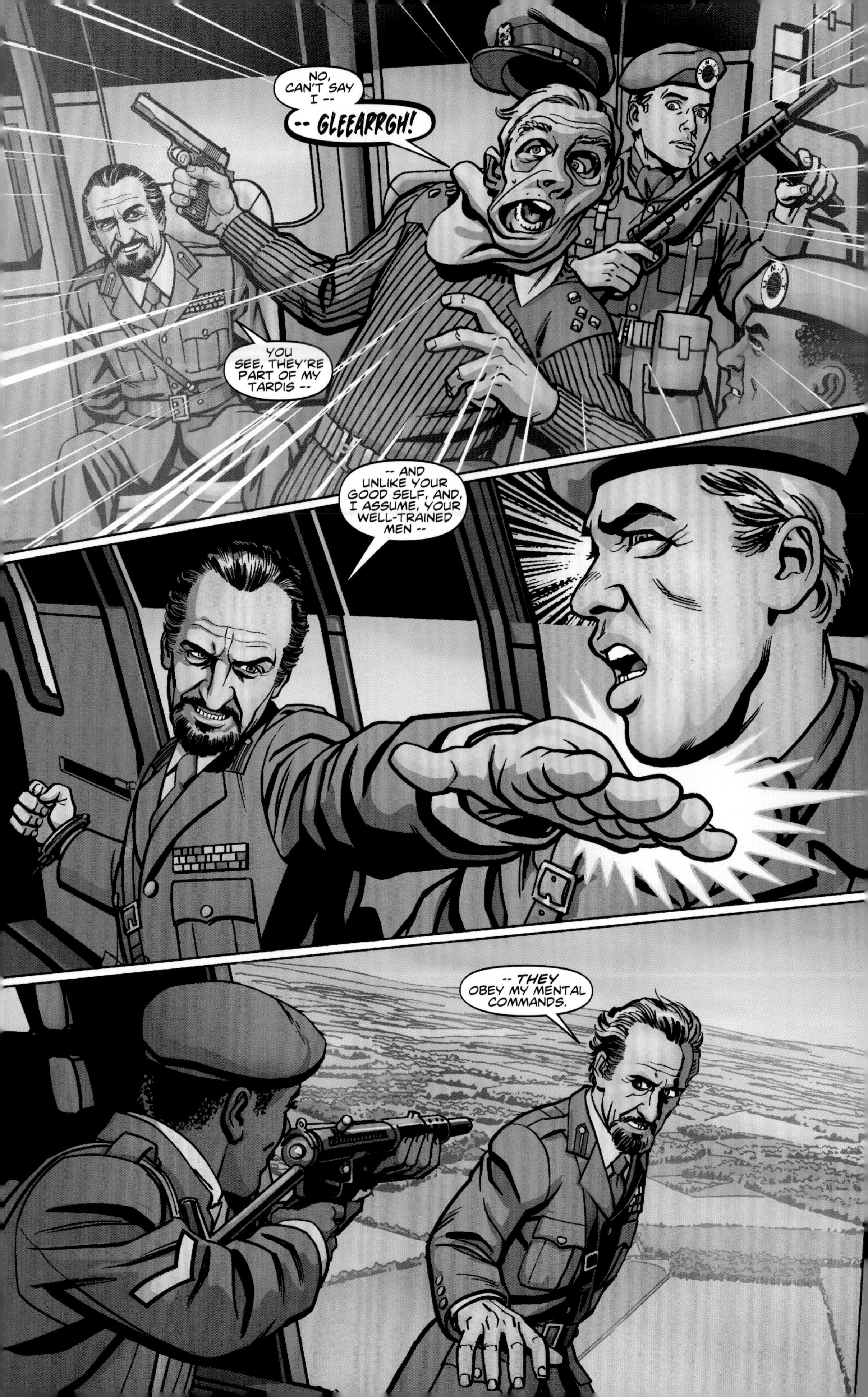
NO, CAN'T SAY I --
-- GLEEARRGH!
YOU SEE, THEY'RE PART OF MY TARDIS --
-- AND UNLIKE YOUR GOOD SELF, AND, I ASSUME, YOUR WELL-TRAINED MEN --
-- THEY OBEY MY MENTAL COMMANDS.

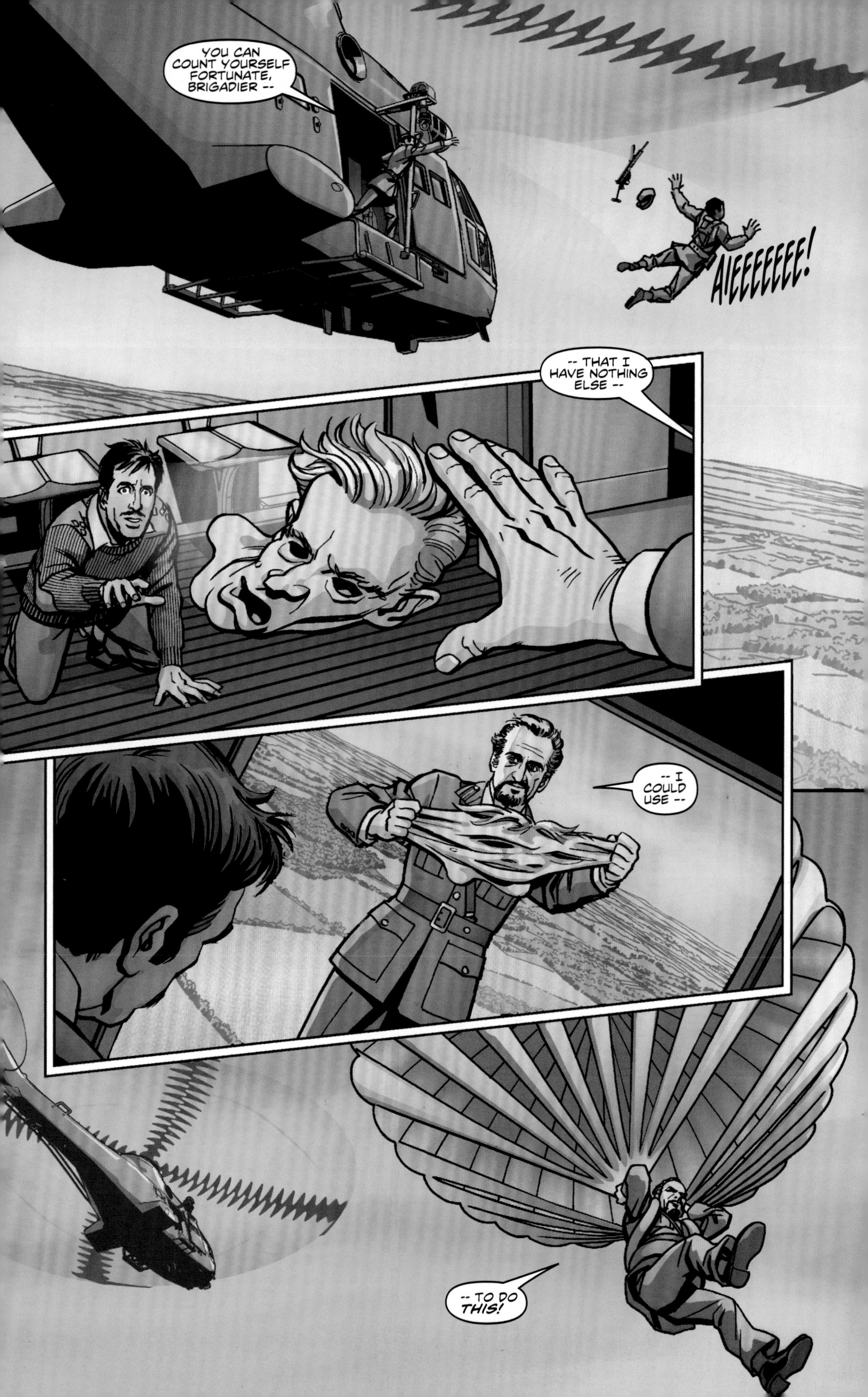
YOU CAN COUNT YOURSELF FORTUNATE, BRIGADIER --
AIEEEEEEE!
-- THAT I HAVE NOTHING ELSE --
-- I COULD USE --
-- TO DO THIS!

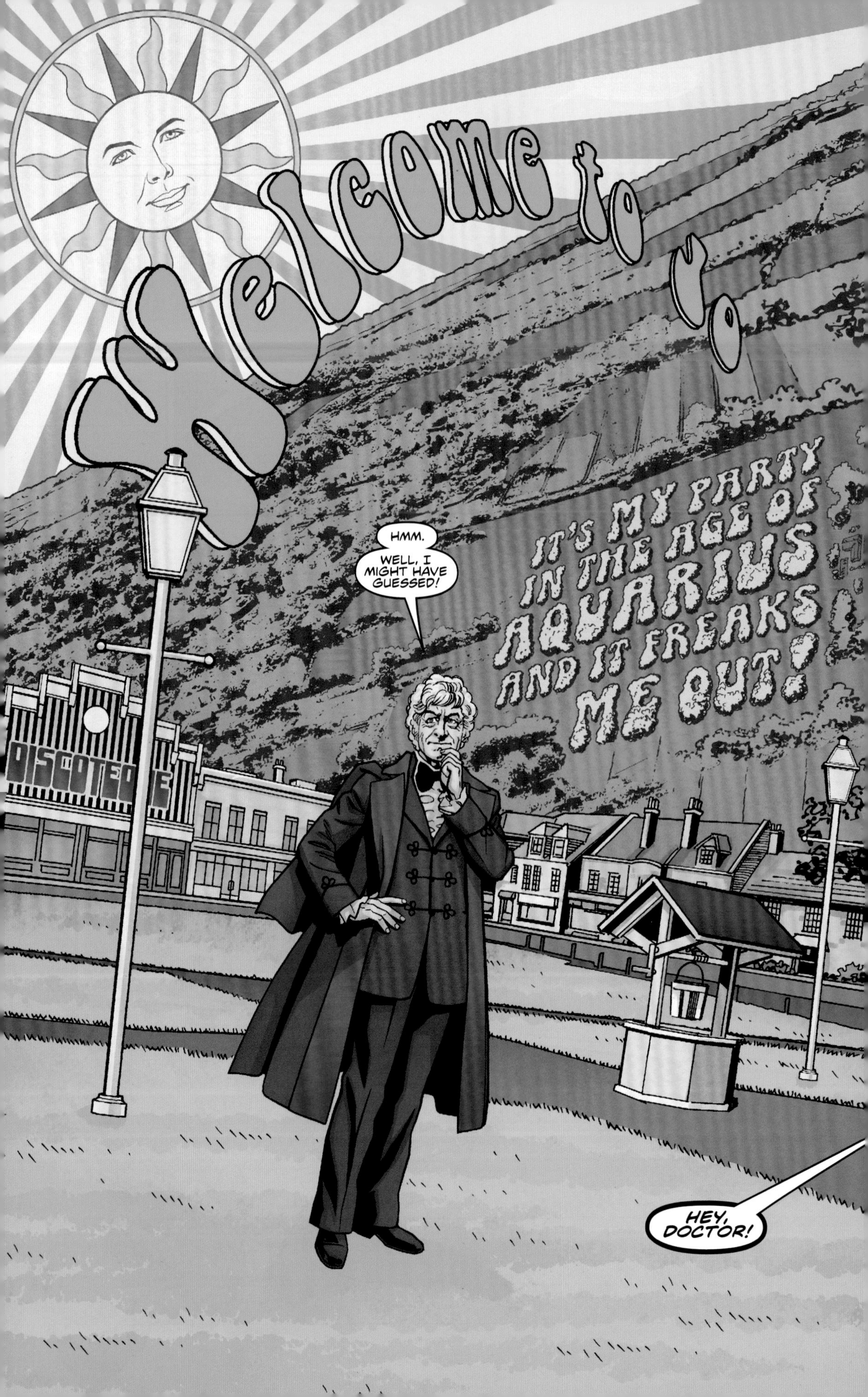
Welcome to
IT'S MY PARTY IN THE AGE OF AQUARIUS AND IT FREAKS ME OUT!
HMM.
WELL, I MIGHT HAVE GUESSED!
HEY, DOCTOR!

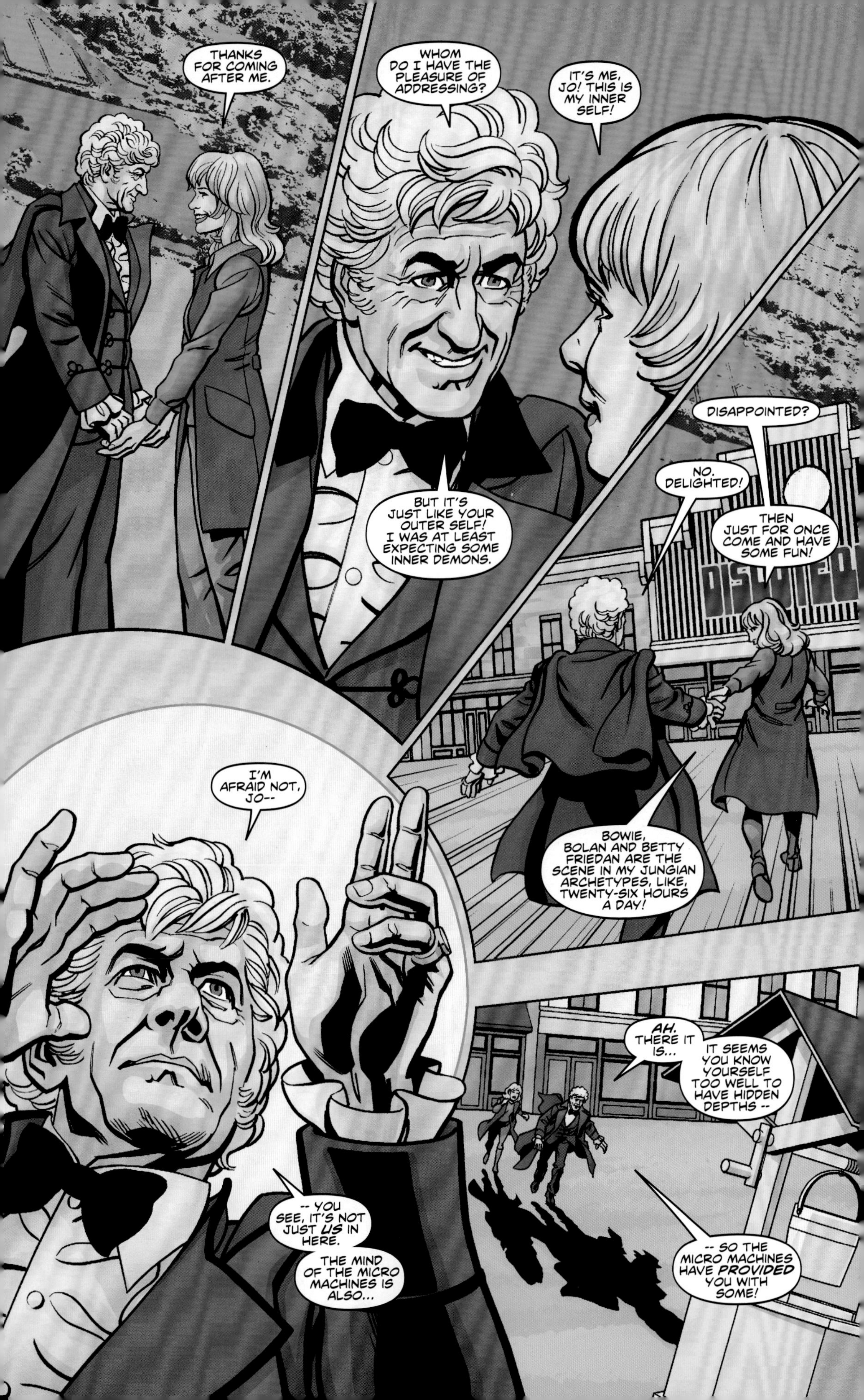
THANKS FOR COMING AFTER ME.
WHOM DO I HAVE THE PLEASURE OF ADDRESSING?
IT'S ME, JO! THIS IS MY INNER SELF!
BUT IT'S JUST LIKE YOUR OUTER SELF! I WAS AT LEAST EXPECTING SOME INNER DEMONS.
DISAPPOINTED?
NO. DELIGHTED!
THEN JUST FOR ONCE COME AND HAVE SOME FUN!
BOWIE, BOLAN AND BETTY FRIEDAN ARE THE SCENE IN MY JUNGIAN ARCHETYPES, LIKE, TWENTY-SIX HOURS A DAY!
I'M AFRAID NOT, JO--
-- YOU SEE, IT'S NOT JUST *US* IN HERE.
THE MIND OF THE MICRO MACHINES IS ALSO...
AH. THERE IT IS...
IT SEEMS YOU KNOW YOURSELF TOO WELL TO HAVE HIDDEN DEPTHS --
-- SO THE MICRO MACHINES HAVE *PROVIDED* YOU WITH SOME!

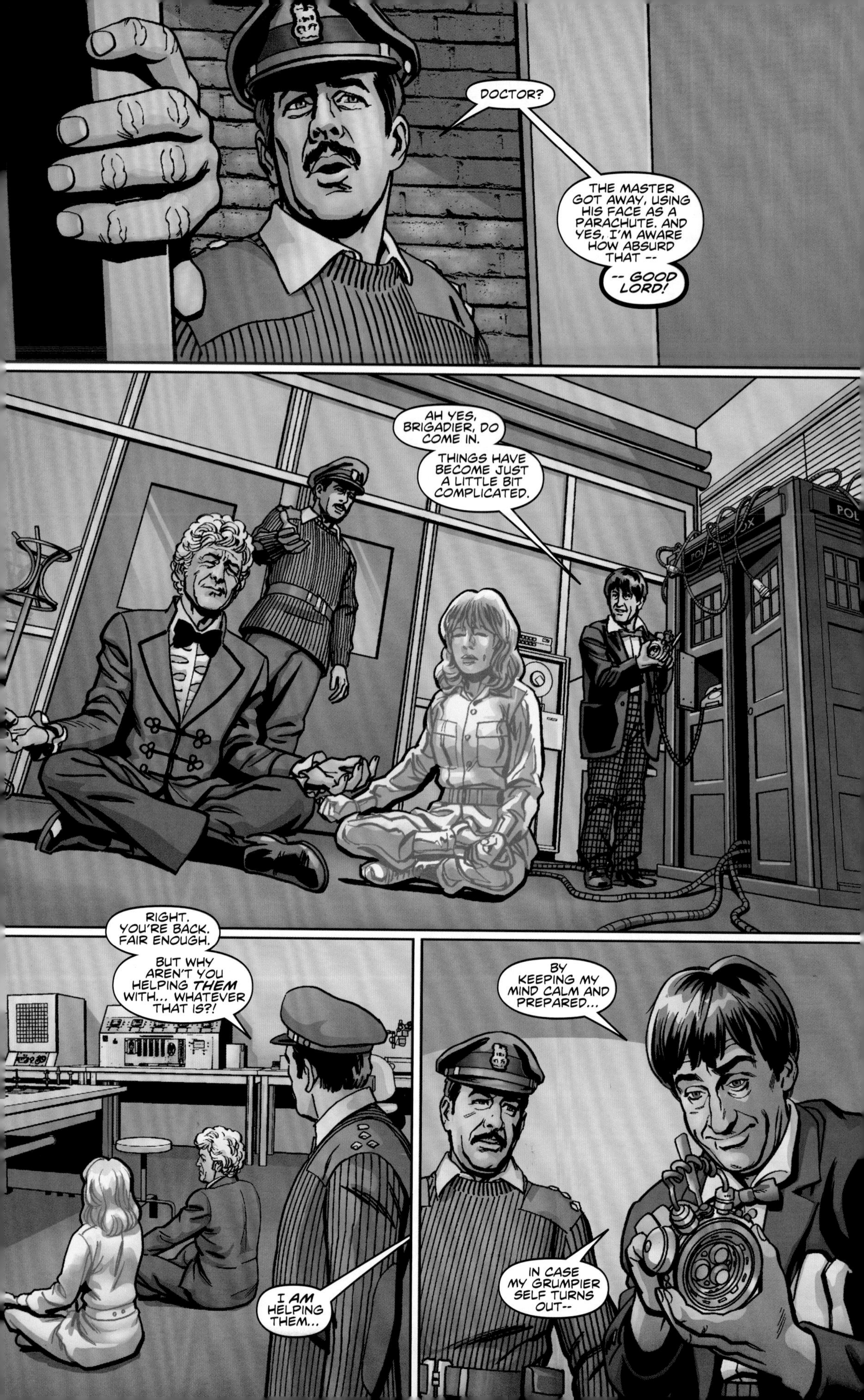
DOCTOR?
THE MASTER GOT AWAY, USING HIS FACE AS A PARACHUTE. AND YES, I'M AWARE HOW ABSURD THAT --
-- GOOD LORD!
AH YES, BRIGADIER, DO COME IN.
THINGS HAVE BECOME JUST A LITTLE BIT COMPLICATED.
RIGHT. YOU'RE BACK. FAIR ENOUGH.
BUT WHY AREN'T YOU HELPING THEM WITH... WHATEVER THAT IS?!
I AM HELPING THEM...
BY KEEPING MY MIND CALM AND PREPARED...
IN CASE MY GRUMPIER SELF TURNS OUT--

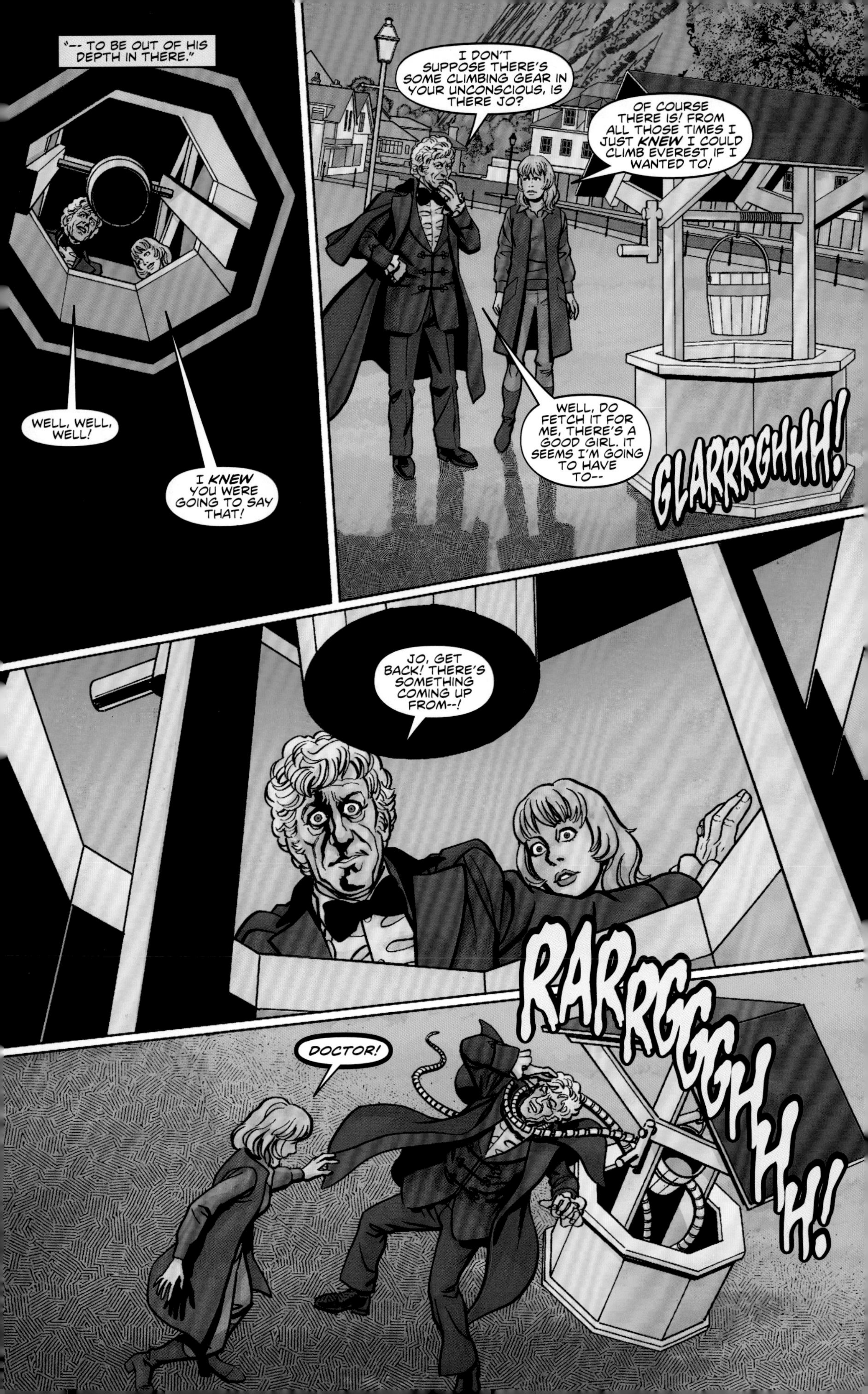
"-- TO BE OUT OF HIS DEPTH IN THERE."
WELL, WELL, WELL!
I KNEW YOU WERE GOING TO SAY THAT!
I DON'T SUPPOSE THERE'S SOME CLIMBING GEAR IN YOUR UNCONSCIOUS, IS THERE JO?
OF COURSE THERE IS! FROM ALL THOSE TIMES I JUST KNEW I COULD CLIMB EVEREST IF I WANTED TO!
WELL, DO FETCH IT FOR ME, THERE'S A GOOD GIRL. IT SEEMS I'M GOING TO HAVE TO--
GLARRRGHHH!
JO, GET BACK! THERE'S SOMETHING COMING UP FROM--!
RARRGGGHHHH!
DOCTOR!

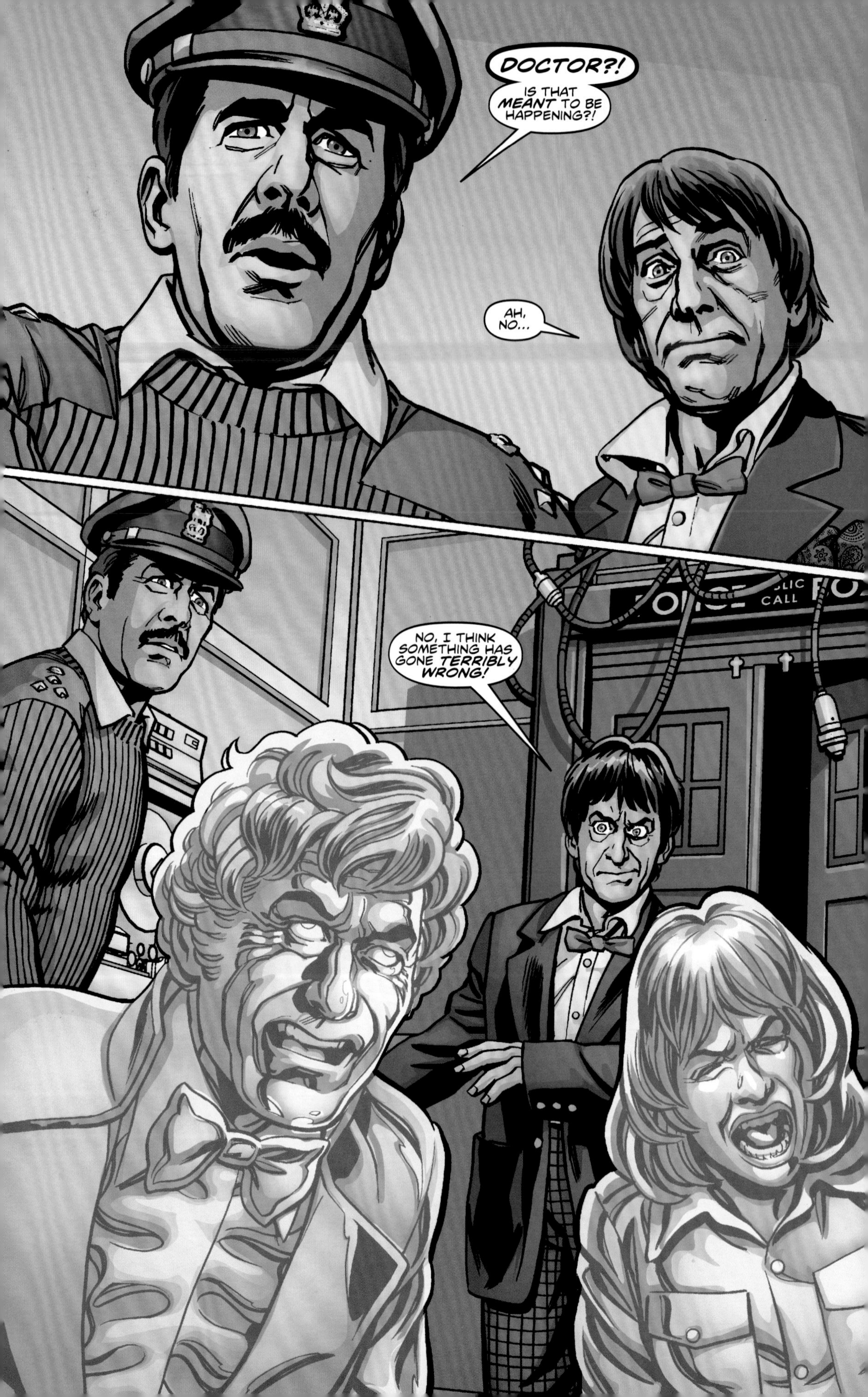
DOCTOR?!
IS THAT MEANT TO BE HAPPENING?!
AH, NO...
NO, I THINK SOMETHING HAS GONE TERRIBLY WRONG!

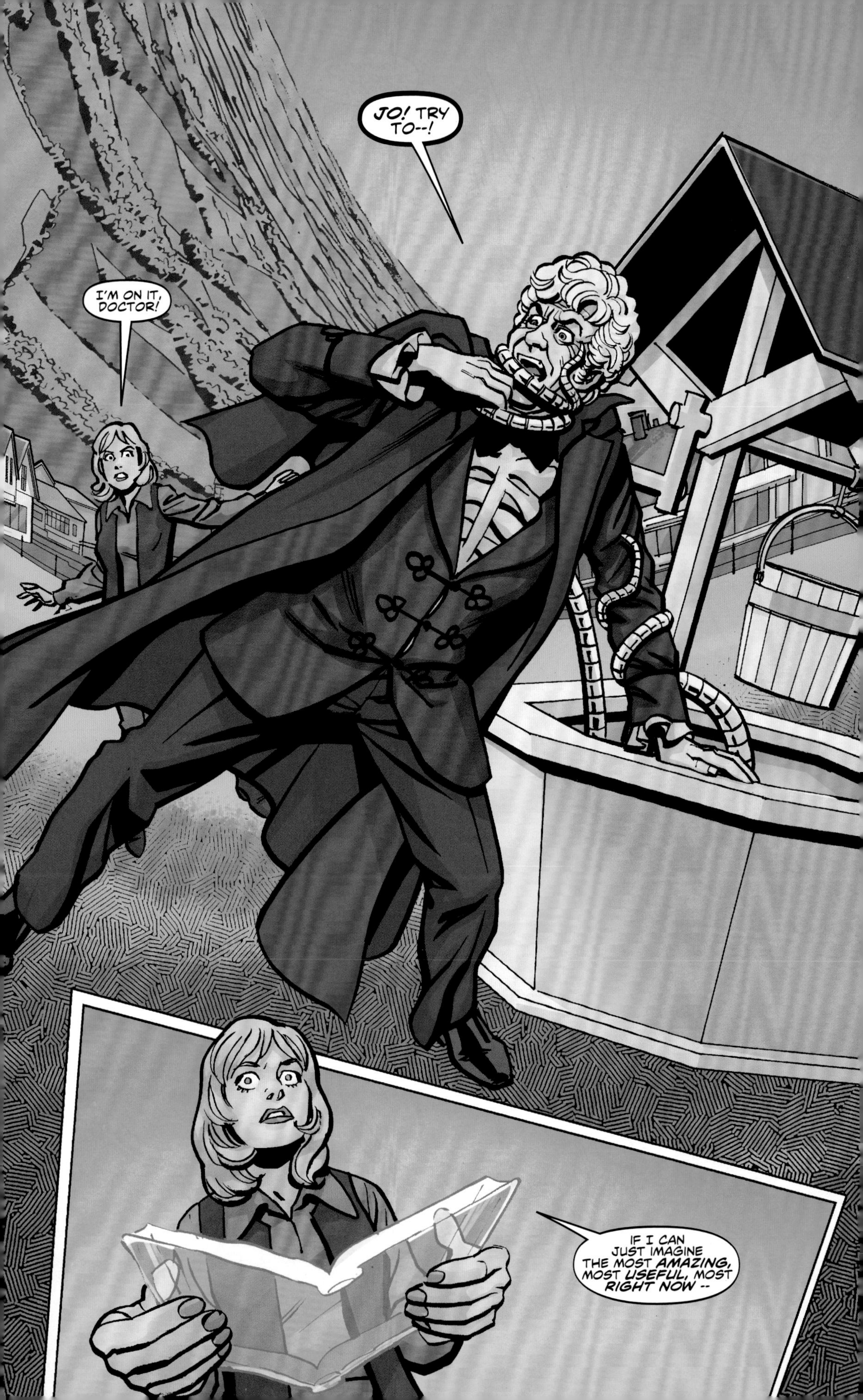
JO! TRY TO--!
I'M ON IT, DOCTOR!
IF I CAN JUST IMAGINE THE MOST AMAZING, MOST USEFUL, MOST RIGHT NOW --

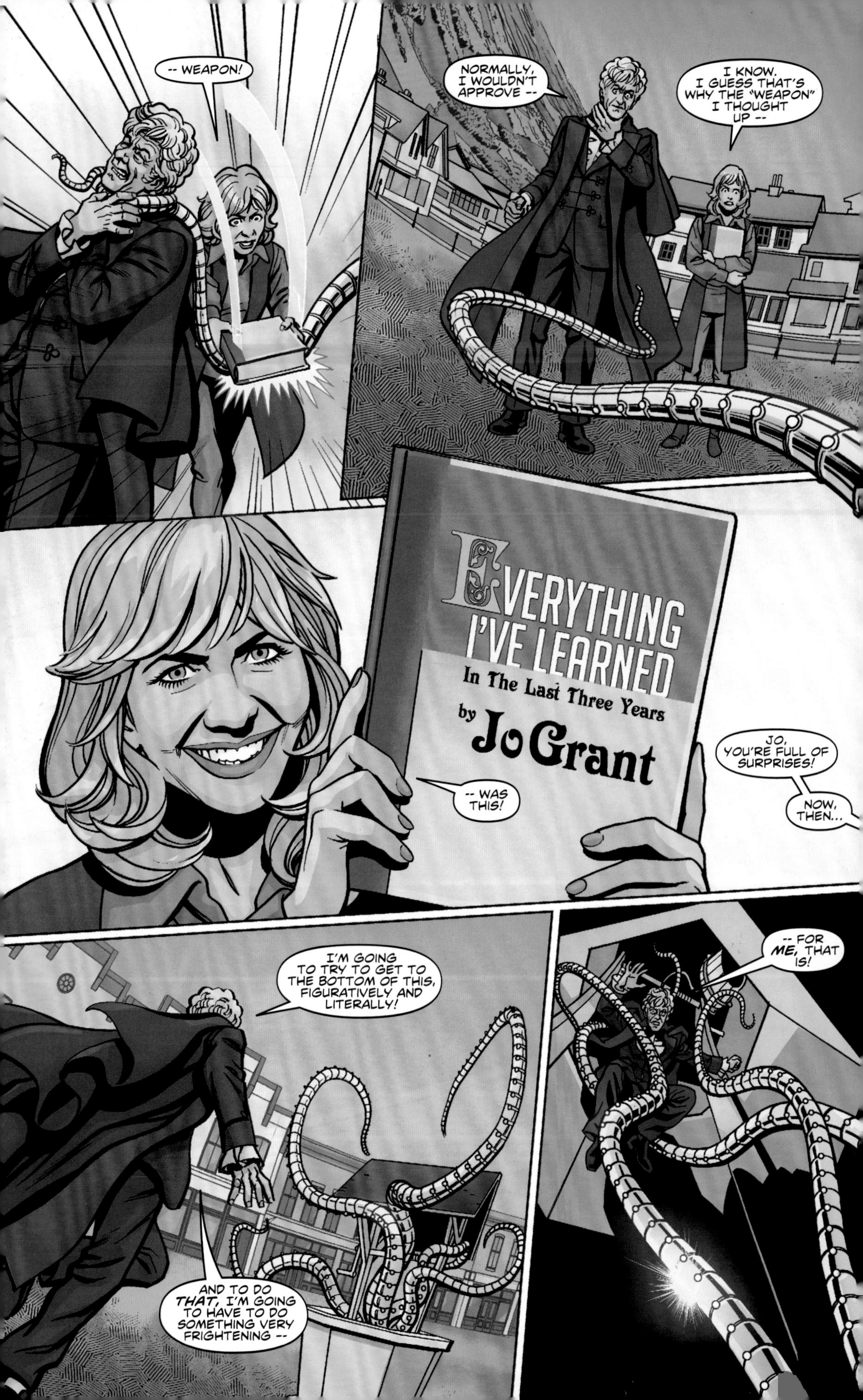

-- WEAPON!
NORMALLY, I WOULDN'T APPROVE --
I KNOW. I GUESS THAT'S WHY THE "WEAPON" I THOUGHT UP --
EVERYTHING I'VE LEARNED
In The Last Three Years
by Jo Grant
-- WAS THIS!
JO, YOU'RE FULL OF SURPRISES!
NOW, THEN...
I'M GOING TO TRY TO GET TO THE BOTTOM OF THIS, FIGURATIVELY AND LITERALLY!
AND TO DO THAT, I'M GOING TO HAVE TO DO SOMETHING VERY FRIGHTENING --
-- FOR ME, THAT IS!

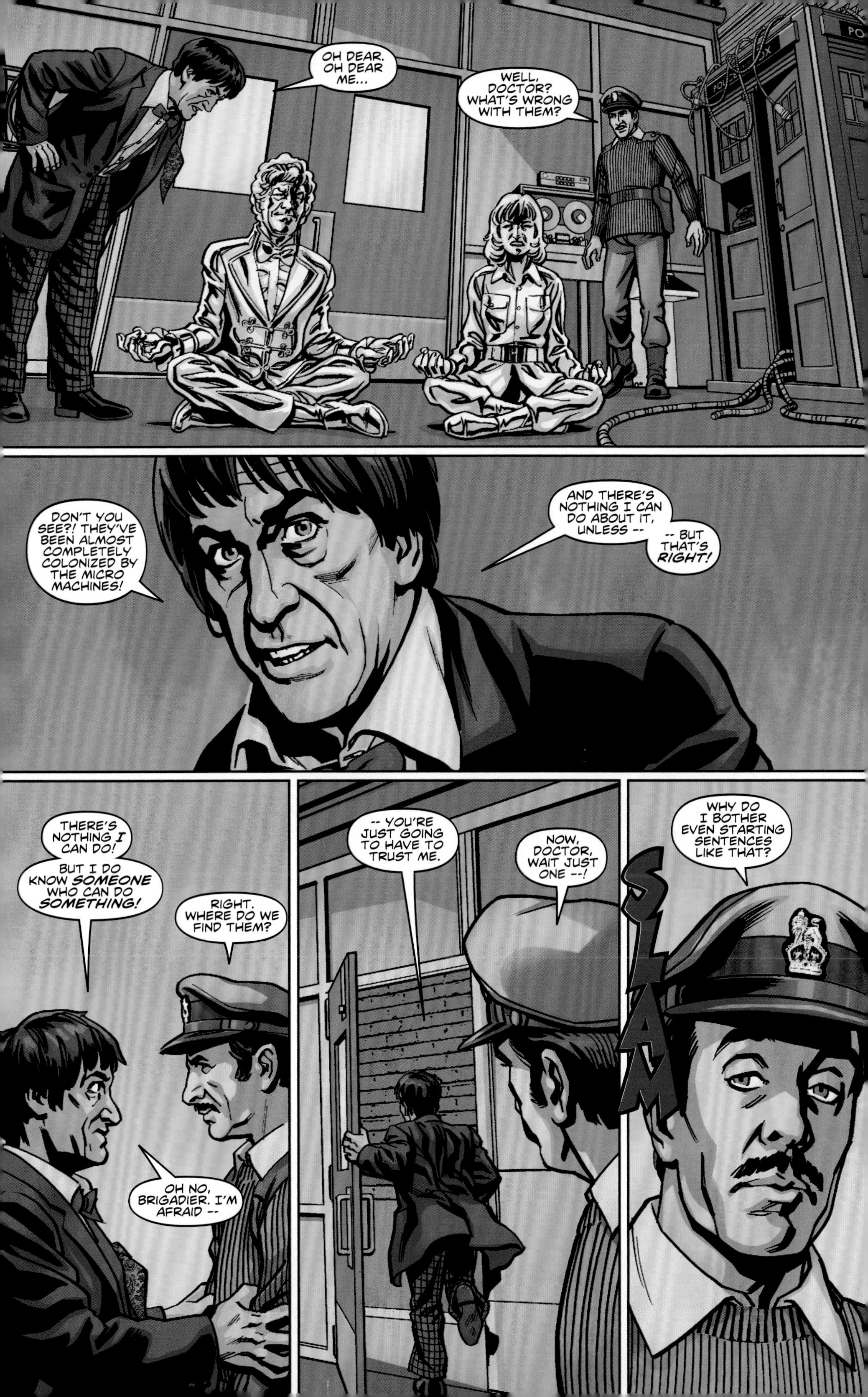
OH DEAR. OH DEAR ME...
WELL, DOCTOR? WHAT'S WRONG WITH THEM?
DON'T YOU SEE?! THEY'VE BEEN ALMOST COMPLETELY COLONIZED BY THE MICRO MACHINES!
AND THERE'S NOTHING I CAN DO ABOUT IT, UNLESS --
-- BUT THAT'S RIGHT!
THERE'S NOTHING I CAN DO!
BUT I DO KNOW SOMEONE WHO CAN DO SOMETHING!
RIGHT. WHERE DO WE FIND THEM?
OH NO, BRIGADIER. I'M AFRAID --
-- YOU'RE JUST GOING TO HAVE TO TRUST ME.
NOW, DOCTOR, WAIT JUST ONE --!
SLAM
WHY DO I BOTHER EVEN STARTING SENTENCES LIKE THAT?

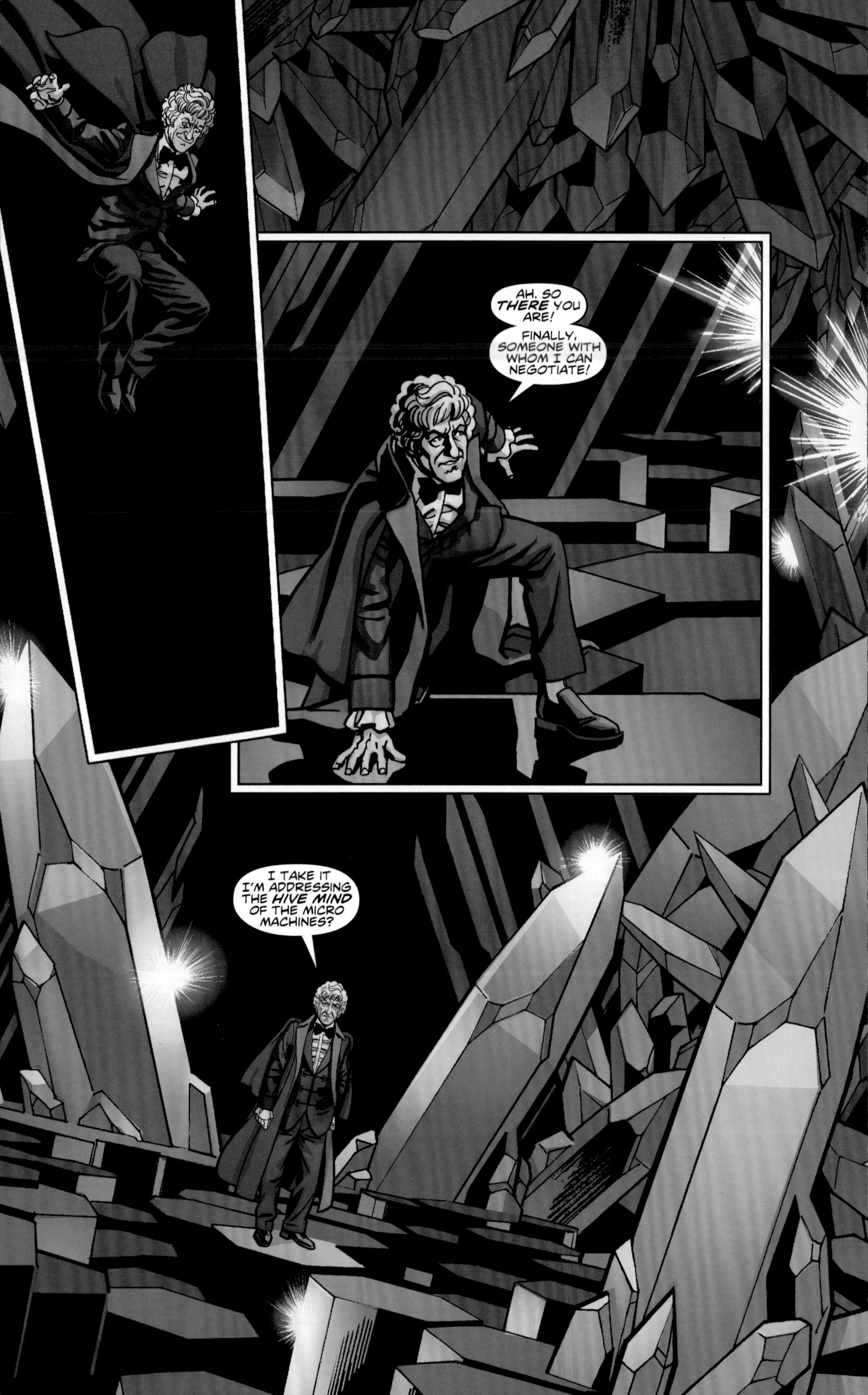
AH. SO THERE YOU ARE!
FINALLY, SOMEONE WITH WHOM I CAN NEGOTIATE!
I TAKE IT I'M ADDRESSING THE HIVE MIND OF THE MICRO MACHINES?

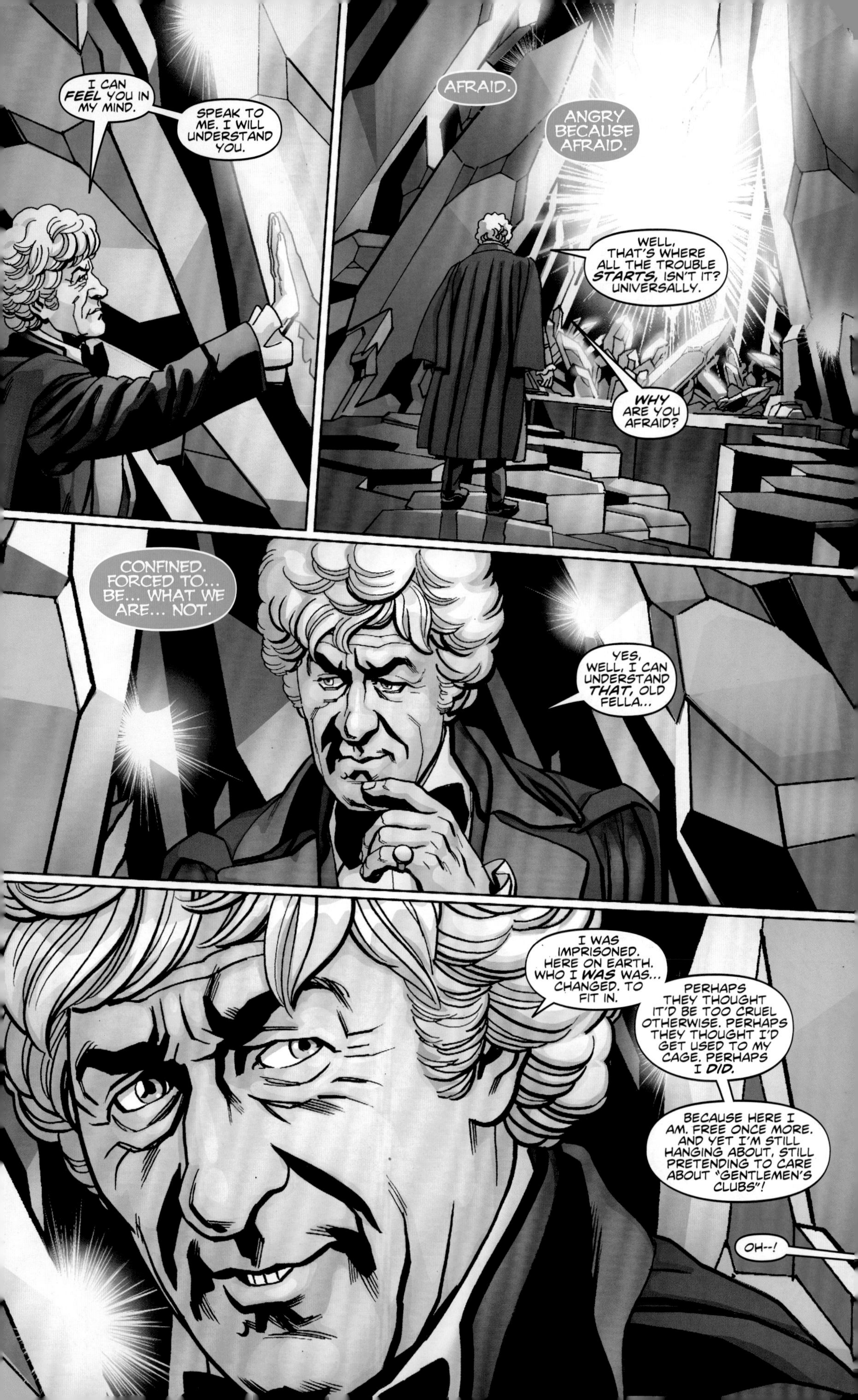
I CAN FEEL YOU IN MY MIND.
SPEAK TO ME. I WILL UNDERSTAND YOU.
AFRAID.
ANGRY BECAUSE AFRAID.
WELL, THAT'S WHERE ALL THE TROUBLE STARTS, ISN'T IT? UNIVERSALLY.
WHY ARE YOU AFRAID?
CONFINED. FORCED TO... BE... WHAT WE ARE... NOT.
YES, WELL, I CAN UNDERSTAND THAT, OLD FELLA...
I WAS IMPRISONED. HERE ON EARTH. WHO I WAS WAS... CHANGED. TO FIT IN.
PERHAPS THEY THOUGHT IT'D BE TOO CRUEL OTHERWISE. PERHAPS THEY THOUGHT I'D GET USED TO MY CAGE. PERHAPS I DID.
BECAUSE HERE I AM. FREE ONCE MORE. AND YET I'M STILL HANGING ABOUT, STILL PRETENDING TO CARE ABOUT "GENTLEMEN'S CLUBS"!
OH--!

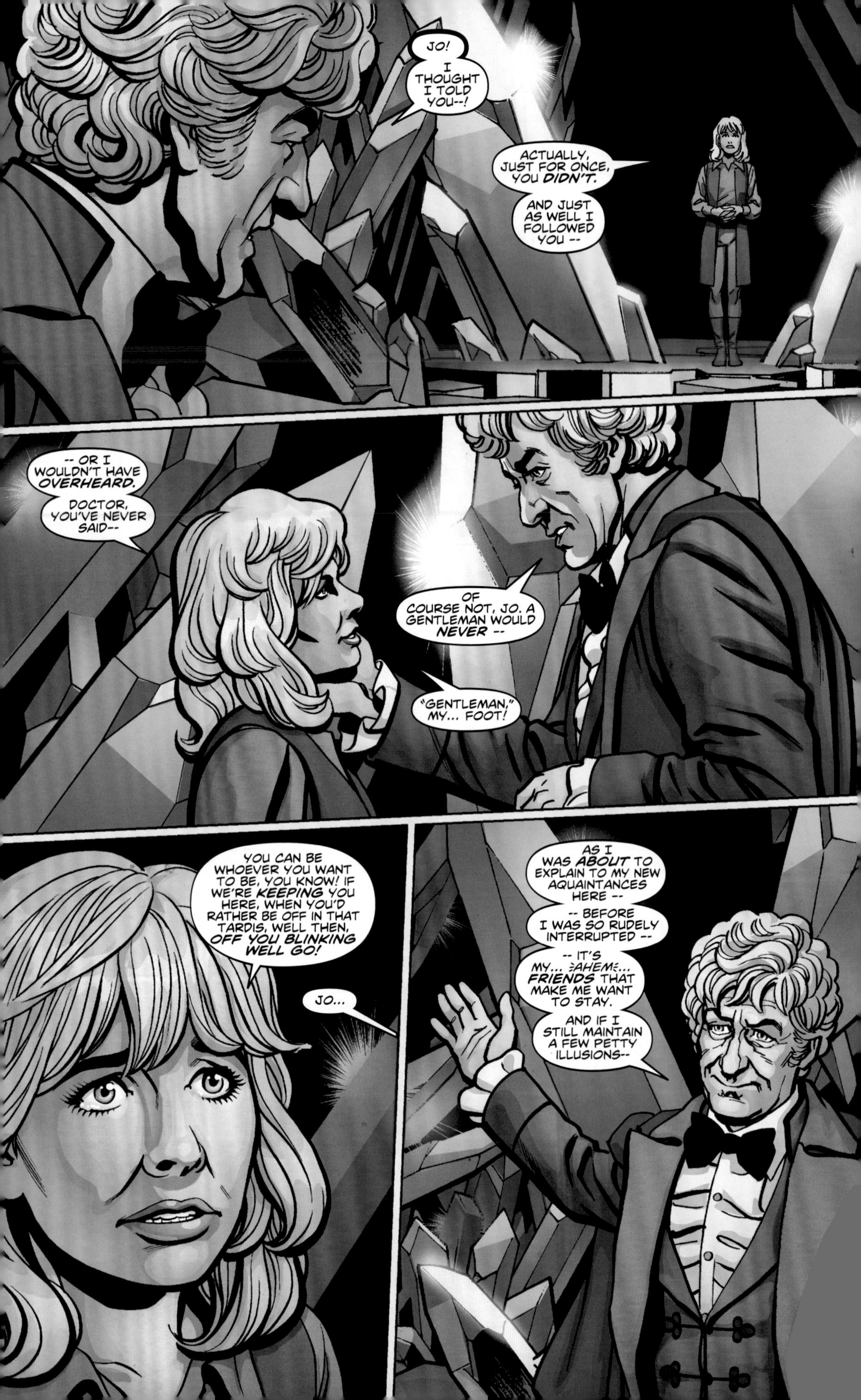
JO! I THOUGHT I TOLD YOU--!
ACTUALLY, JUST FOR ONCE, YOU DIDN'T.
AND JUST AS WELL I FOLLOWED YOU --
-- OR I WOULDN'T HAVE OVERHEARD.
DOCTOR, YOU'VE NEVER SAID--
OF COURSE NOT, JO. A GENTLEMAN WOULD NEVER --
"GENTLEMAN," MY... FOOT!
YOU CAN BE WHOEVER YOU WANT TO BE, YOU KNOW! IF WE'RE KEEPING YOU HERE, WHEN YOU'D RATHER BE OFF IN THAT TARDIS, WELL THEN, OFF YOU BLINKING WELL GO!
JO...
AS I WAS ABOUT TO EXPLAIN TO MY NEW AQUAINTANCES HERE --
-- BEFORE I WAS SO RUDELY INTERRUPTED --
-- IT'S MY... AHEM... FRIENDS THAT MAKE ME WANT TO STAY.
AND IF I STILL MAINTAIN A FEW PETTY ILLUSIONS--

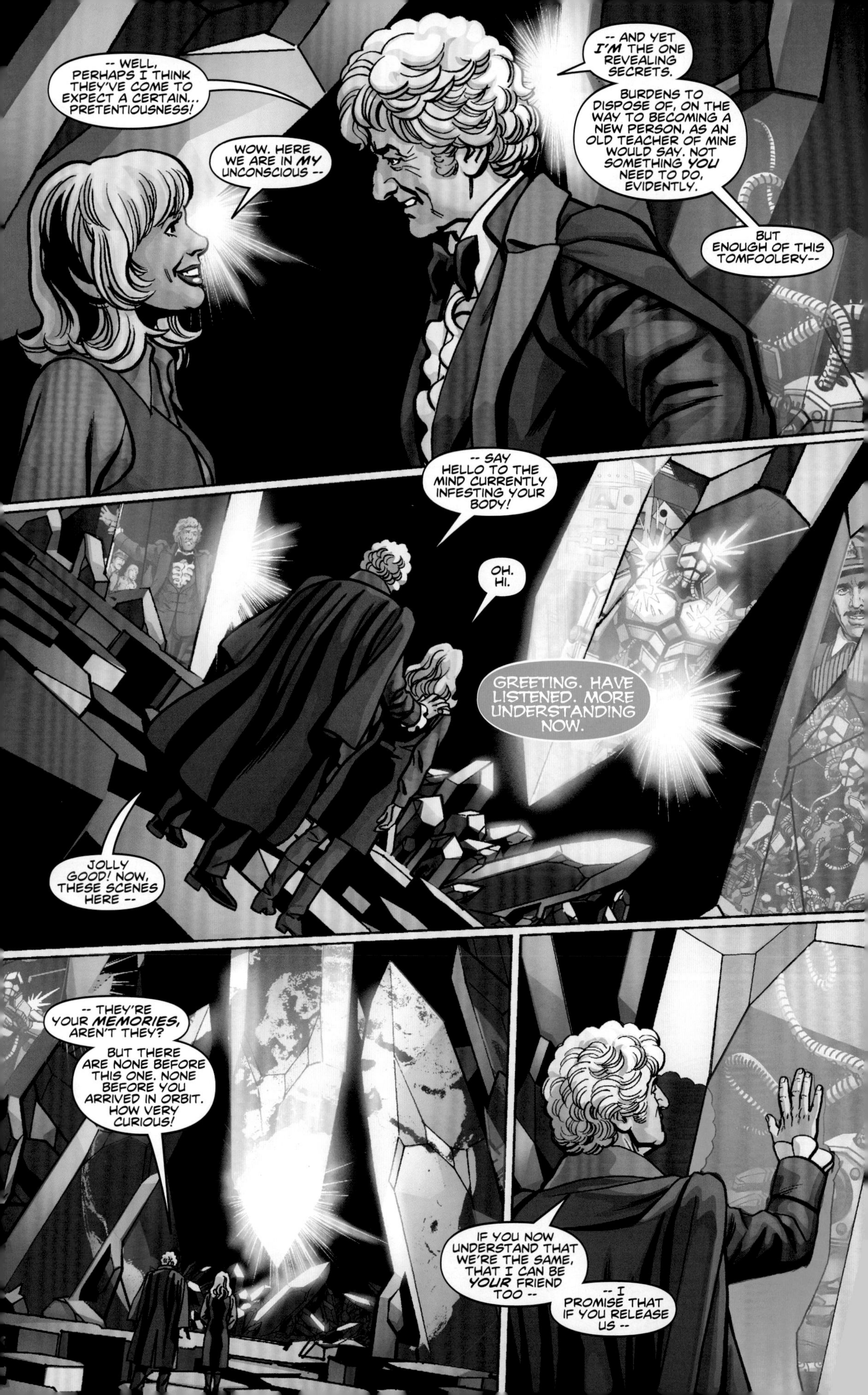
-- WELL, PERHAPS I THINK THEY'VE COME TO EXPECT A CERTAIN... PRETENTIOUSNESS!
WOW. HERE WE ARE IN MY UNCONSCIOUS --
-- AND YET I'M THE ONE REVEALING SECRETS.
BURDENS TO DISPOSE OF, ON THE WAY TO BECOMING A NEW PERSON, AS AN OLD TEACHER OF MINE WOULD SAY. NOT SOMETHING YOU NEED TO DO, EVIDENTLY.
BUT ENOUGH OF THIS TOMFOOLERY--
-- SAY HELLO TO THE MIND CURRENTLY INFESTING YOUR BODY!
OH. HI.
GREETING. HAVE LISTENED. MORE UNDERSTANDING NOW.
JOLLY GOOD! NOW, THESE SCENES HERE --
-- THEY'RE YOUR MEMORIES, AREN'T THEY?
BUT THERE ARE NONE BEFORE THIS ONE. NONE BEFORE YOU ARRIVED IN ORBIT. HOW VERY CURIOUS!
IF YOU NOW UNDERSTAND THAT WE'RE THE SAME, THAT I CAN BE YOUR FRIEND TOO --
-- I PROMISE THAT IF YOU RELEASE US --

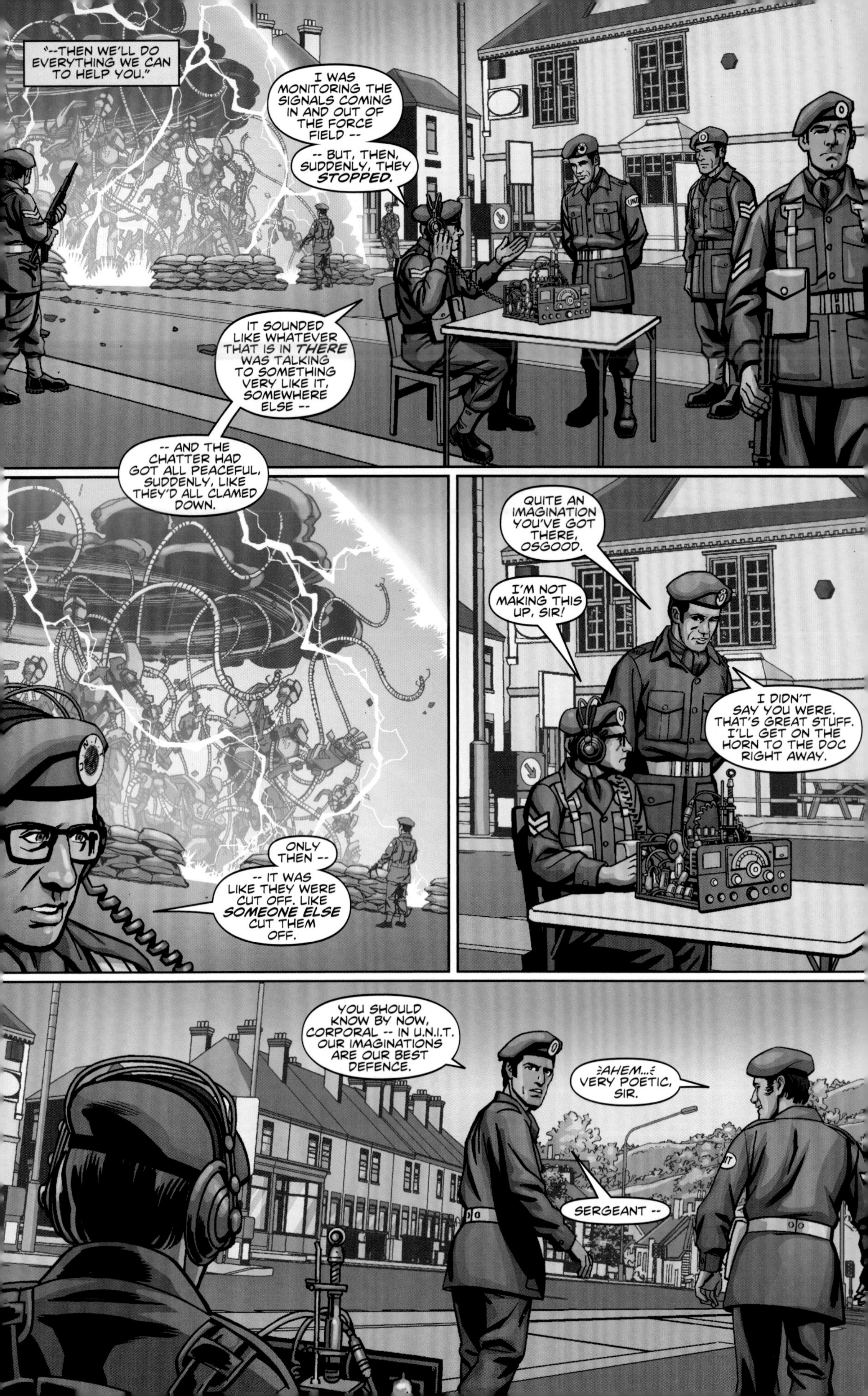
"--THEN WE'LL DO EVERYTHING WE CAN TO HELP YOU."
I WAS MONITORING THE SIGNALS COMING IN AND OUT OF THE FORCE FIELD --
-- BUT, THEN, SUDDENLY, THEY STOPPED.
IT SOUNDED LIKE WHATEVER THAT IS IN THERE WAS TALKING TO SOMETHING VERY LIKE IT, SOMEWHERE ELSE --
-- AND THE CHATTER HAD GOT ALL PEACEFUL, SUDDENLY, LIKE THEY'D ALL CLAMED DOWN.
ONLY THEN --
-- IT WAS LIKE THEY WERE CUT OFF. LIKE SOMEONE ELSE CUT THEM OFF.
QUITE AN IMAGINATION YOU'VE GOT THERE, OSGOOD.
I'M NOT MAKING THIS UP, SIR!
I DIDN'T SAY YOU WERE. THAT'S GREAT STUFF. I'LL GET ON THE HORN TO THE DOC RIGHT AWAY.
YOU SHOULD KNOW BY NOW, CORPORAL -- IN U.N.I.T. OUR IMAGINATIONS ARE OUR BEST DEFENCE.
AHEM... VERY POETIC, SIR.
SERGEANT --

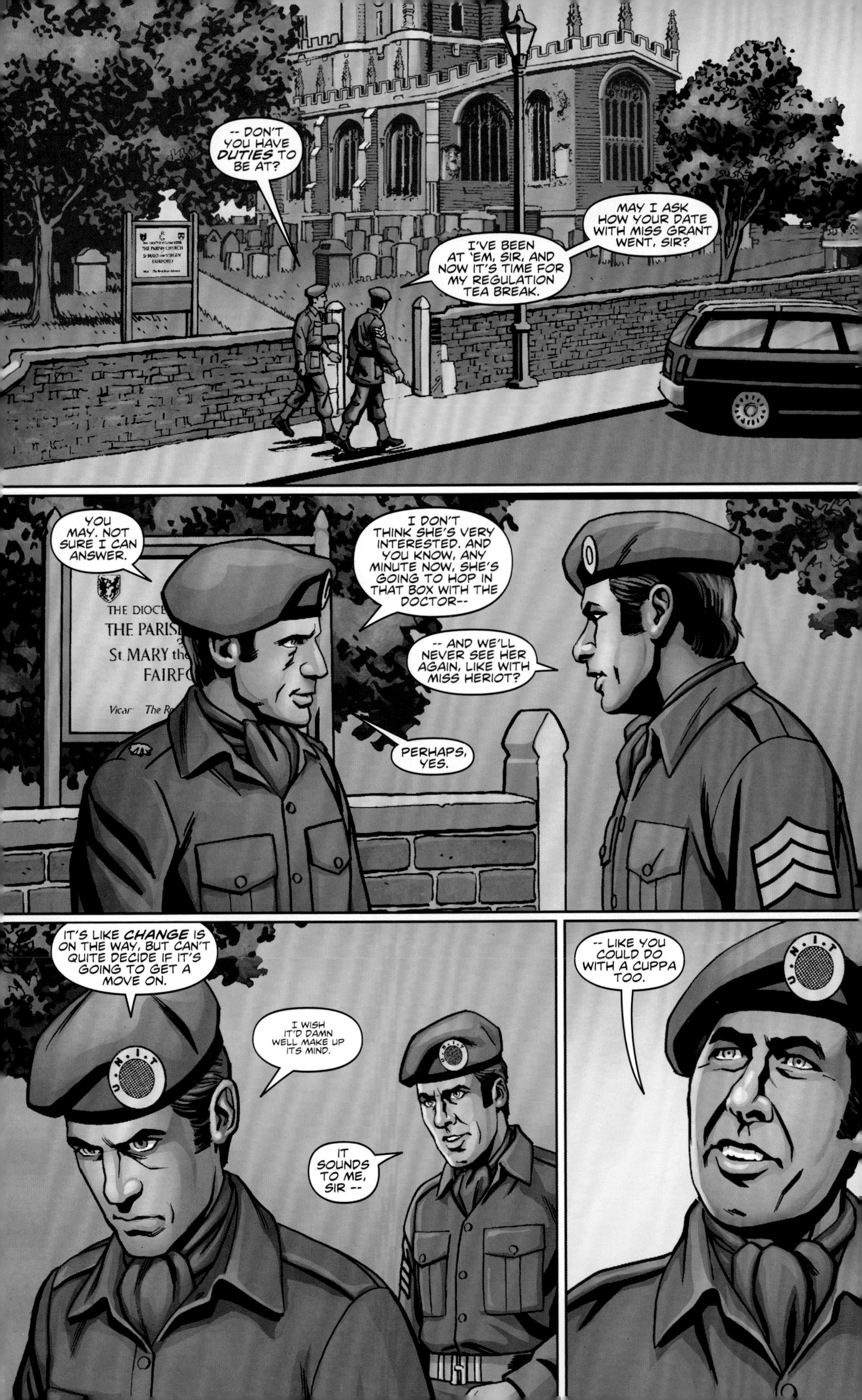
-- DON'T YOU HAVE *DUTIES* TO BE AT?
I'VE BEEN AT 'EM, SIR, AND NOW IT'S TIME FOR MY REGULATION TEA BREAK.
MAY I ASK HOW YOUR DATE WITH MISS GRANT WENT, SIR?
YOU MAY. NOT SURE I CAN ANSWER.
I DON'T THINK SHE'S VERY INTERESTED. AND YOU KNOW, ANY MINUTE NOW, SHE'S GOING TO HOP IN THAT BOX WITH THE DOCTOR--
-- AND WE'LL NEVER SEE HER AGAIN, LIKE WITH MISS HERIOT?
PERHAPS, YES.
IT'S LIKE *CHANGE* IS ON THE WAY, BUT CAN'T QUITE DECIDE IF IT'S GOING TO GET A MOVE ON.
I WISH IT'D DAMN WELL MAKE UP ITS MIND.
IT SOUNDS TO ME, SIR --
-- LIKE YOU COULD DO WITH A CUPPA TOO.

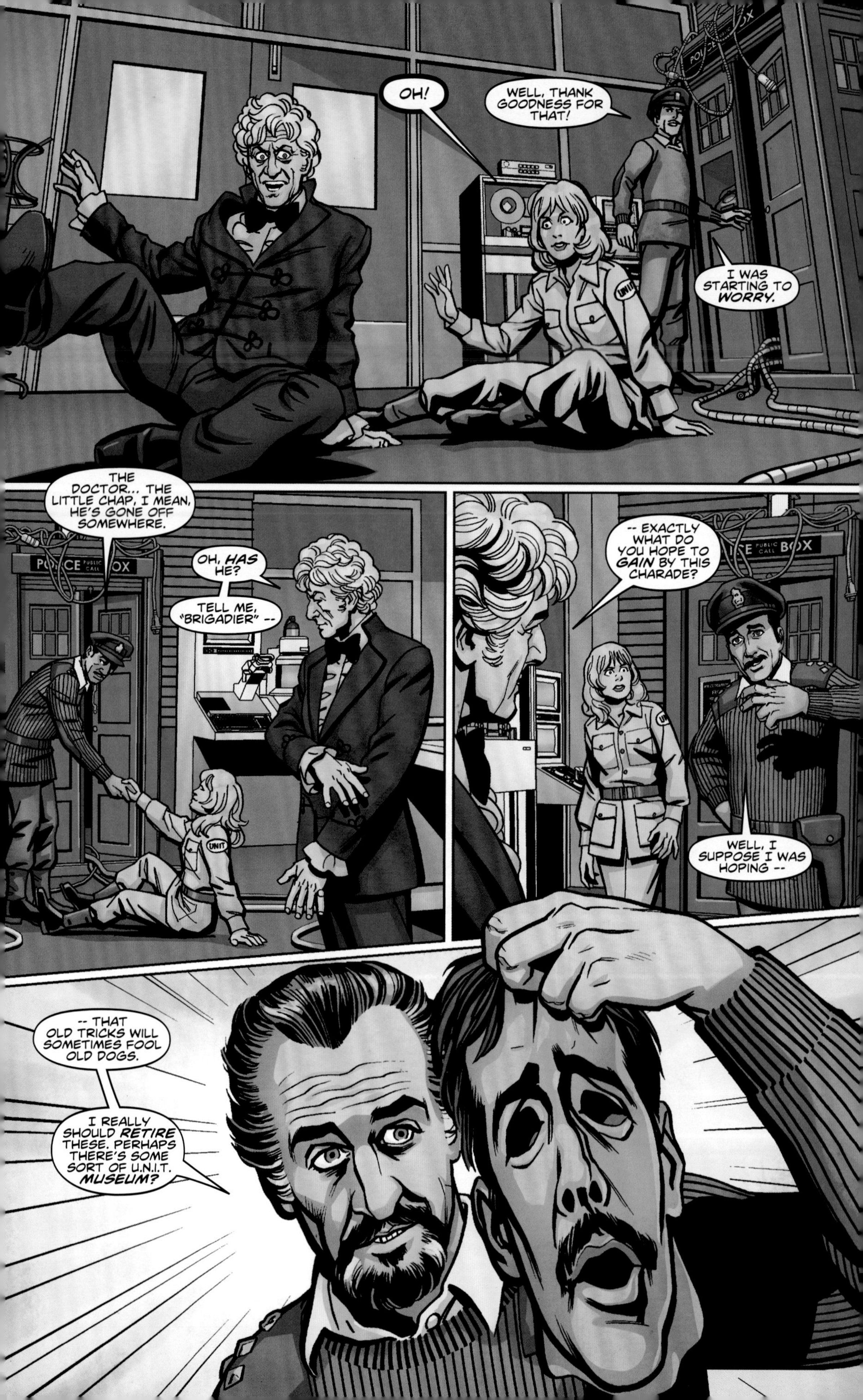
OH!
WELL, THANK GOODNESS FOR THAT!
I WAS STARTING TO WORRY.
THE DOCTOR... THE LITTLE CHAP, I MEAN, HE'S GONE OFF SOMEWHERE.
OH, HAS HE?
TELL ME, "BRIGADIER" --
-- EXACTLY WHAT DO YOU HOPE TO GAIN BY THIS CHARADE?
WELL, I SUPPOSE I WAS HOPING --
-- THAT OLD TRICKS WILL SOMETIMES FOOL OLD DOGS.
I REALLY SHOULD RETIRE THESE. PERHAPS THERE'S SOME SORT OF U.N.I.T. MUSEUM?

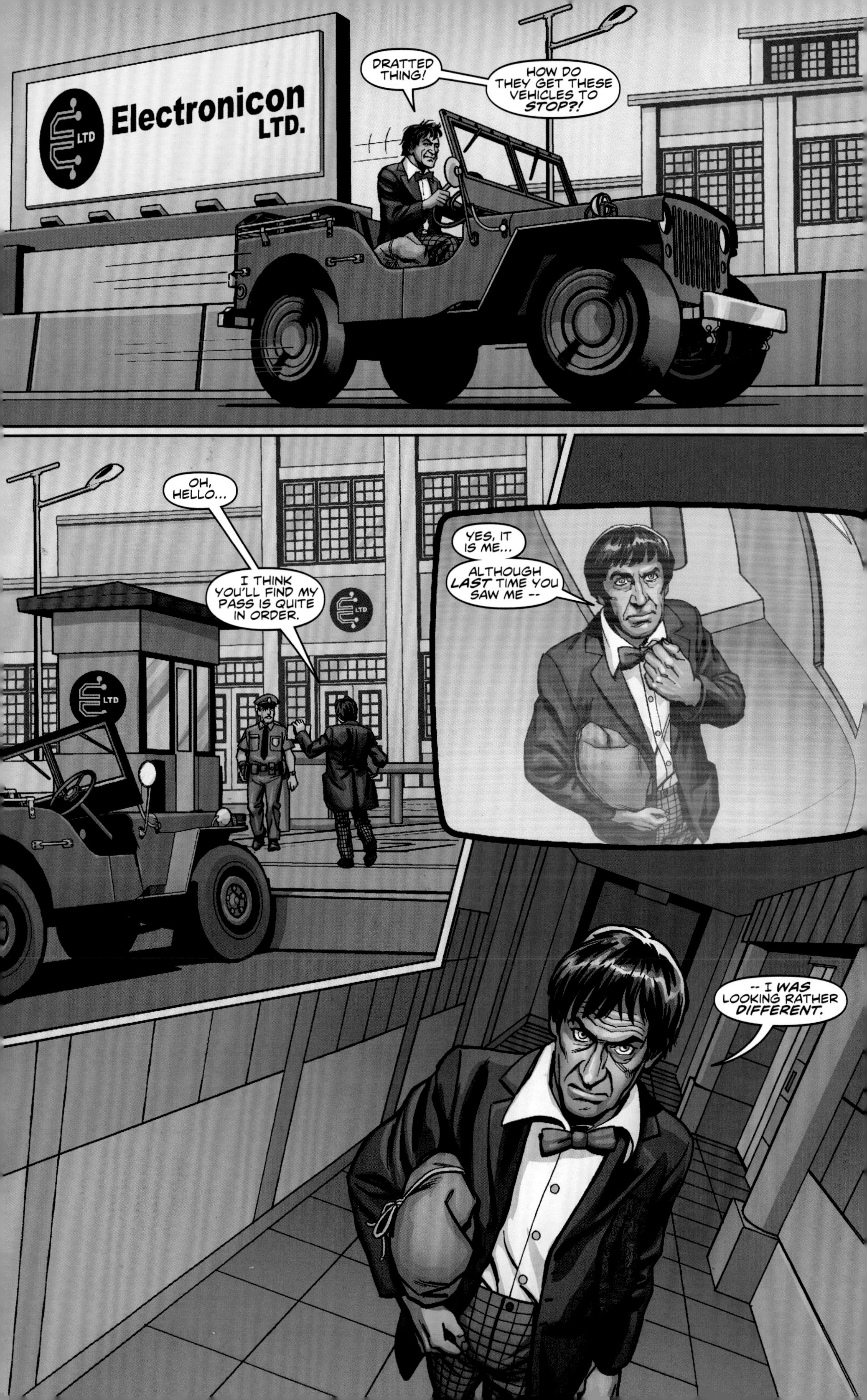
Electronicon
LTD.
LTD
DRATTED THING!
HOW DO THEY GET THESE VEHICLES TO STOP?!
OH, HELLO...
I THINK YOU'LL FIND MY PASS IS QUITE IN ORDER.
LTD
LTD
YES, IT IS ME...
ALTHOUGH LAST TIME YOU SAW ME --
-- I WAS LOOKING RATHER DIFFERENT.

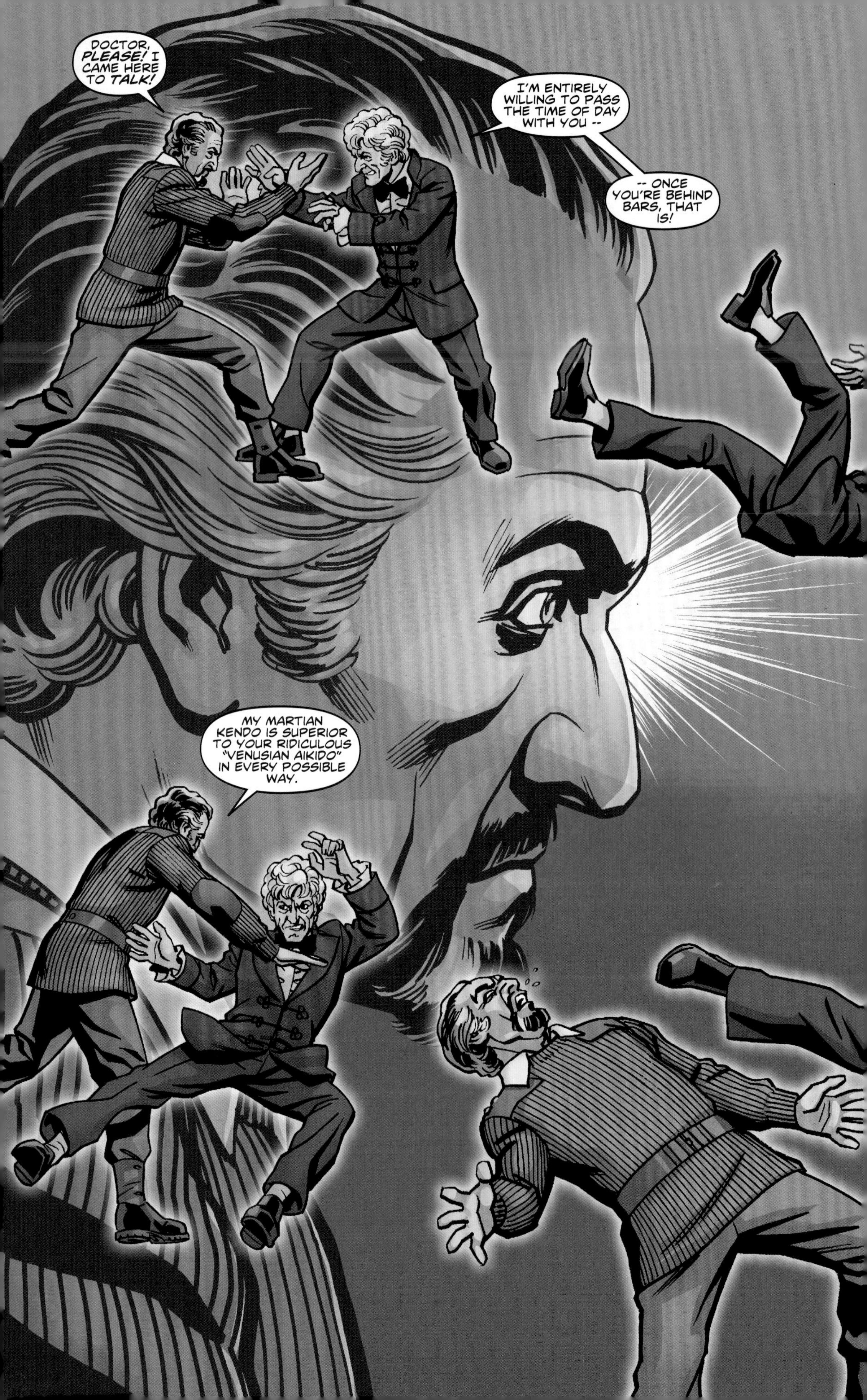
DOCTOR, PLEASE! I CAME HERE TO TALK!
I'M ENTIRELY WILLING TO PASS THE TIME OF DAY WITH YOU --
-- ONCE YOU'RE BEHIND BARS, THAT IS!
MY MARTIAN KENDO IS SUPERIOR TO YOUR RIDICULOUS "VENUSIAN AIKIDO" IN EVERY POSSIBLE WAY.

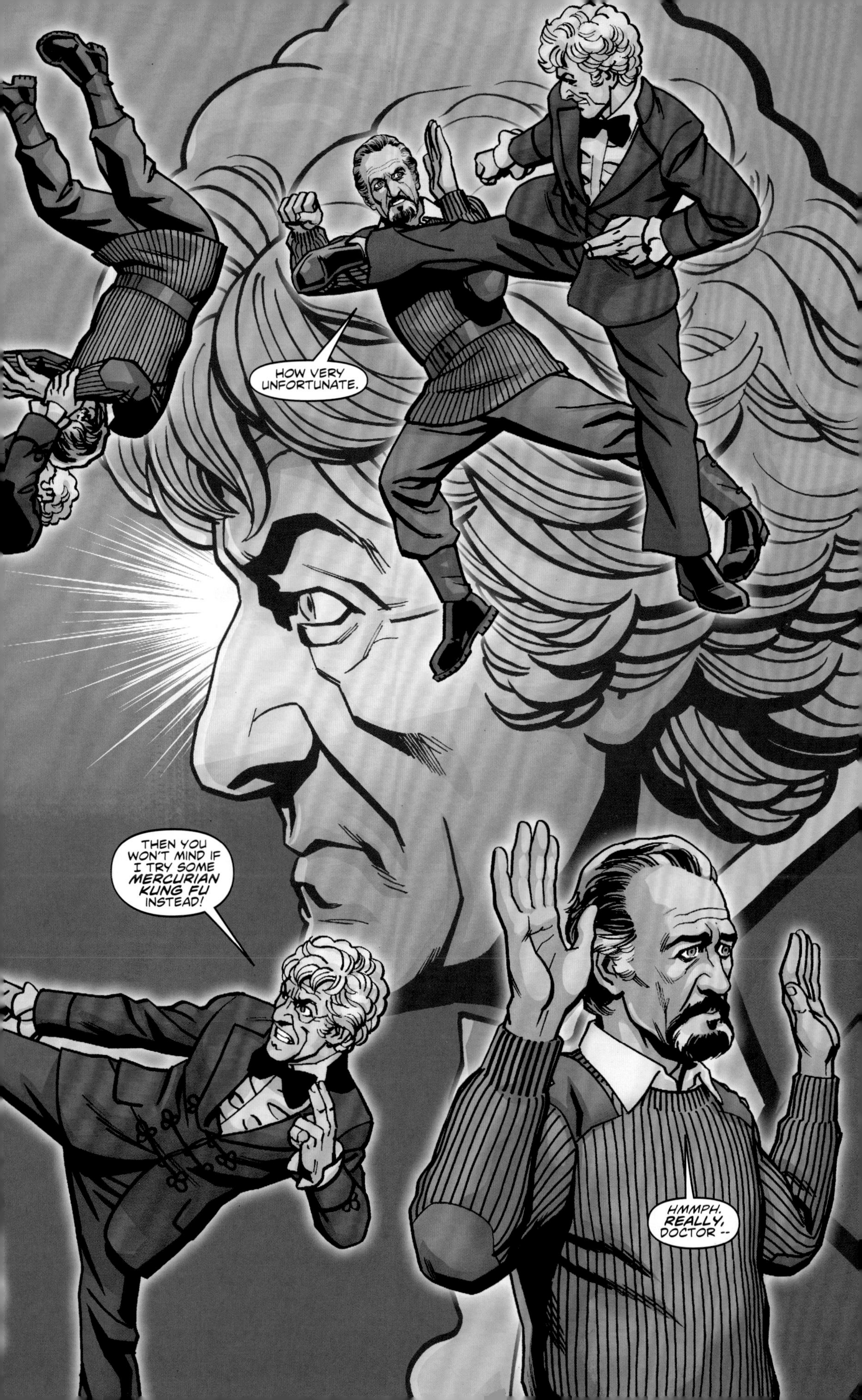
HOW VERY UNFORTUNATE.
THEN YOU WON'T MIND IF I TRY SOME *MERCURIAN KUNG FU* INSTEAD!
HMMPH. *REALLY,* DOCTOR --

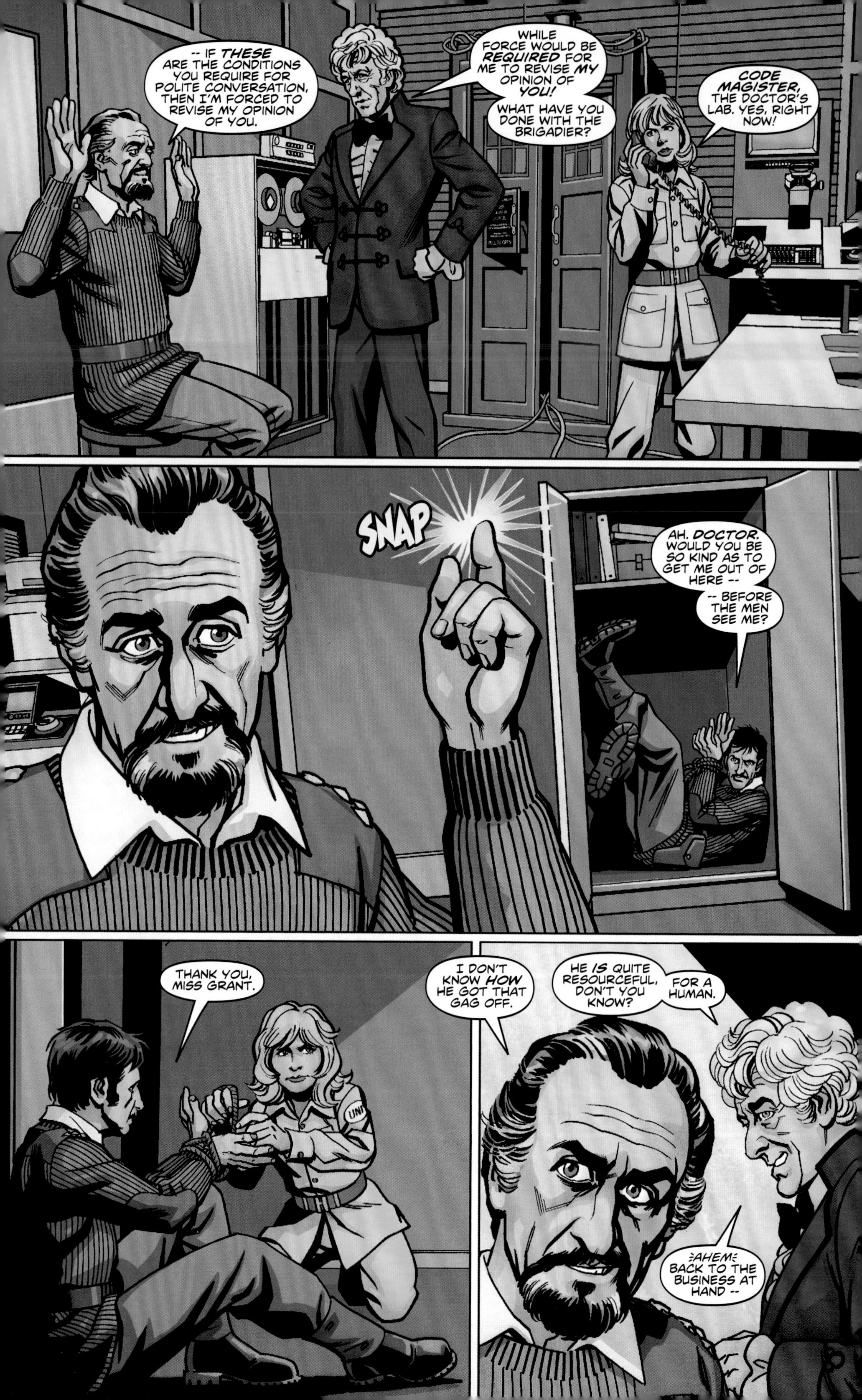
-- IF THESE ARE THE CONDITIONS YOU REQUIRE FOR POLITE CONVERSATION, THEN I'M FORCED TO REVISE MY OPINION OF YOU.
WHILE FORCE WOULD BE REQUIRED FOR ME TO REVISE MY OPINION OF YOU!
WHAT HAVE YOU DONE WITH THE BRIGADIER?
CODE MAGISTER, THE DOCTOR'S LAB. YES, RIGHT NOW!
SNAP
AH. DOCTOR. WOULD YOU BE SO KIND AS TO GET ME OUT OF HERE --
-- BEFORE THE MEN SEE ME?
THANK YOU, MISS GRANT.
I DON'T KNOW HOW HE GOT THAT GAG OFF.
HE IS QUITE RESOURCEFUL, DON'T YOU KNOW?
FOR A HUMAN.
AHEM
BACK TO THE BUSINESS AT HAND --

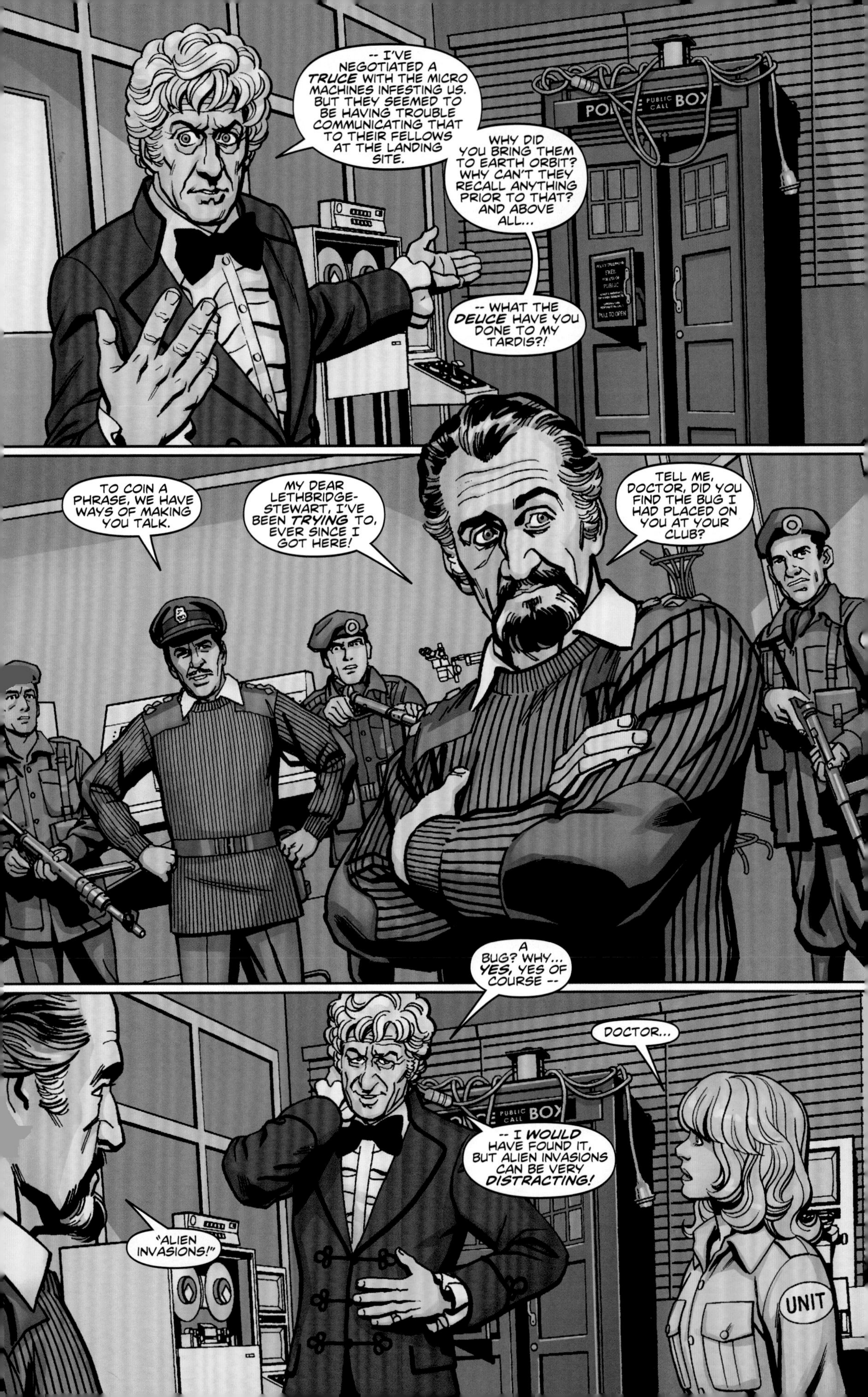
-- I'VE NEGOTIATED A TRUCE WITH THE MICRO MACHINES INFESTING US. BUT THEY SEEMED TO BE HAVING TROUBLE COMMUNICATING THAT TO THEIR FELLOWS AT THE LANDING SITE.
WHY DID YOU BRING THEM TO EARTH ORBIT? WHY CAN'T THEY RECALL ANYTHING PRIOR TO THAT? AND ABOVE ALL...
-- WHAT THE DEUCE HAVE YOU DONE TO MY TARDIS?!
POLICE PUBLIC CALL BOX
TO COIN A PHRASE, WE HAVE WAYS OF MAKING YOU TALK.
MY DEAR LETHBRIDGE-STEWART, I'VE BEEN TRYING TO, EVER SINCE I GOT HERE!
TELL ME, DOCTOR, DID YOU FIND THE BUG I HAD PLACED ON YOU AT YOUR CLUB?
A BUG? WHY... YES, YES OF COURSE --
DOCTOR...
-- I WOULD HAVE FOUND IT, BUT ALIEN INVASIONS CAN BE VERY DISTRACTING!
"ALIEN INVASIONS!"
UNIT

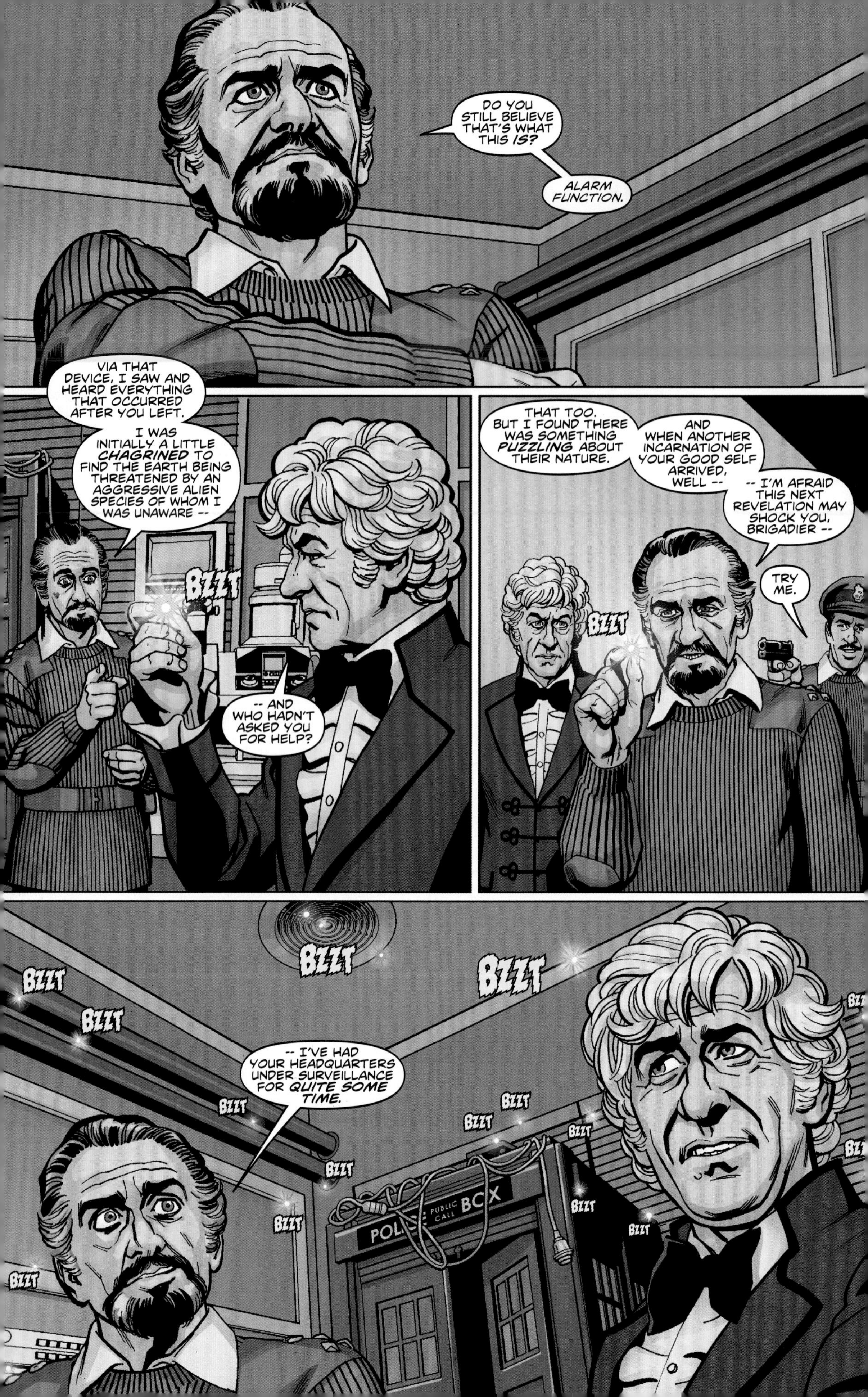
DO YOU STILL BELIEVE THAT'S WHAT THIS *IS?*
ALARM FUNCTION.
VIA THAT DEVICE, I SAW AND HEARD EVERYTHING THAT OCCURRED AFTER YOU LEFT.
I WAS INITIALLY A LITTLE *CHAGRINED* TO FIND THE EARTH BEING THREATENED BY AN AGGRESSIVE ALIEN SPECIES OF WHOM I WAS UNAWARE --
BZZT
-- AND WHO HADN'T ASKED YOU FOR HELP?
THAT TOO. BUT I FOUND THERE WAS SOMETHING *PUZZLING* ABOUT THEIR NATURE.
AND WHEN ANOTHER INCARNATION OF YOUR GOOD SELF ARRIVED, WELL --
-- I'M AFRAID THIS NEXT REVELATION MAY SHOCK YOU, BRIGADIER --
TRY ME.
BZZT
BZZT
BZZT
BZZT
BZZT
-- I'VE HAD YOUR HEADQUARTERS UNDER SURVEILLANCE FOR *QUITE SOME TIME.*
BZZT
BZZT
BZZT
BZZT
BZZT
BZZT
BZZT
BZZT
POLICE PUBLIC CALL BOX

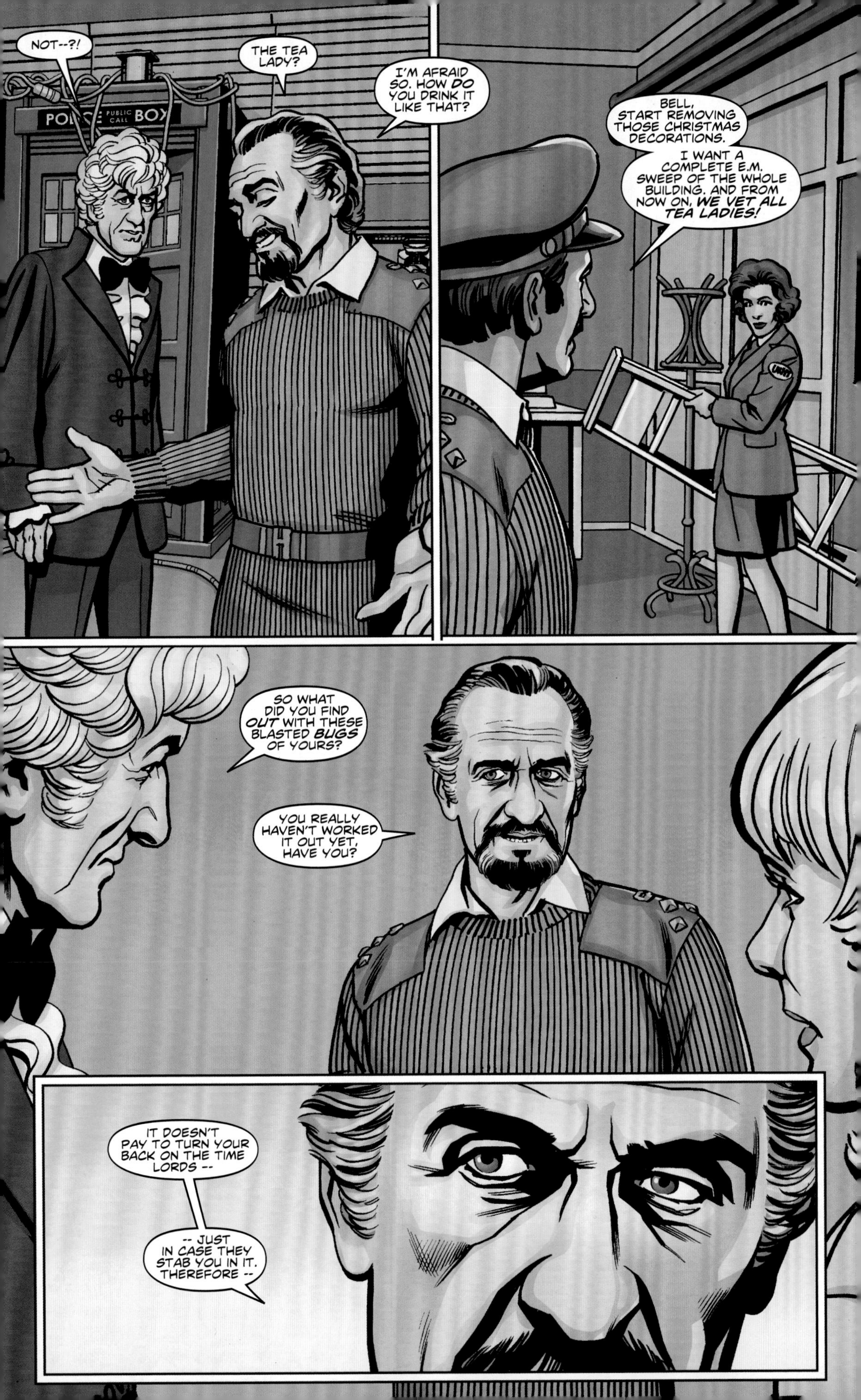
NOT--?!
THE TEA LADY?
I'M AFRAID SO. HOW DO YOU DRINK IT LIKE THAT?
POLICE PUBLIC CALL BOX
BELL, START REMOVING THOSE CHRISTMAS DECORATIONS.
I WANT A COMPLETE E.M. SWEEP OF THE WHOLE BUILDING. AND FROM NOW ON, WE VET ALL TEA LADIES!
SO WHAT DID YOU FIND OUT WITH THESE BLASTED BUGS OF YOURS?
YOU REALLY HAVEN'T WORKED IT OUT YET, HAVE YOU?
IT DOESN'T PAY TO TURN YOUR BACK ON THE TIME LORDS --
-- JUST IN CASE THEY STAB YOU IN IT. THEREFORE --

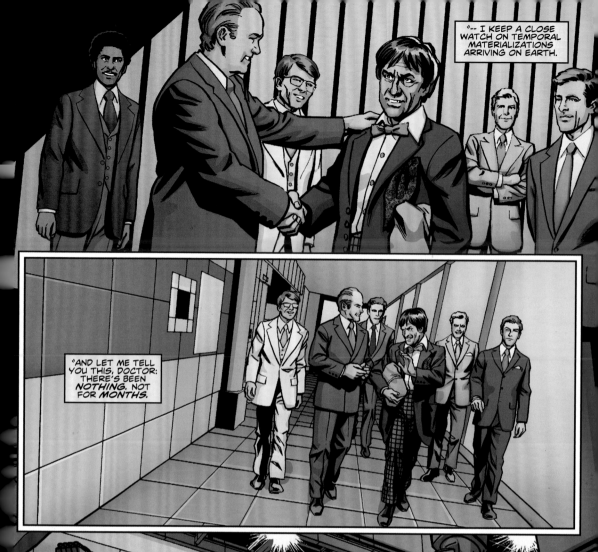

"-- I KEEP A CLOSE WATCH ON TEMPORAL MATERIALIZATIONS ARRIVING ON EARTH.

"AND LET ME TELL YOU THIS, DOCTOR: THERE'S BEEN *NOTHING.* NOT FOR *MONTHS.*

"SO HOW, *EXACTLY,* DID YOUR FORMER SELF GET HERE?"

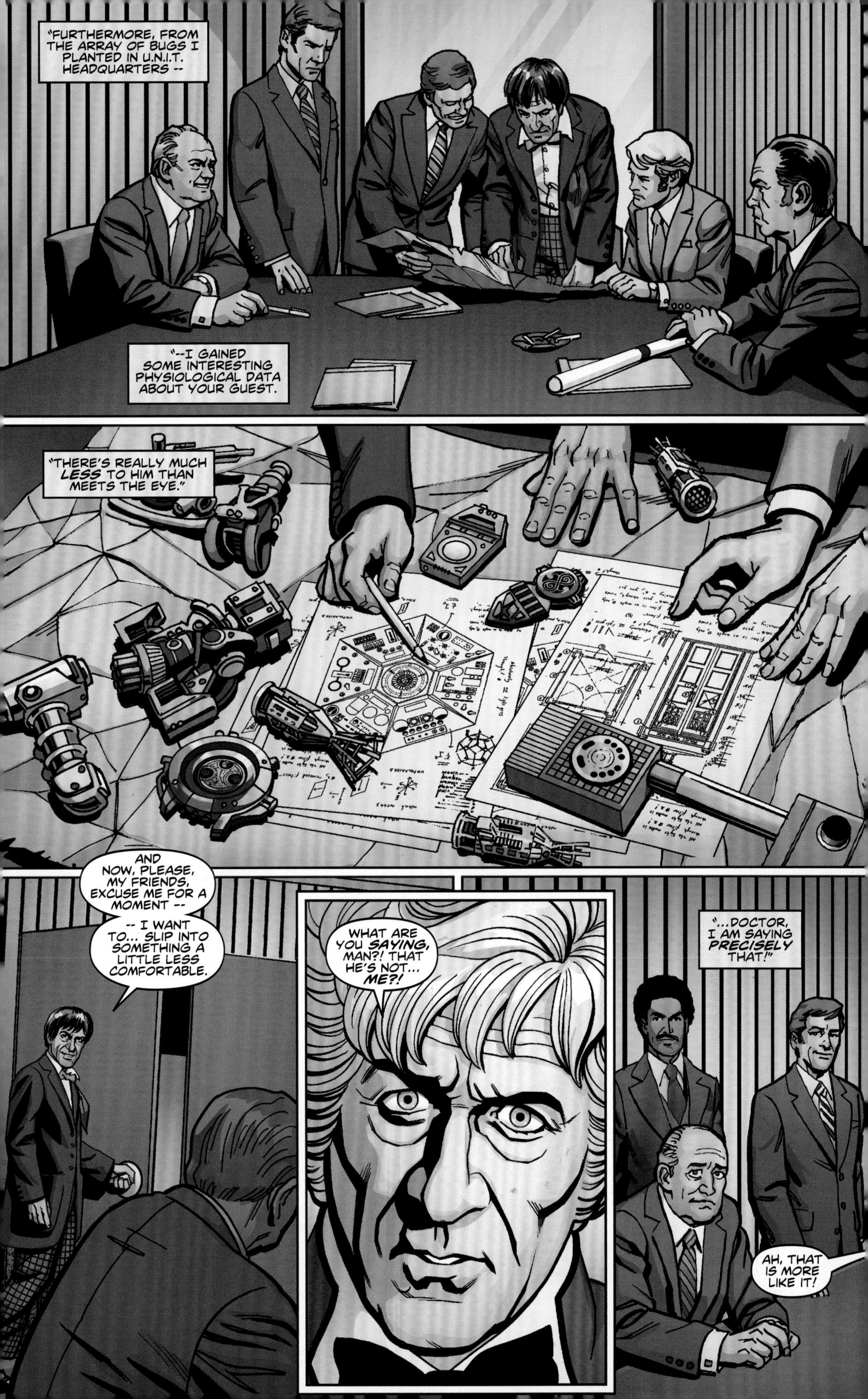
"FURTHERMORE, FROM THE ARRAY OF BUGS I PLANTED IN U.N.I.T. HEADQUARTERS --
"--I GAINED SOME INTERESTING PHYSIOLOGICAL DATA ABOUT YOUR GUEST.
"THERE'S REALLY MUCH LESS TO HIM THAN MEETS THE EYE."
AND NOW, PLEASE, MY FRIENDS, EXCUSE ME FOR A MOMENT --
-- I WANT TO... SLIP INTO SOMETHING A LITTLE LESS COMFORTABLE.
WHAT ARE YOU SAYING, MAN?! THAT HE'S NOT... ME?!
"...DOCTOR, I AM SAYING PRECISELY THAT!"
AH, THAT IS MORE LIKE IT!

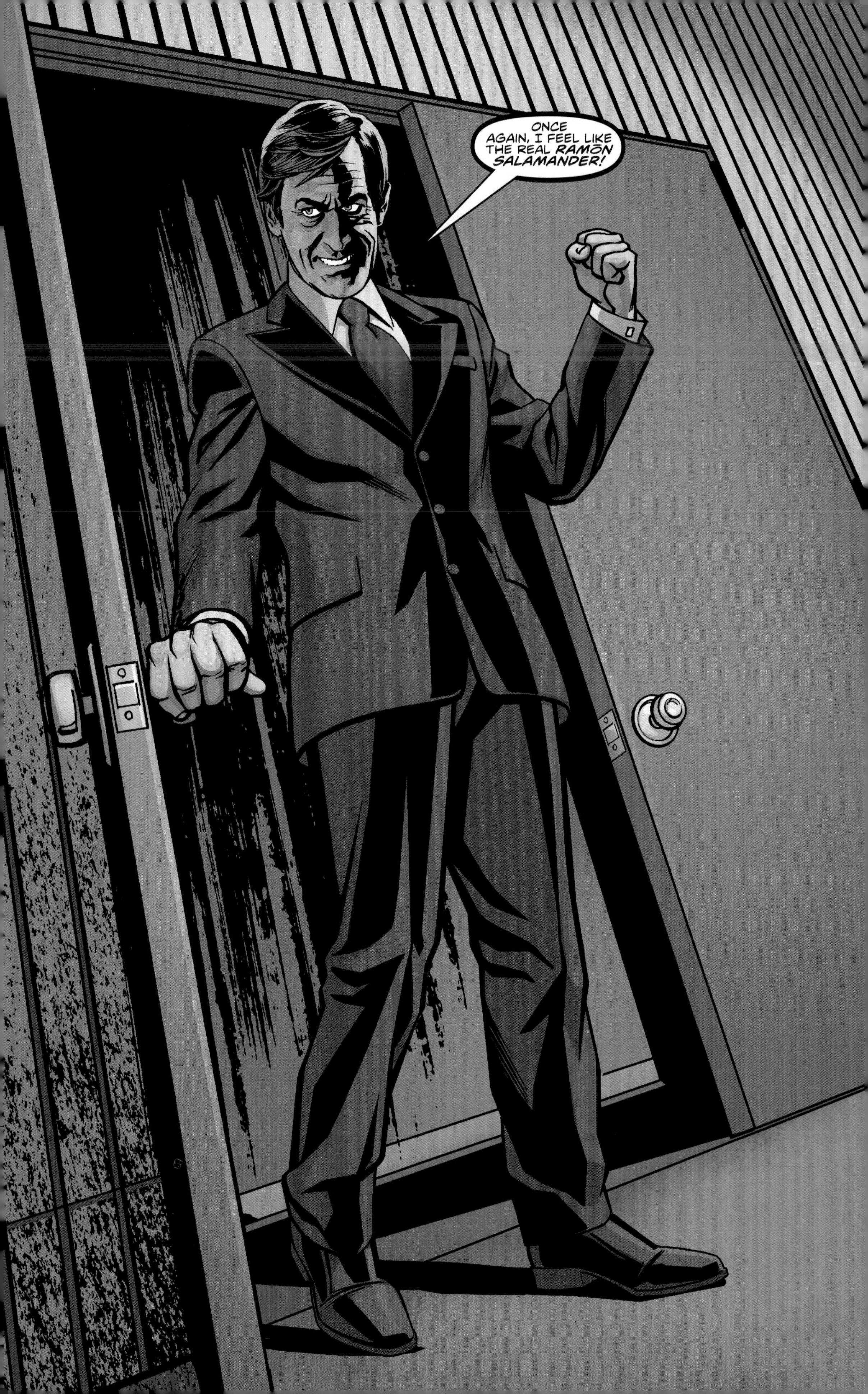
ONCE AGAIN, I FEEL LIKE THE REAL RAMŌN SALAMANDER!

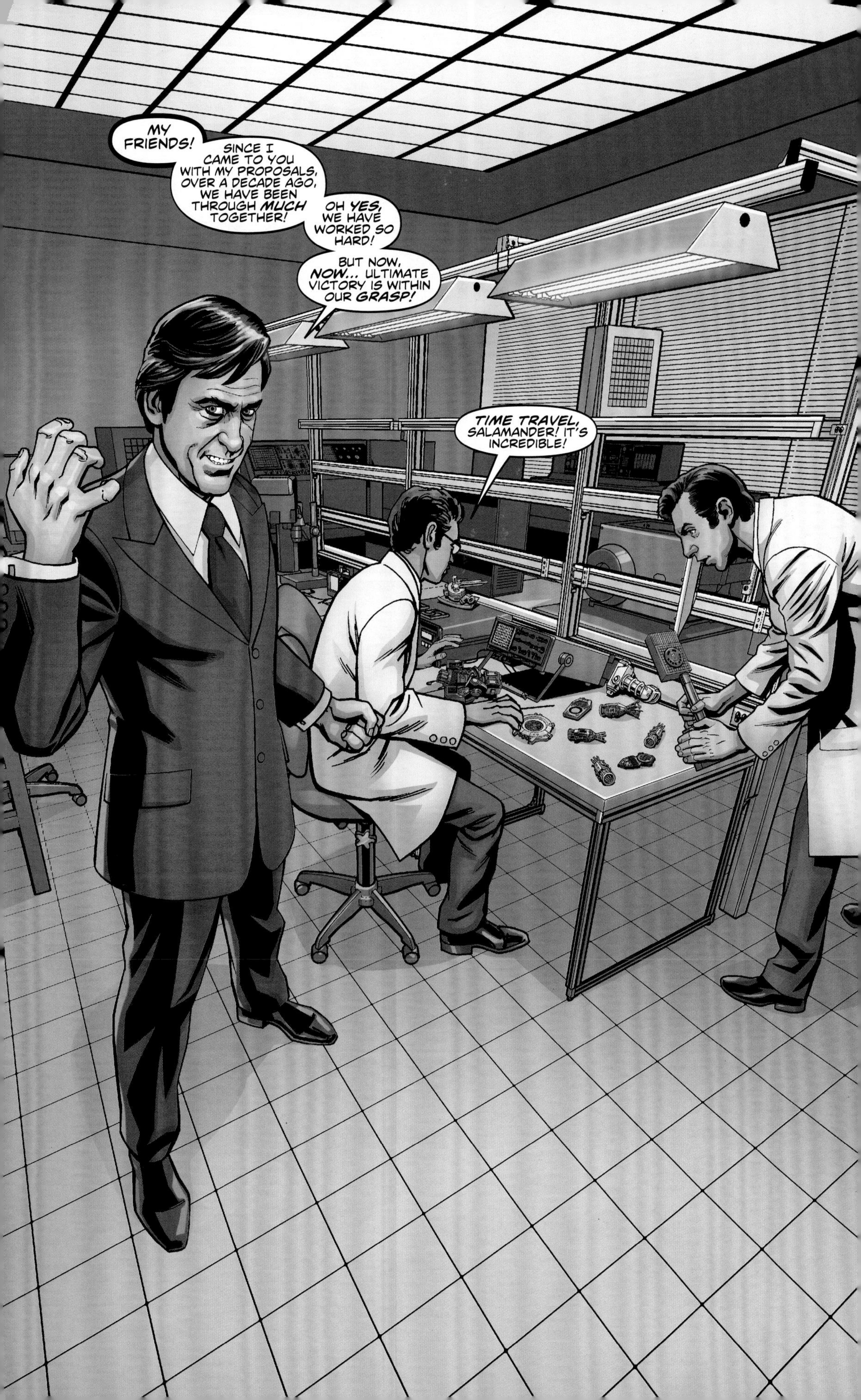
MY FRIENDS!
SINCE I CAME TO YOU WITH MY PROPOSALS, OVER A DECADE AGO, WE HAVE BEEN THROUGH MUCH TOGETHER!
OH YES, WE HAVE WORKED SO HARD!
BUT NOW, NOW... ULTIMATE VICTORY IS WITHIN OUR GRASP!
TIME TRAVEL, SALAMANDER! IT'S INCREDIBLE!

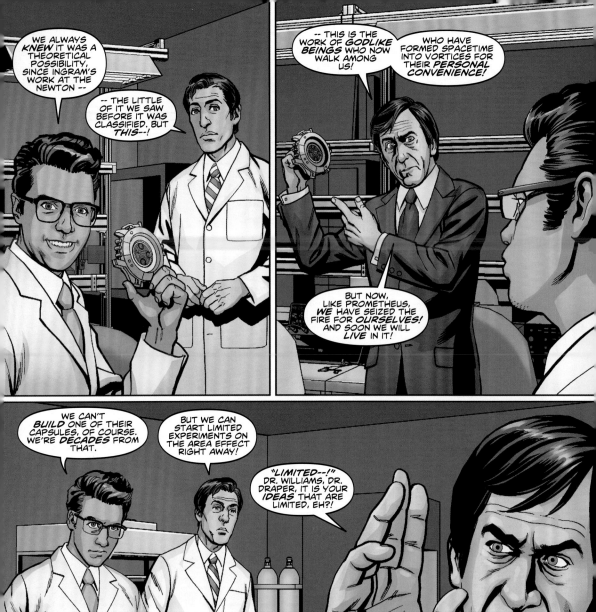

WE ALWAYS *KNEW* IT WAS A THEORETICAL POSSIBILITY, SINCE INGRAM'S WORK AT THE NEWTON --

-- THE LITTLE OF IT WE SAW BEFORE IT WAS CLASSIFIED. BUT *THIS*--!

-- THIS IS THE WORK OF *GODLIKE BEINGS* WHO NOW WALK AMONG US!

WHO HAVE FORMED SPACETIME INTO VORTICES FOR THEIR *PERSONAL CONVENIENCE!*

BUT NOW, LIKE PROMETHEUS, *WE* HAVE SEIZED THE FIRE FOR *OURSELVES!* AND SOON WE WILL *LIVE* IN IT!

WE CAN'T *BUILD* ONE OF THEIR CAPSULES, OF COURSE. WE'RE *DECADES* FROM THAT.

BUT WE CAN START LIMITED EXPERIMENTS ON THE AREA EFFECT RIGHT AWAY!

"*LIMITED*--!" DR. WILLIAMS, DR. DRAPER, IT IS YOUR *IDEAS* THAT ARE LIMITED, EH?!

THIS TECHNOLOGY HAS SOMETHING OF THE *MIND* ABOUT IT, AS WITH MY OWN MICRO MACHINES.

IF WE SUIT ITS AIMS, IT *WILL* AID US!

IT WILL SEE *I* AM ITS NATURAL INHERITOR!

I, THE FUTURE MAN, AWAKENED --

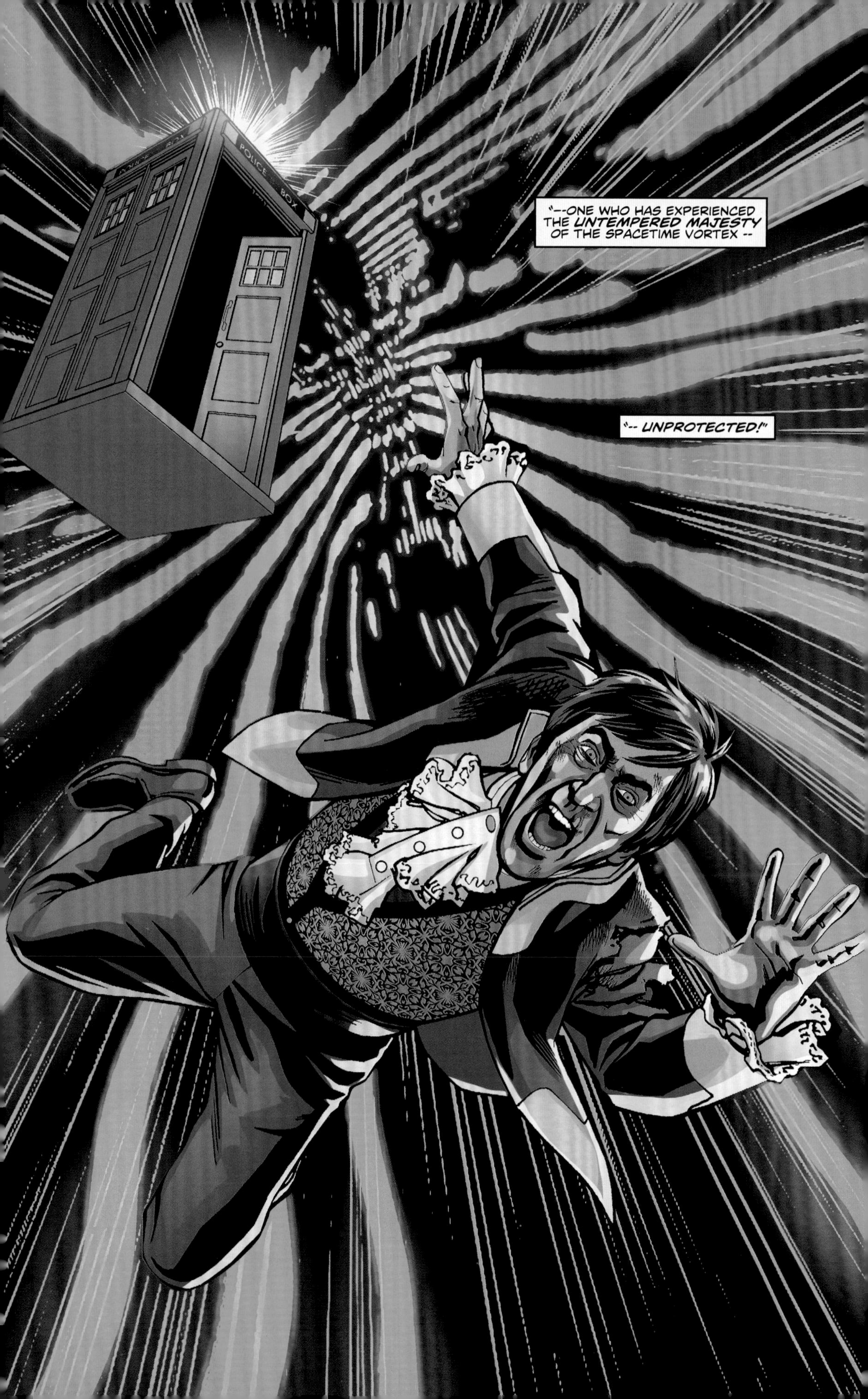

"--ONE WHO HAS EXPERIENCED THE UNTEMPERED MAJESTY OF THE SPACETIME VORTEX --
"-- UNPROTECTED!"

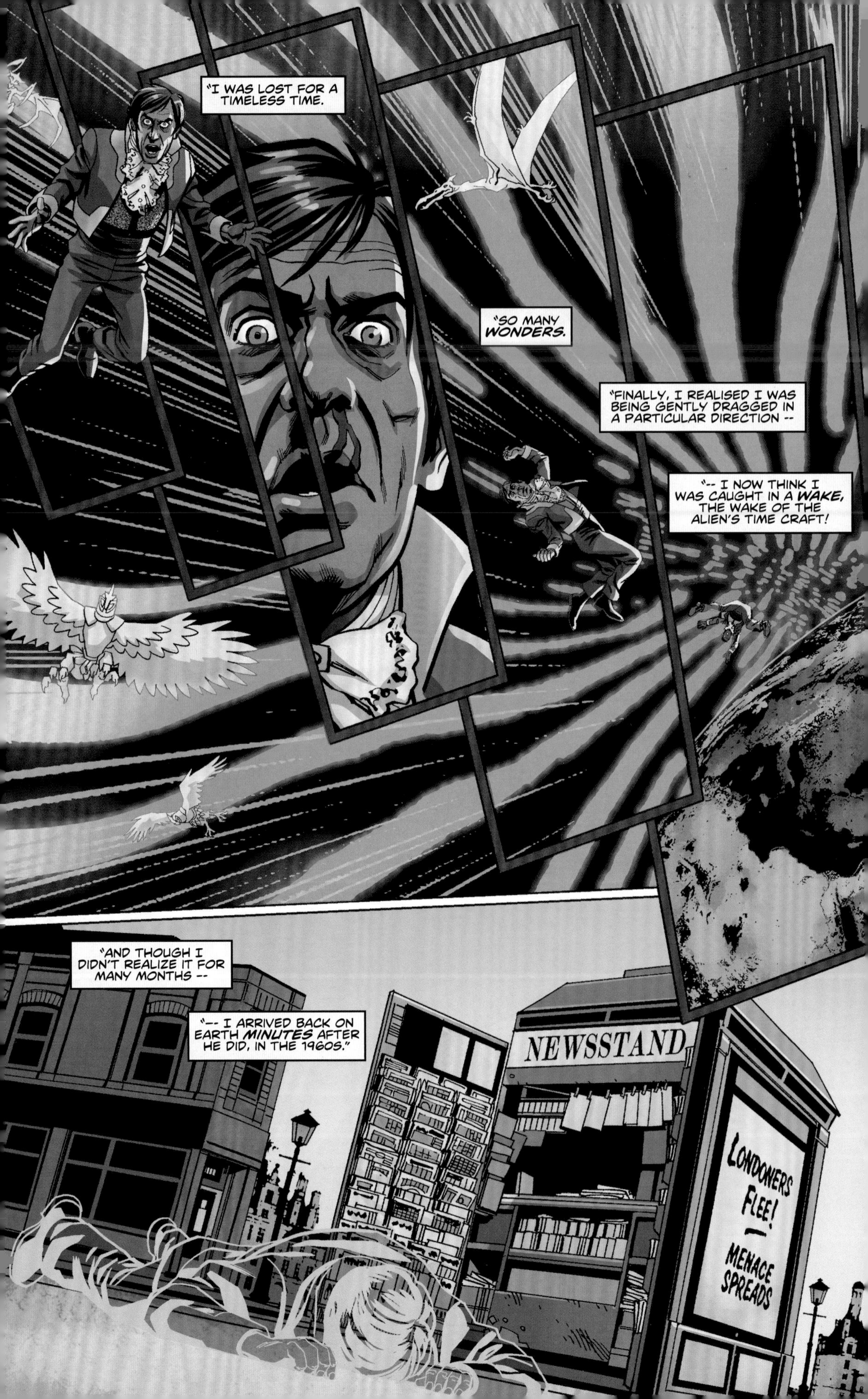
"I WAS LOST FOR A TIMELESS TIME.
"SO MANY WONDERS.
"FINALLY, I REALISED I WAS BEING GENTLY DRAGGED IN A PARTICULAR DIRECTION --
"-- I NOW THINK I WAS CAUGHT IN A WAKE, THE WAKE OF THE ALIEN'S TIME CRAFT!
"AND THOUGH I DIDN'T REALIZE IT FOR MANY MONTHS --
"-- I ARRIVED BACK ON EARTH MINUTES AFTER HE DID, IN THE 1960S."
NEWSSTAND
LONDONERS FLEE! — MENACE SPREADS

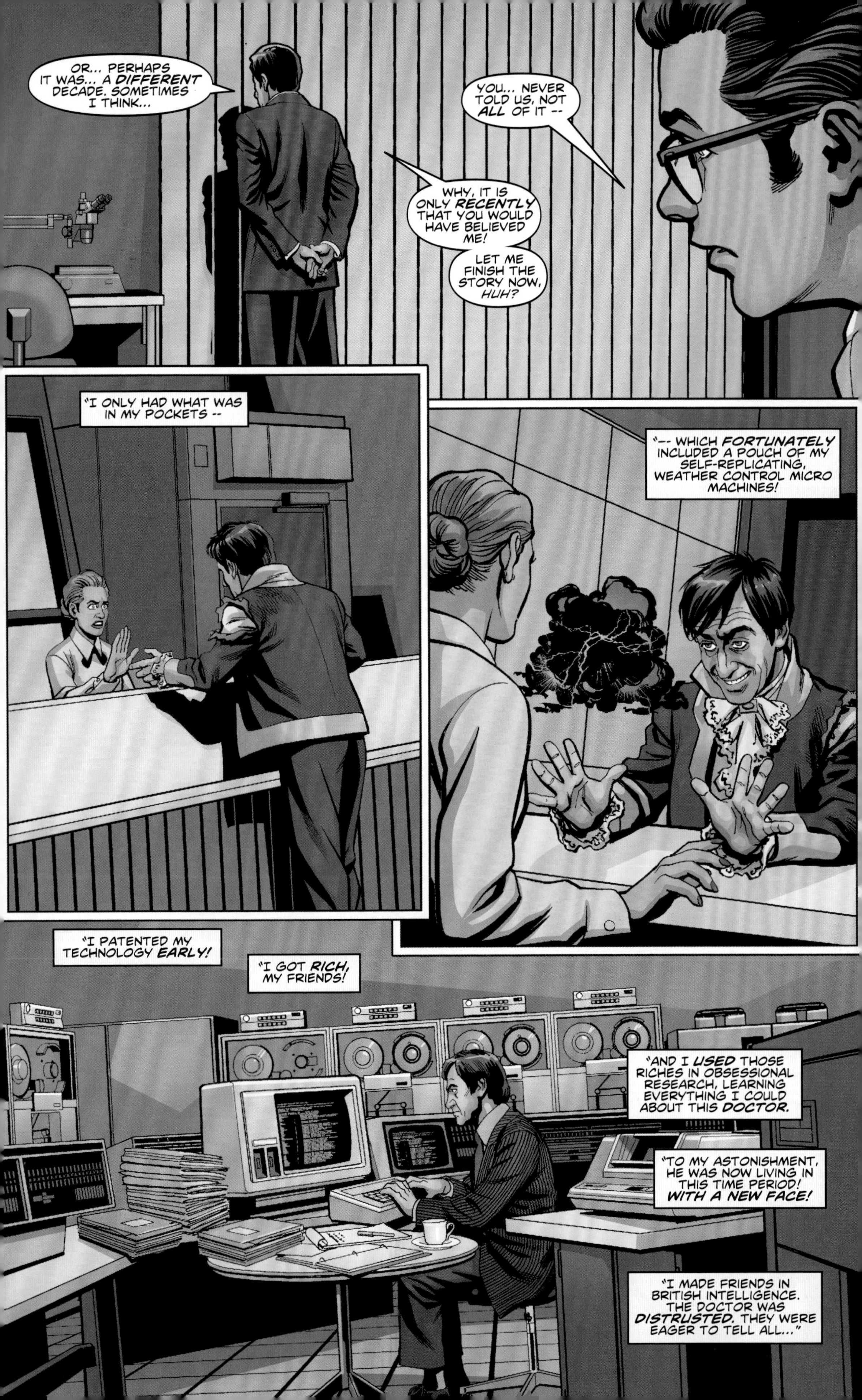
OR... PERHAPS IT WAS... A DIFFERENT DECADE. SOMETIMES I THINK...
YOU... NEVER TOLD US, NOT ALL OF IT --
WHY, IT IS ONLY RECENTLY THAT YOU WOULD HAVE BELIEVED ME!
LET ME FINISH THE STORY NOW, HUH?
"I ONLY HAD WHAT WAS IN MY POCKETS --
"-- WHICH FORTUNATELY INCLUDED A POUCH OF MY SELF-REPLICATING, WEATHER CONTROL MICRO MACHINES!
"I PATENTED MY TECHNOLOGY EARLY!
"I GOT RICH, MY FRIENDS!
"AND I USED THOSE RICHES IN OBSESSIONAL RESEARCH, LEARNING EVERYTHING I COULD ABOUT THIS DOCTOR.
"TO MY ASTONISHMENT, HE WAS NOW LIVING IN THIS TIME PERIOD! WITH A NEW FACE!
"I MADE FRIENDS IN BRITISH INTELLIGENCE. THE DOCTOR WAS DISTRUSTED. THEY WERE EAGER TO TELL ALL..."

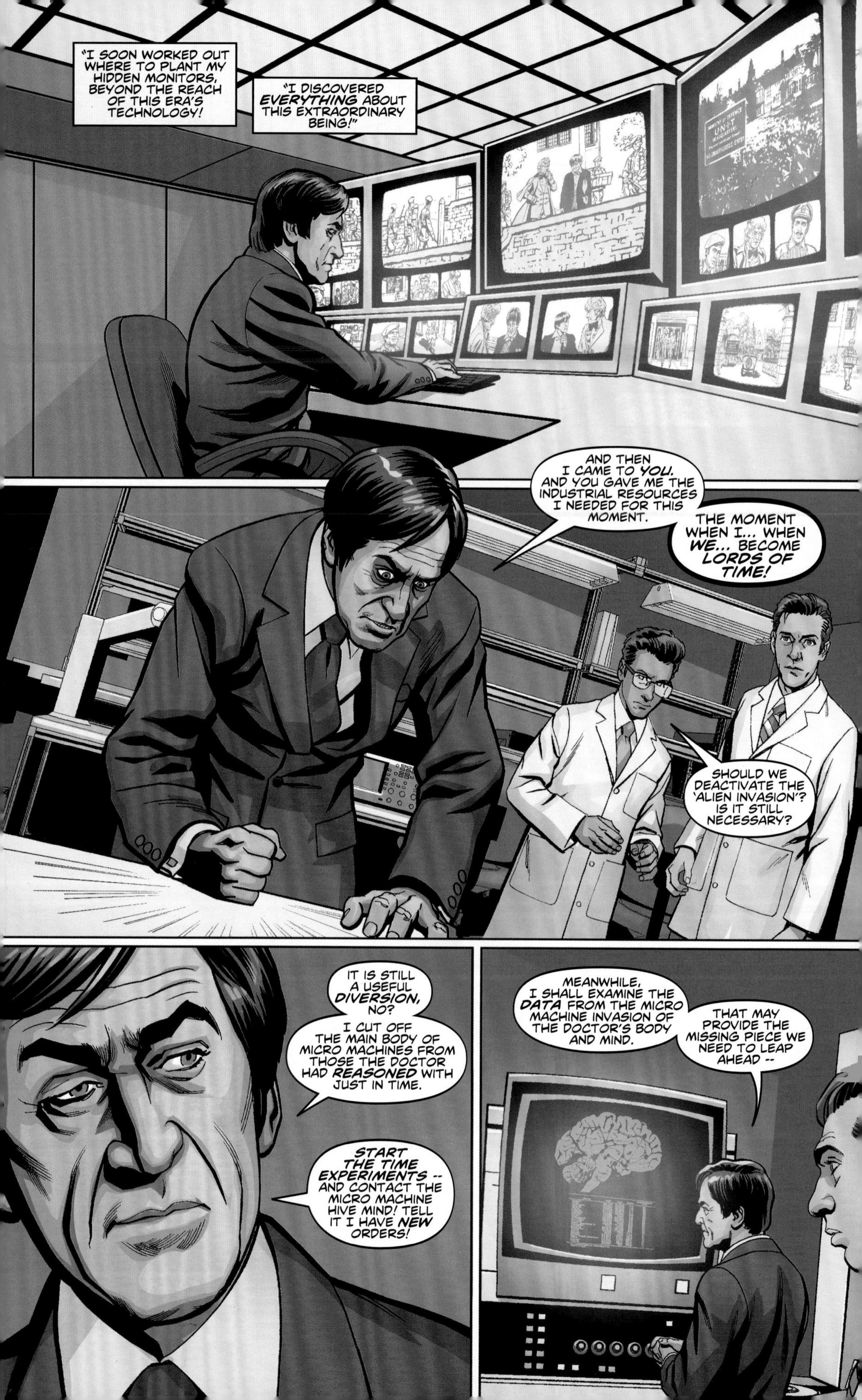
"I SOON WORKED OUT WHERE TO PLANT MY HIDDEN MONITORS, BEYOND THE REACH OF THIS ERA'S TECHNOLOGY!
"I DISCOVERED *EVERYTHING* ABOUT THIS EXTRAORDINARY BEING!"
AND THEN I CAME TO *YOU.* AND YOU GAVE ME THE INDUSTRIAL RESOURCES I NEEDED FOR THIS MOMENT.
THE MOMENT WHEN I... WHEN *WE*... BECOME *LORDS OF TIME!*
SHOULD WE DEACTIVATE THE 'ALIEN INVASION'? IS IT STILL NECESSARY?
IT IS STILL A USEFUL *DIVERSION,* NO?
I CUT OFF THE MAIN BODY OF MICRO MACHINES FROM THOSE THE DOCTOR HAD *REASONED* WITH JUST IN TIME.
START THE TIME EXPERIMENTS -- AND CONTACT THE MICRO MACHINE HIVE MIND! TELL IT I HAVE *NEW* ORDERS!
MEANWHILE, I SHALL EXAMINE THE *DATA* FROM THE MICRO MACHINE INVASION OF THE DOCTOR'S BODY AND MIND.
THAT MAY PROVIDE THE MISSING PIECE WE NEED TO LEAP AHEAD --

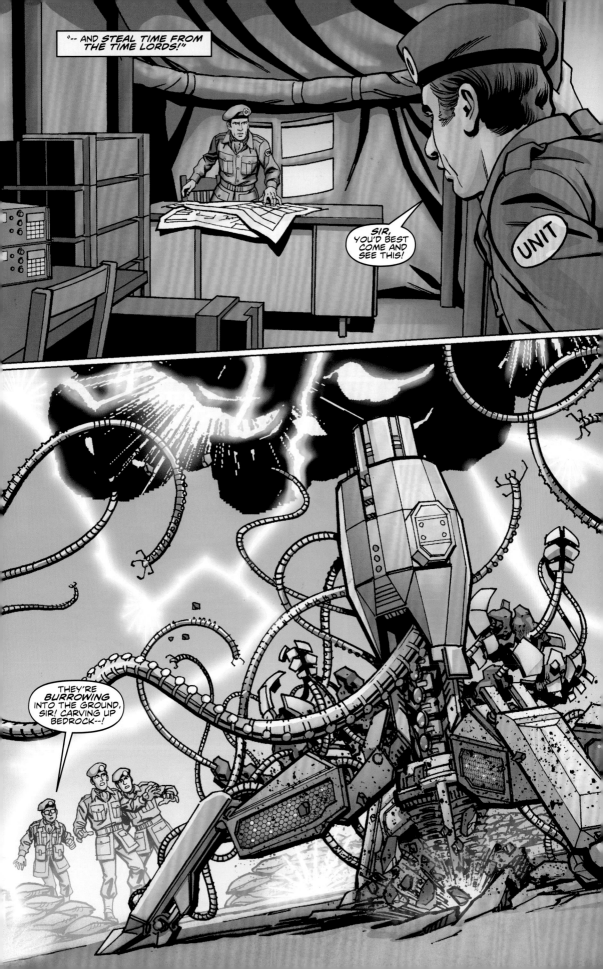

"-- AND STEAL TIME FROM THE TIME LORDS!"

SIR, YOU'D BEST COME AND SEE THIS!

UNIT

THEY'RE BURROWING INTO THE GROUND, SIR! CARVING UP BEDROCK--!

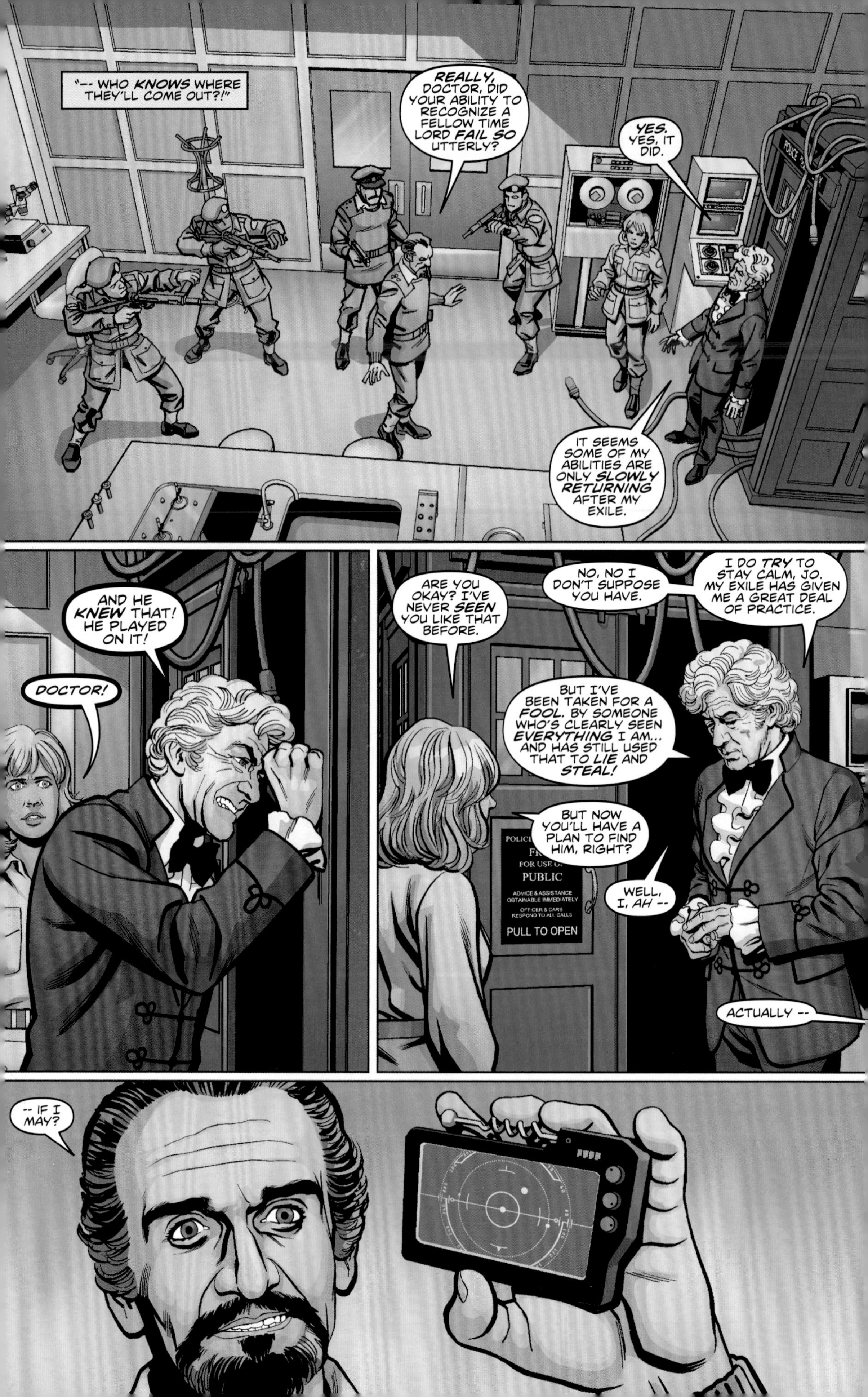
"-- WHO KNOWS WHERE THEY'LL COME OUT?!"
REALLY, DOCTOR, DID YOUR ABILITY TO RECOGNIZE A FELLOW TIME LORD FAIL SO UTTERLY?
YES. YES, IT DID.
IT SEEMS SOME OF MY ABILITIES ARE ONLY SLOWLY RETURNING AFTER MY EXILE.
AND HE KNEW THAT! HE PLAYED ON IT!
DOCTOR!
ARE YOU OKAY? I'VE NEVER SEEN YOU LIKE THAT BEFORE.
NO, NO I DON'T SUPPOSE YOU HAVE.
I DO TRY TO STAY CALM, JO. MY EXILE HAS GIVEN ME A GREAT DEAL OF PRACTICE.
BUT I'VE BEEN TAKEN FOR A FOOL. BY SOMEONE WHO'S CLEARLY SEEN EVERYTHING I AM... AND HAS STILL USED THAT TO LIE AND STEAL!
BUT NOW YOU'LL HAVE A PLAN TO FIND HIM, RIGHT?
WELL, I, AH --
ACTUALLY --
-- IF I MAY?

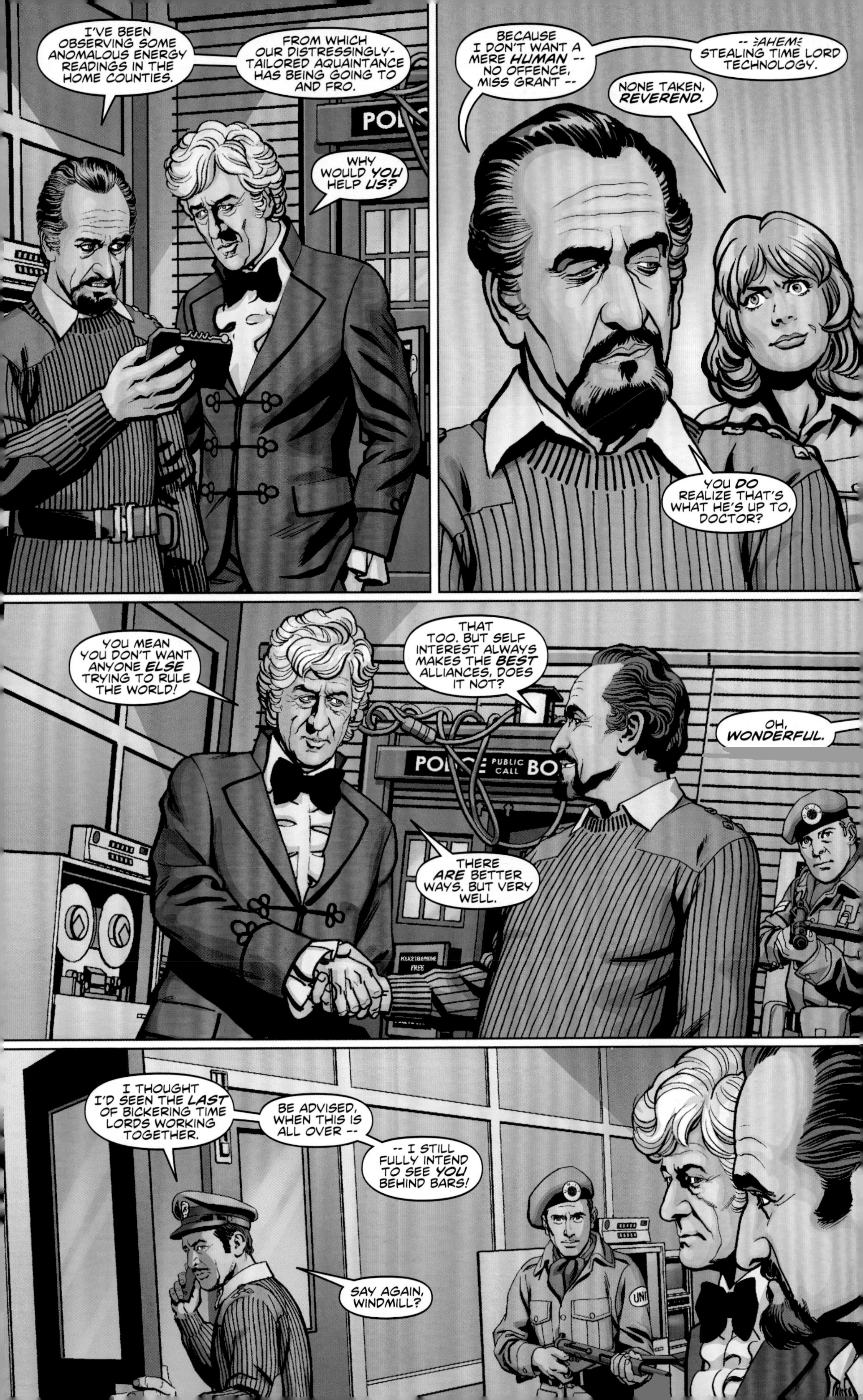
I'VE BEEN OBSERVING SOME ANOMALOUS ENERGY READINGS IN THE HOME COUNTIES.
FROM WHICH OUR DISTRESSINGLY-TAILORED AQUAINTANCE HAS BEING GOING TO AND FRO.
WHY WOULD YOU HELP US?
BECAUSE I DON'T WANT A MERE HUMAN -- NO OFFENCE, MISS GRANT --
-- AHEM STEALING TIME LORD TECHNOLOGY.
NONE TAKEN, REVEREND.
YOU DO REALIZE THAT'S WHAT HE'S UP TO, DOCTOR?
YOU MEAN YOU DON'T WANT ANYONE ELSE TRYING TO RULE THE WORLD!
THAT TOO. BUT SELF INTEREST ALWAYS MAKES THE BEST ALLIANCES, DOES IT NOT?
OH, WONDERFUL.
THERE ARE BETTER WAYS. BUT VERY WELL.
I THOUGHT I'D SEEN THE LAST OF BICKERING TIME LORDS WORKING TOGETHER.
BE ADVISED, WHEN THIS IS ALL OVER --
-- I STILL FULLY INTEND TO SEE YOU BEHIND BARS!
SAY AGAIN, WINDMILL?

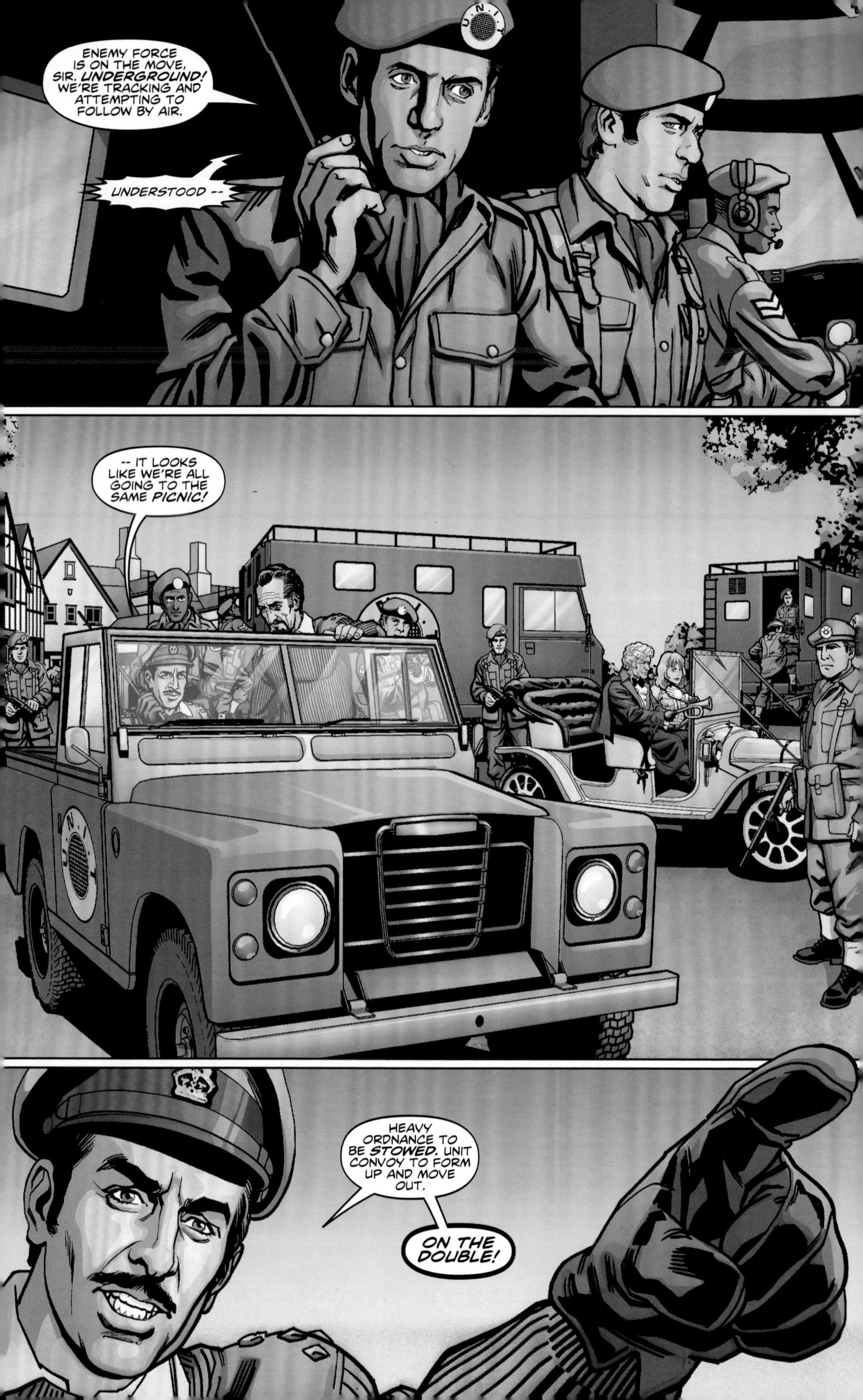
ENEMY FORCE IS ON THE MOVE, SIR. UNDERGROUND! WE'RE TRACKING AND ATTEMPTING TO FOLLOW BY AIR.
UNDERSTOOD --
-- IT LOOKS LIKE WE'RE ALL GOING TO THE SAME PICNIC!
U.N.I.T
HEAVY ORDNANCE TO BE STOWED. UNIT CONVOY TO FORM UP AND MOVE OUT.
ON THE DOUBLE!

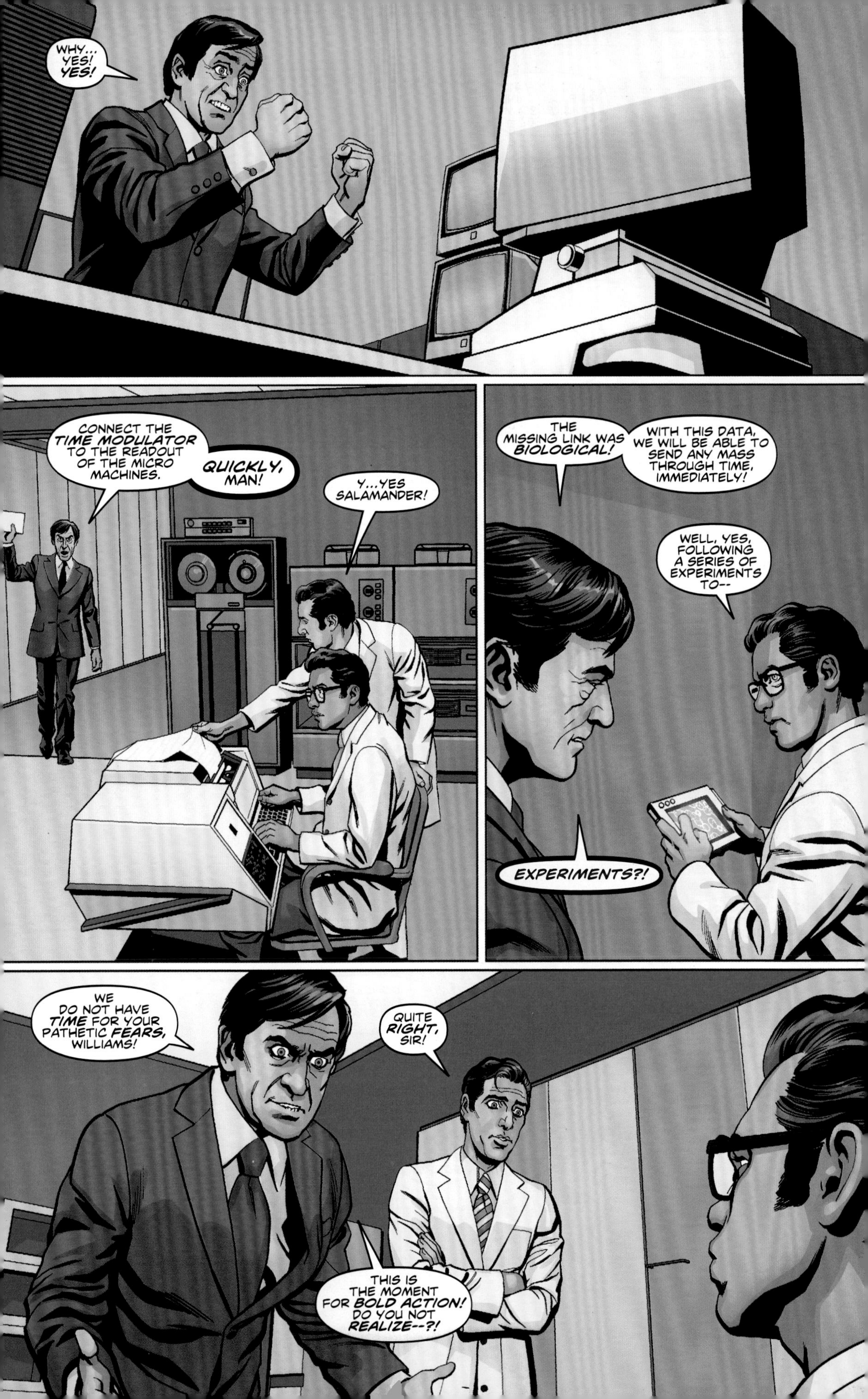
WHY... YES! YES!
CONNECT THE TIME MODULATOR TO THE READOUT OF THE MICRO MACHINES.
QUICKLY, MAN!
Y...YES SALAMANDER!
THE MISSING LINK WAS BIOLOGICAL!
WITH THIS DATA, WE WILL BE ABLE TO SEND ANY MASS THROUGH TIME, IMMEDIATELY!
WELL, YES, FOLLOWING A SERIES OF EXPERIMENTS TO--
EXPERIMENTS?!
WE DO NOT HAVE TIME FOR YOUR PATHETIC FEARS, WILLIAMS!
QUITE RIGHT, SIR!
THIS IS THE MOMENT FOR BOLD ACTION! DO YOU NOT REALIZE--?!

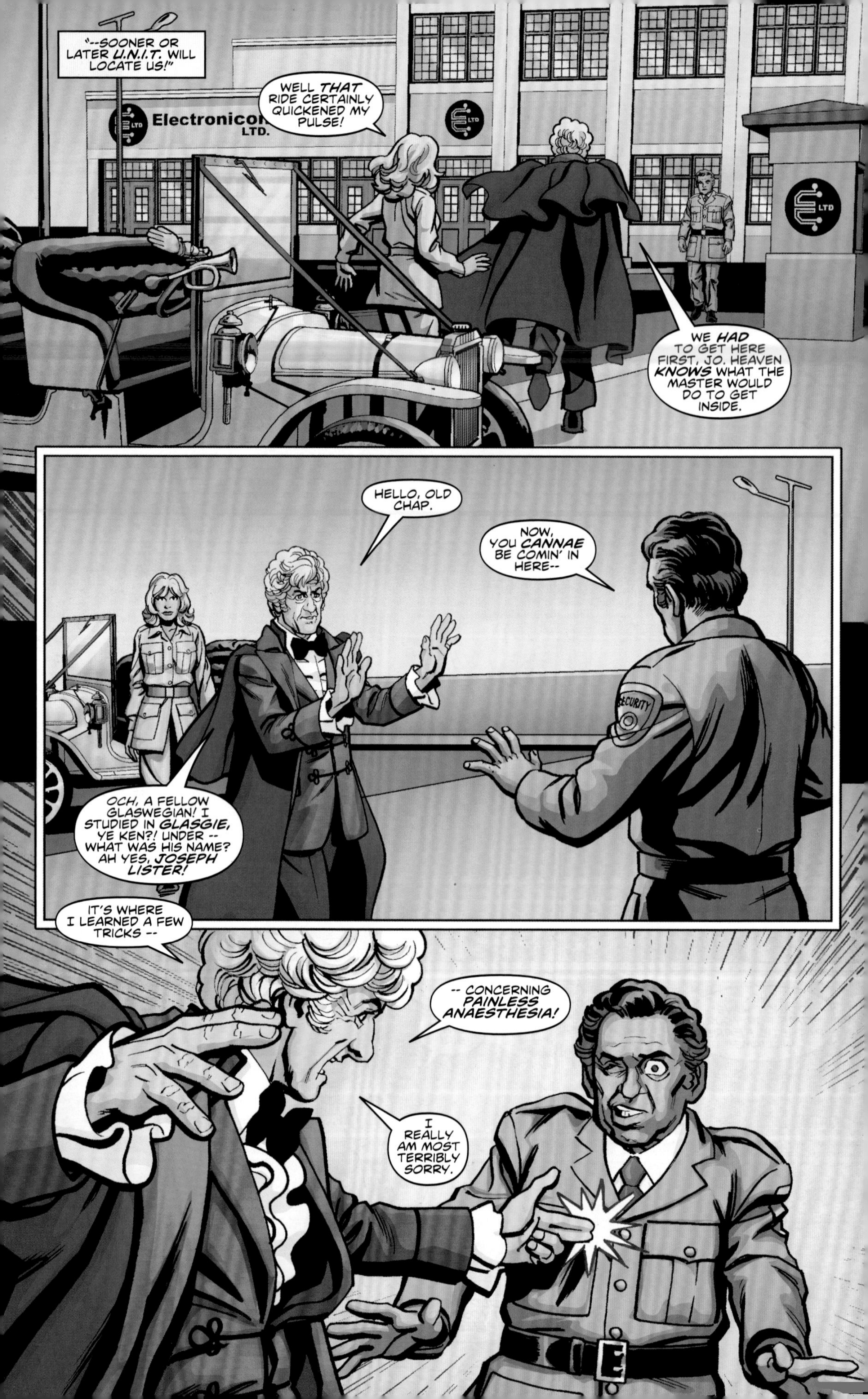
"--SOONER OR LATER U.N.I.T. WILL LOCATE US!"
Electronicom LTD.
WELL THAT RIDE CERTAINLY QUICKENED MY PULSE!
WE HAD TO GET HERE FIRST, JO. HEAVEN KNOWS WHAT THE MASTER WOULD DO TO GET INSIDE.
HELLO, OLD CHAP.
NOW, YOU CANNAE BE COMIN' IN HERE--
OCH, A FELLOW GLASWEGIAN! I STUDIED IN GLASGIE, YE KEN?! UNDER -- WHAT WAS HIS NAME? AH YES, JOSEPH LISTER!
SECURITY
IT'S WHERE I LEARNED A FEW TRICKS --
-- CONCERNING PAINLESS ANAESTHESIA!
I REALLY AM MOST TERRIBLY SORRY.

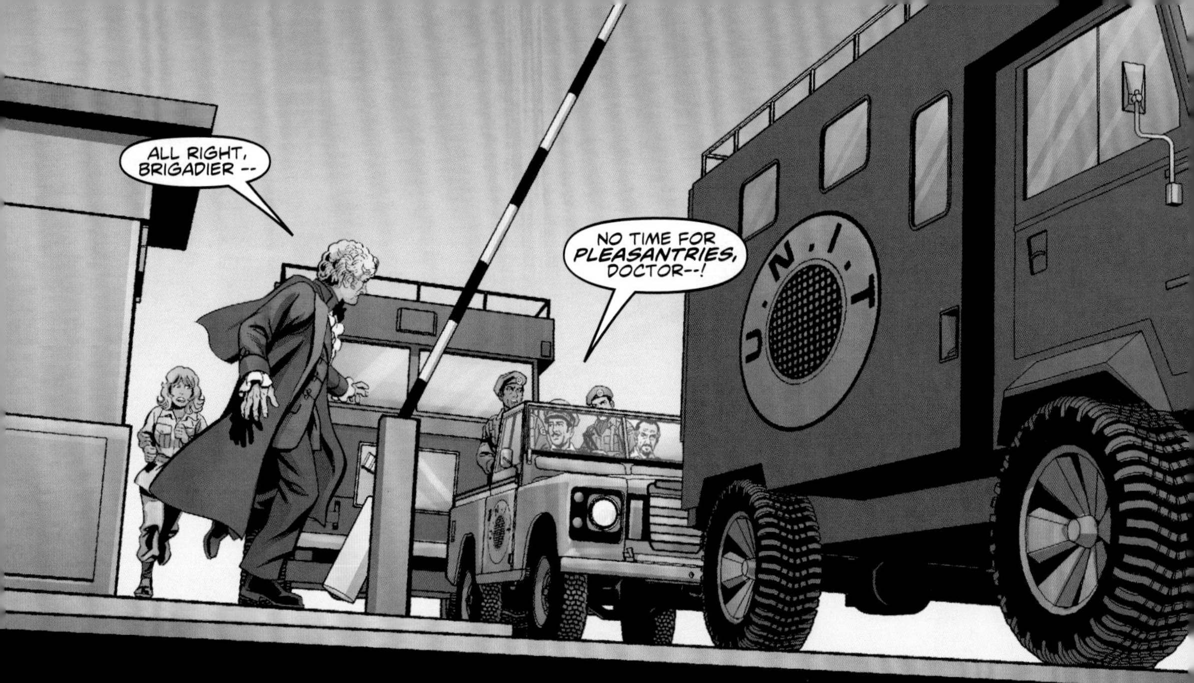
ALL RIGHT, BRIGADIER --
NO TIME FOR PLEASANTRIES, DOCTOR--!
U.N.I.T

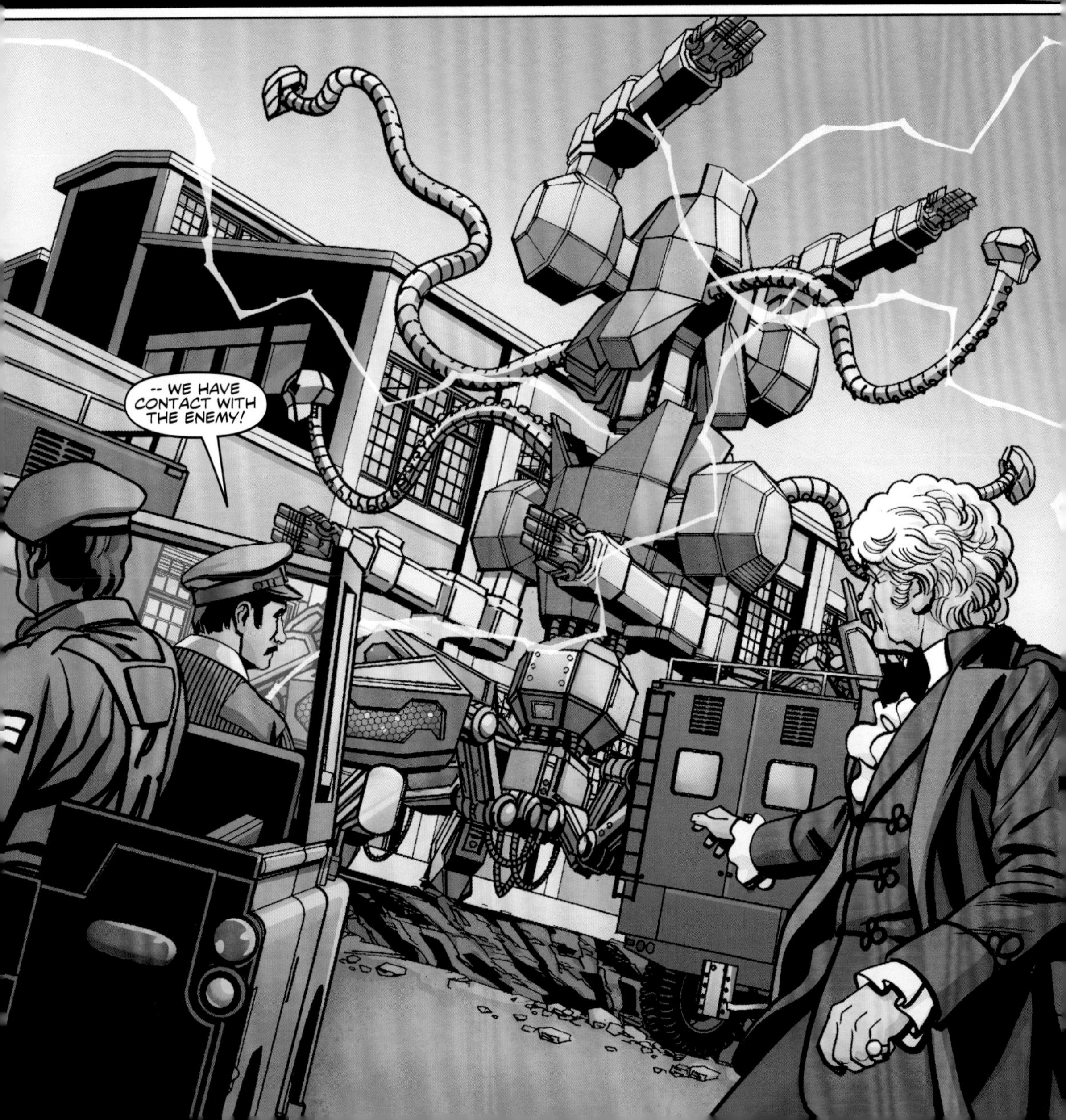
-- WE HAVE CONTACT WITH THE ENEMY!

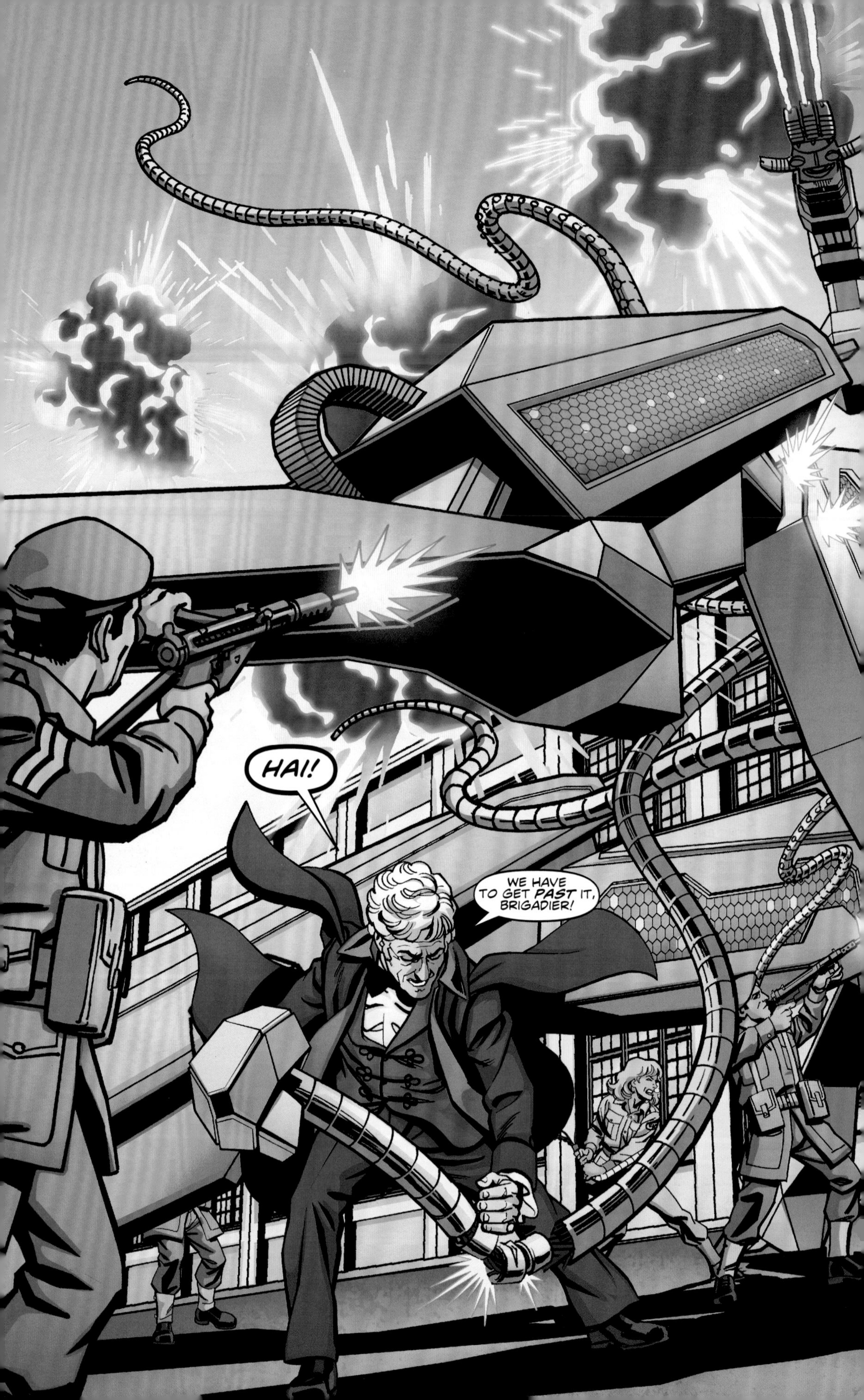
HAI!
WE HAVE TO GET PAST IT, BRIGADIER!

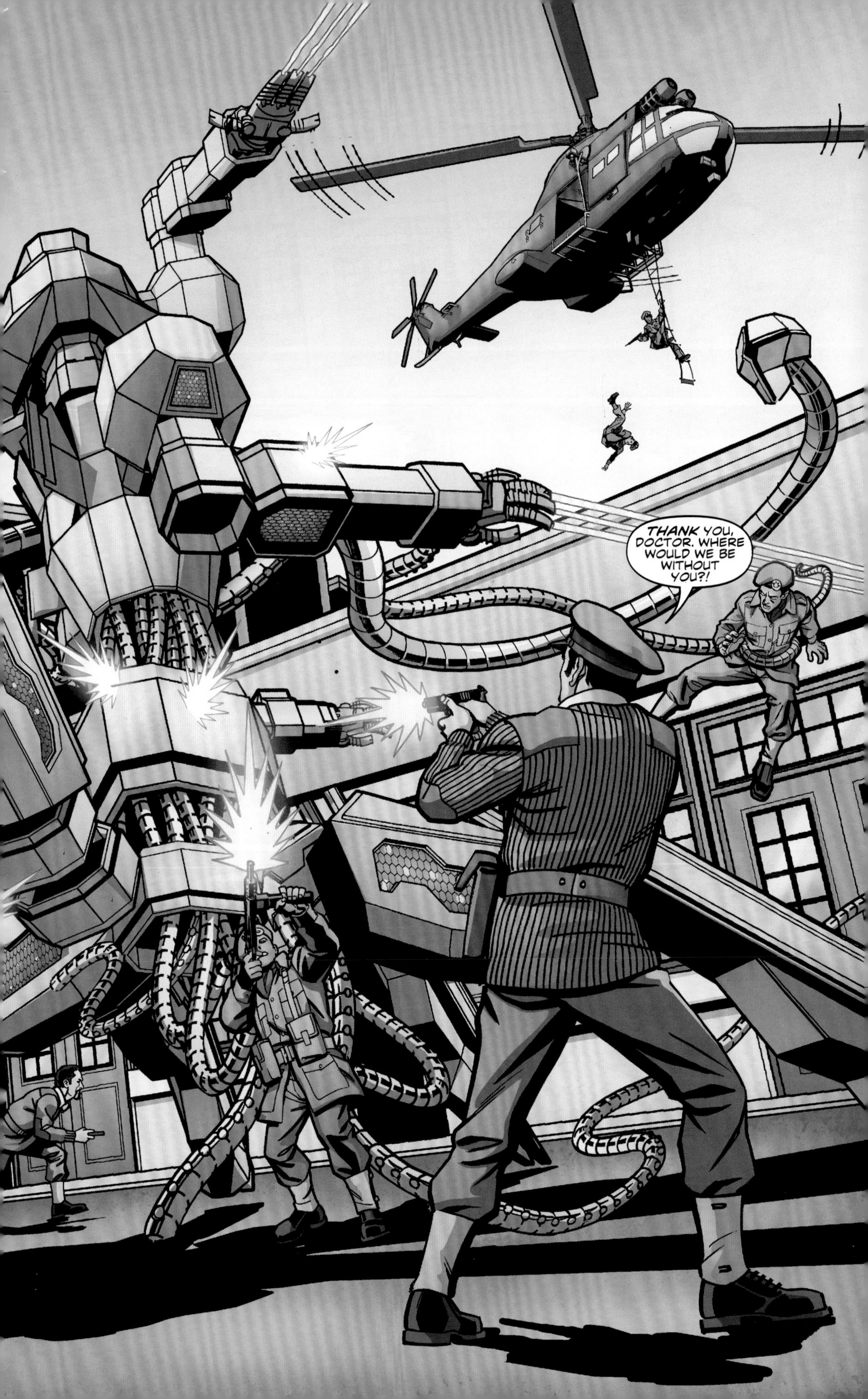
THANK YOU, DOCTOR. WHERE WOULD WE BE WITHOUT YOU?!

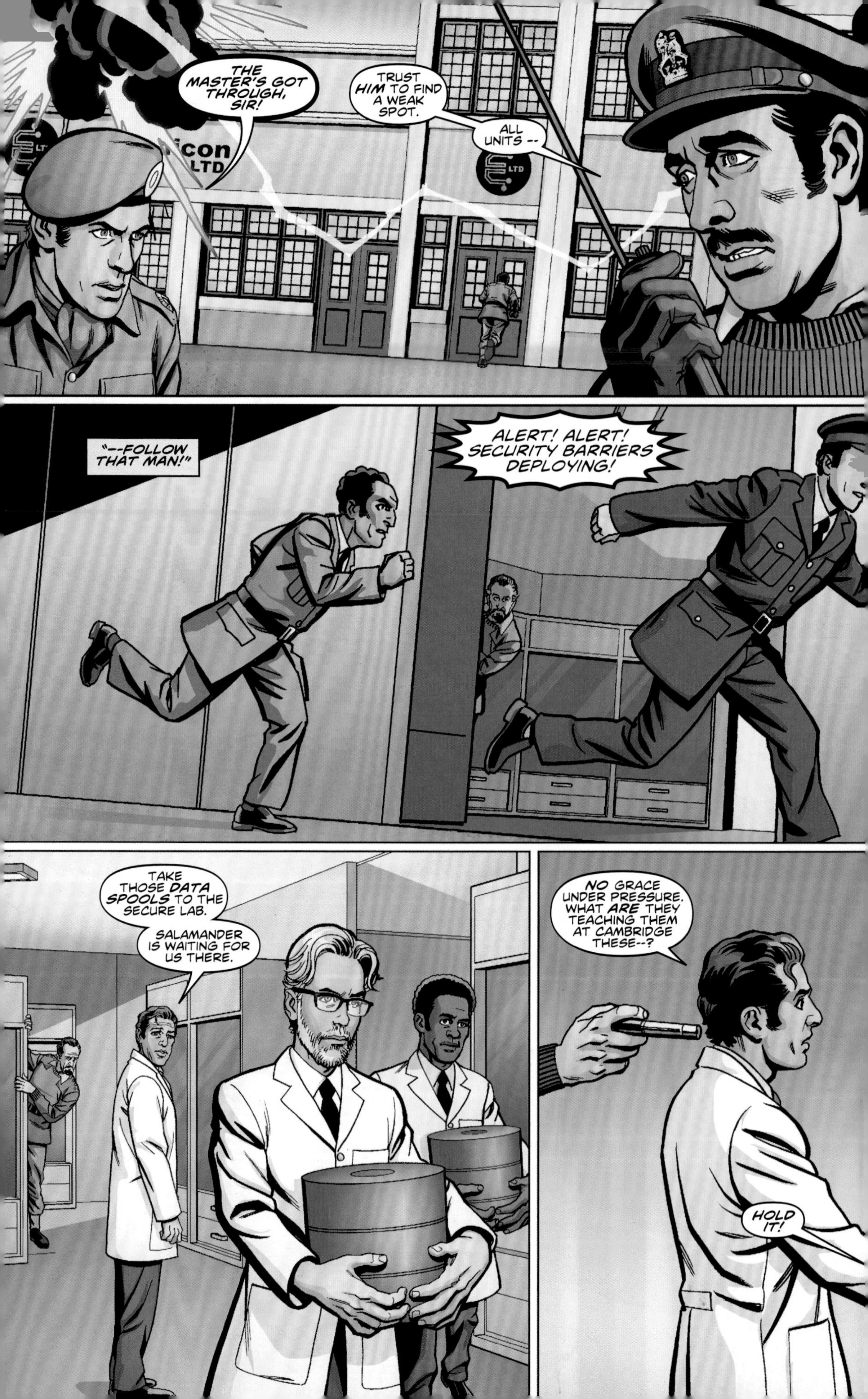
THE MASTER'S GOT THROUGH, SIR!
TRUST HIM TO FIND A WEAK SPOT.
ALL UNITS --
"--FOLLOW THAT MAN!"
ALERT! ALERT! SECURITY BARRIERS DEPLOYING!
TAKE THOSE DATA SPOOLS TO THE SECURE LAB.
SALAMANDER IS WAITING FOR US THERE.
NO GRACE UNDER PRESSURE. WHAT ARE THEY TEACHING THEM AT CAMBRIDGE THESE--?
HOLD IT!

GLAD I WAS THE ONE TO FIND YOU.

I'M SURE YOU KNOW I'M *QUITE* CAPABLE OF SHOOTING YOU WHERE YOU STAND.

WH-- WHAT?!

NO NEED FOR *THAT*, CAPTAIN YATES.

I HAVE MERELY *APPREHENDED* THIS MAN, WHO CAN GAIN US ACCESS TO OUR TARGET.

I -- I WOULD *NEVER*--!

OH *DEAR*, WOULDN'T YOU?

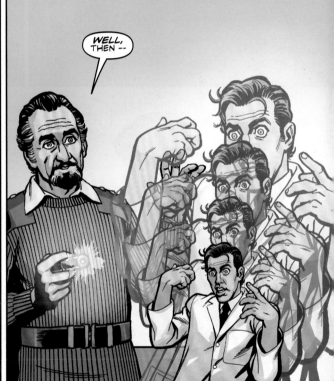

WELL, THEN --

-- BACK TO PLAN A.

I SAID--!

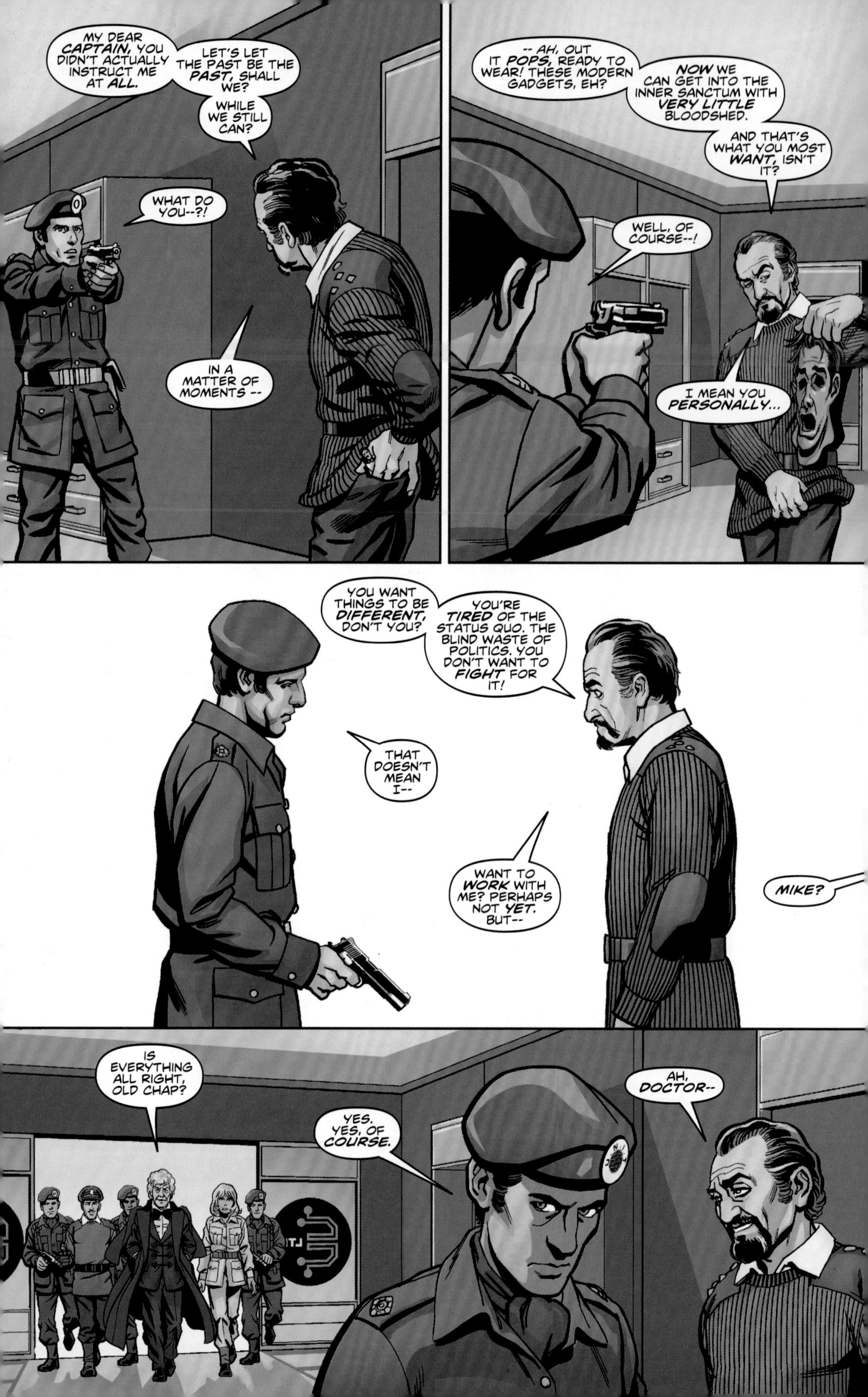
MY DEAR CAPTAIN, YOU DIDN'T ACTUALLY INSTRUCT ME AT ALL.
LET'S LET THE PAST BE THE PAST, SHALL WE?
WHILE WE STILL CAN?
WHAT DO YOU--?!
IN A MATTER OF MOMENTS --
-- AH, OUT IT POPS, READY TO WEAR! THESE MODERN GADGETS, EH?
NOW WE CAN GET INTO THE INNER SANCTUM WITH VERY LITTLE BLOODSHED.
AND THAT'S WHAT YOU MOST WANT, ISN'T IT?
WELL, OF COURSE--!
I MEAN YOU PERSONALLY...
YOU WANT THINGS TO BE DIFFERENT, DON'T YOU?
YOU'RE TIRED OF THE STATUS QUO. THE BLIND WASTE OF POLITICS. YOU DON'T WANT TO FIGHT FOR IT!
THAT DOESN'T MEAN I--
WANT TO WORK WITH ME? PERHAPS NOT YET. BUT--
MIKE?
IS EVERYTHING ALL RIGHT, OLD CHAP?
YES. YES, OF COURSE.
AH, DOCTOR--

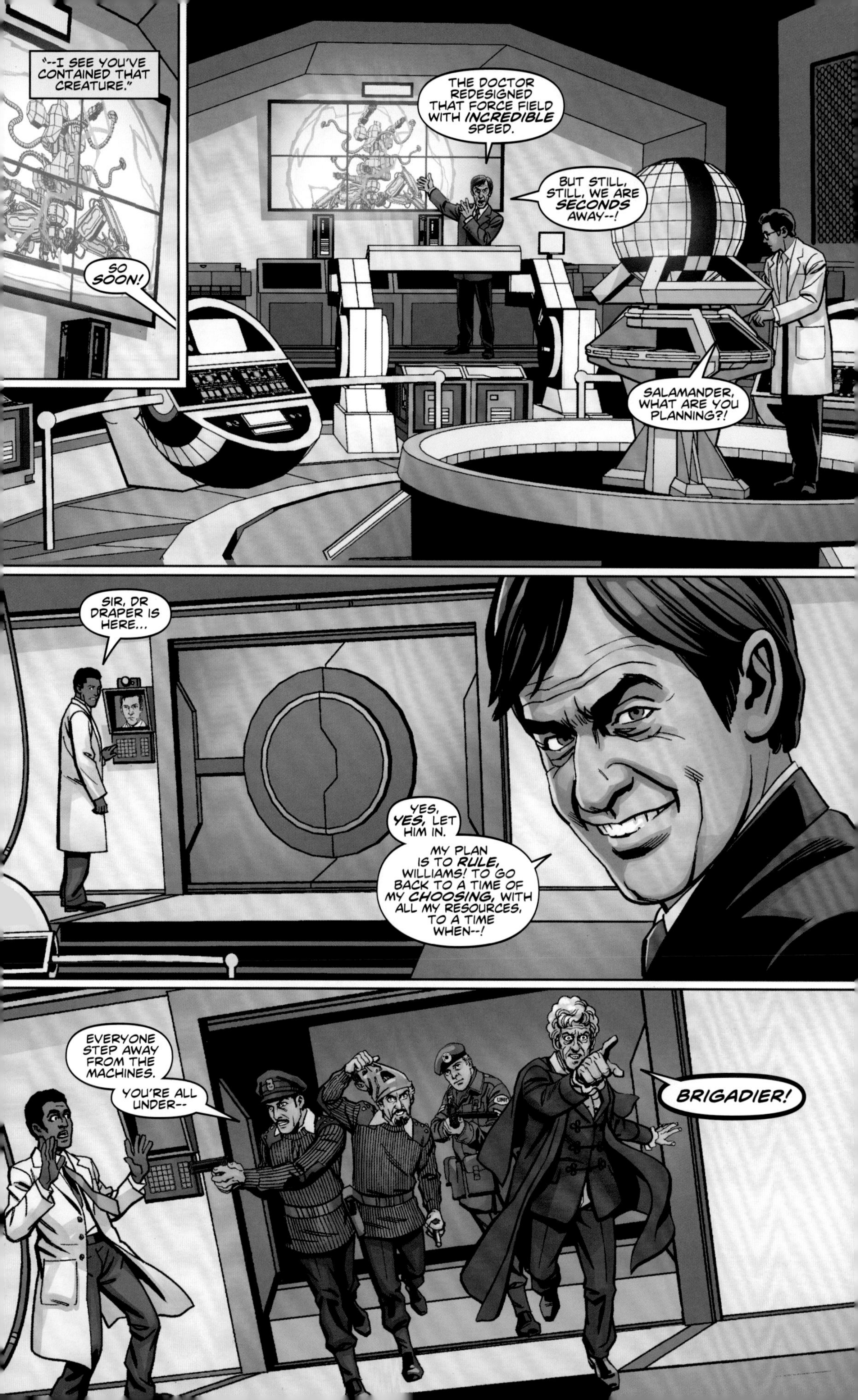
"--I SEE YOU'VE CONTAINED THAT CREATURE."
SO SOON!
THE DOCTOR REDESIGNED THAT FORCE FIELD WITH INCREDIBLE SPEED.
BUT STILL, STILL, WE ARE SECONDS AWAY--!
SALAMANDER, WHAT ARE YOU PLANNING?!
SIR, DR DRAPER IS HERE...
YES, YES, LET HIM IN.
MY PLAN IS TO RULE, WILLIAMS! TO GO BACK TO A TIME OF MY CHOOSING, WITH ALL MY RESOURCES, TO A TIME WHEN--!
EVERYONE STEP AWAY FROM THE MACHINES.
YOU'RE ALL UNDER--
BRIGADIER!

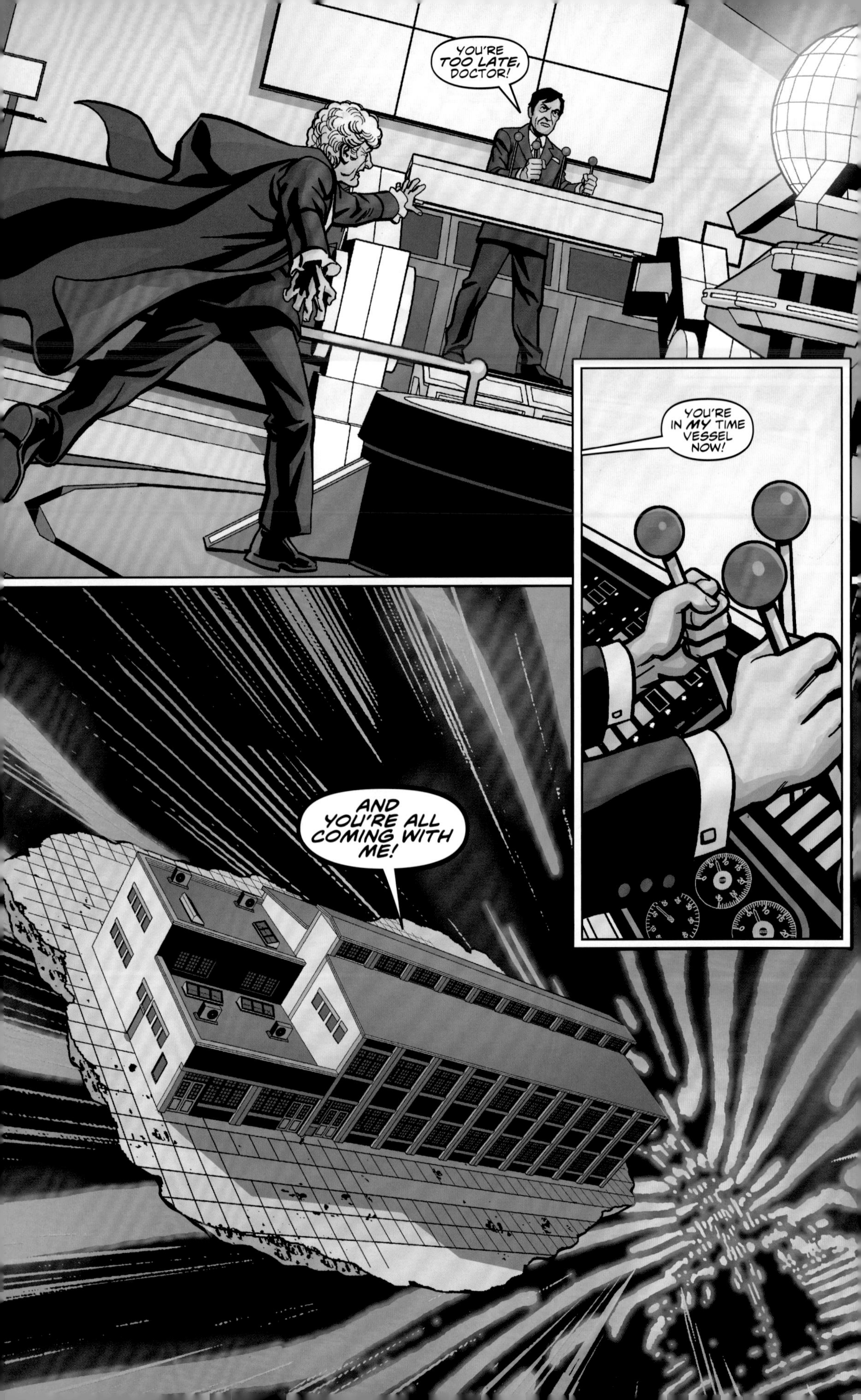
YOU'RE TOO LATE, DOCTOR!
YOU'RE IN MY TIME VESSEL NOW!
AND YOU'RE ALL COMING WITH ME!

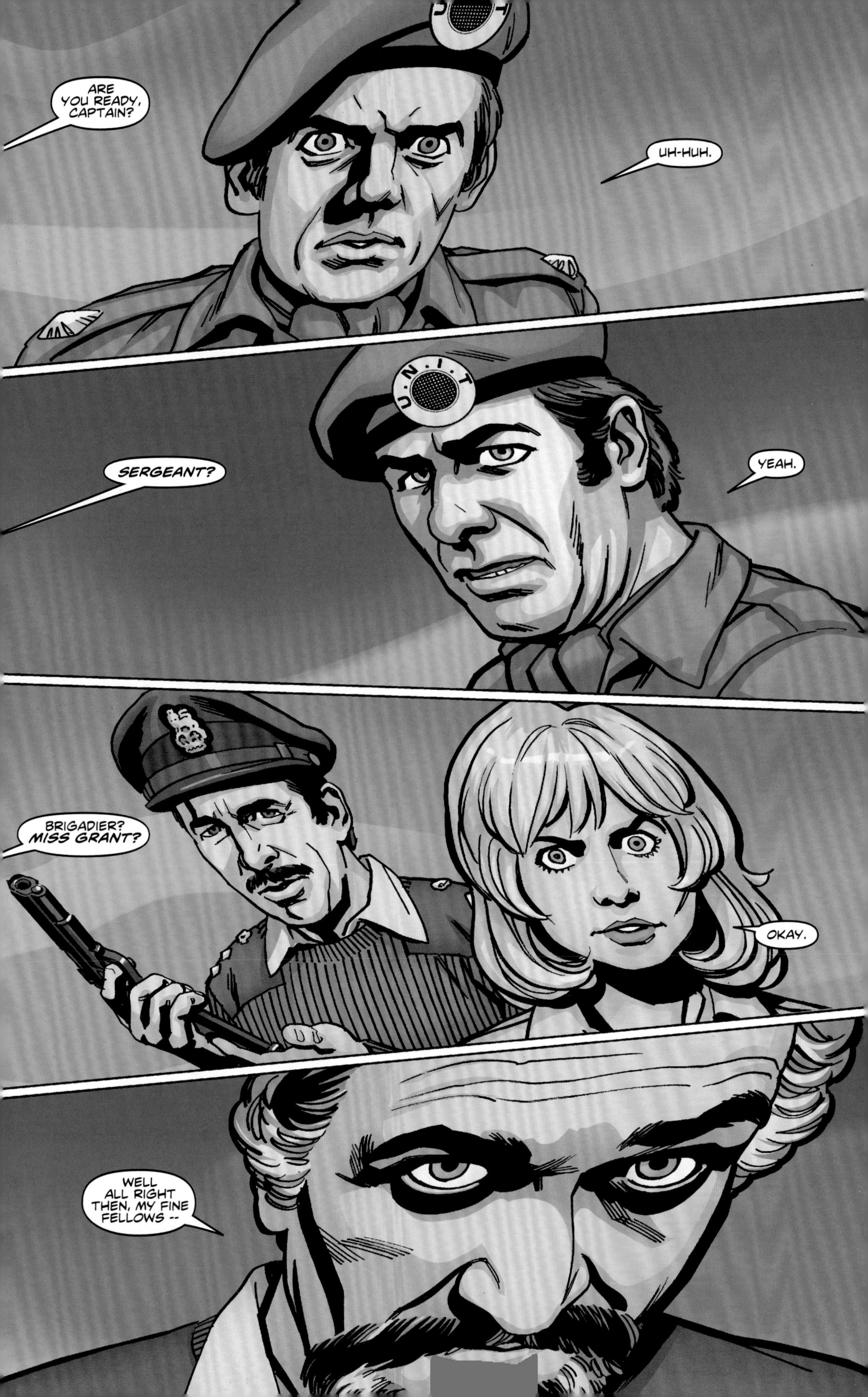
ARE YOU READY, CAPTAIN?
UH-HUH.
SERGEANT?
YEAH.
BRIGADIER? MISS GRANT?
OKAY.
WELL ALL RIGHT THEN, MY FINE FELLOWS --

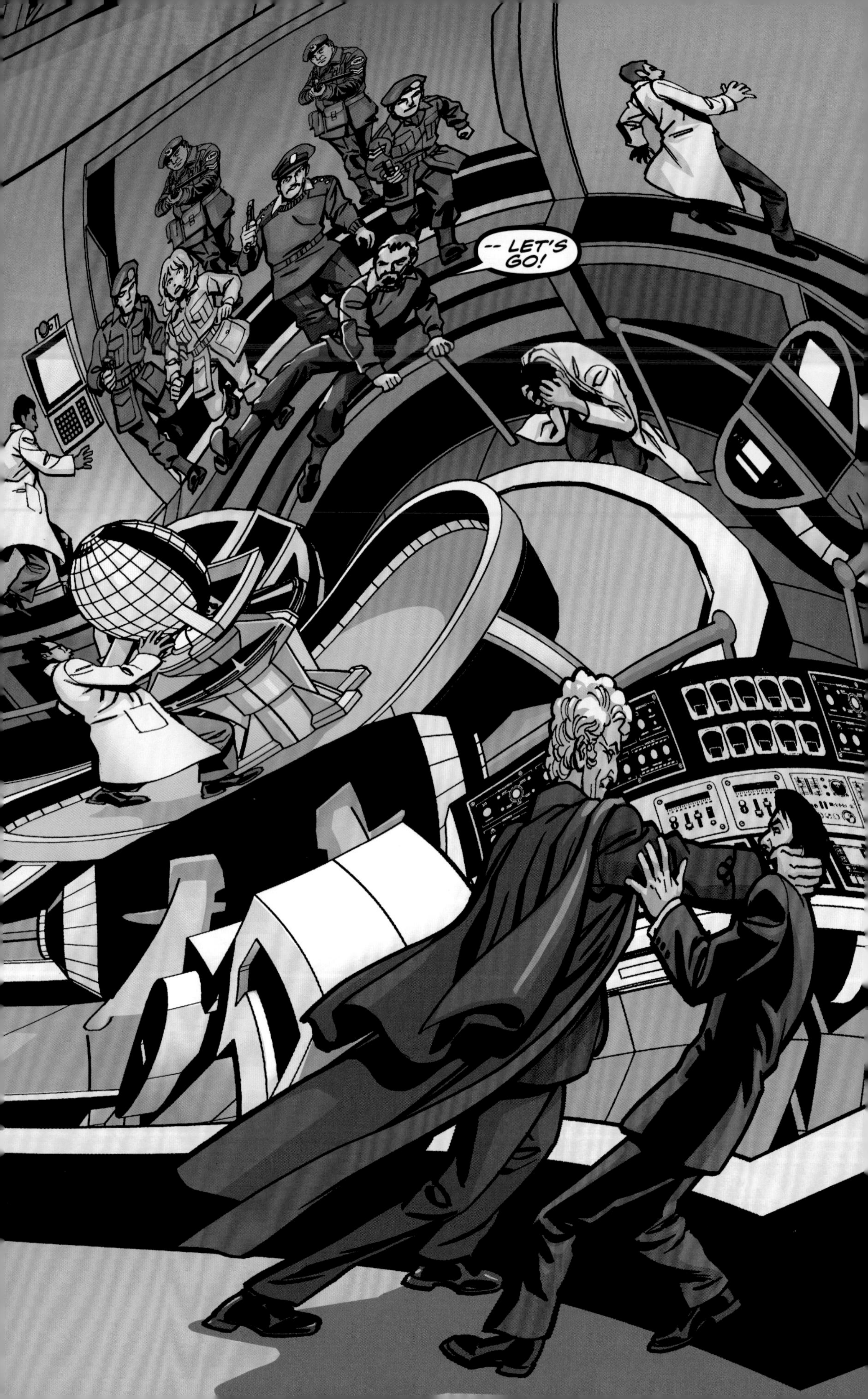
-- LET'S GO!

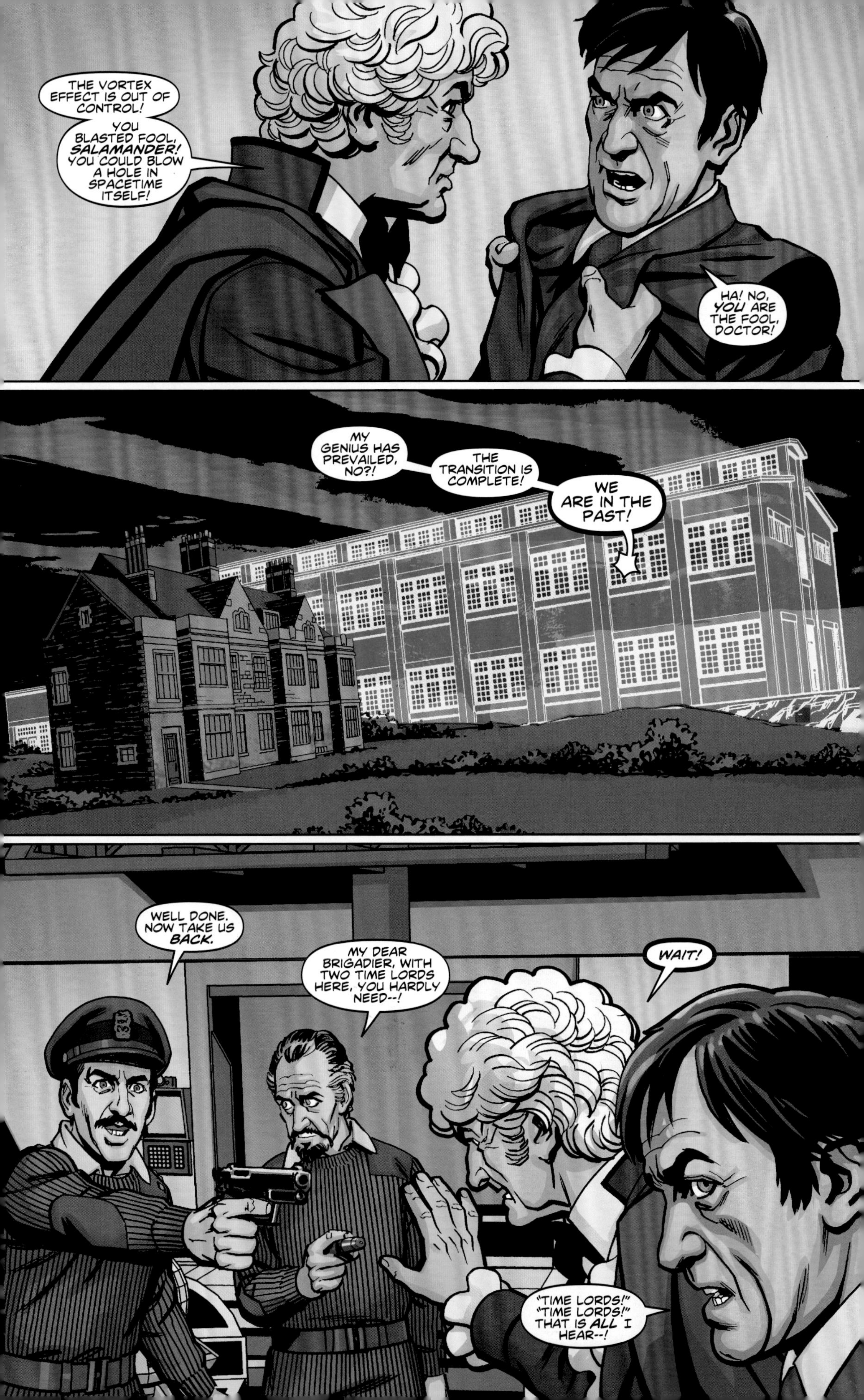
THE VORTEX EFFECT IS OUT OF CONTROL!
YOU BLASTED FOOL, SALAMANDER! YOU COULD BLOW A HOLE IN SPACETIME ITSELF!
HA! NO, YOU ARE THE FOOL, DOCTOR!
MY GENIUS HAS PREVAILED, NO?!
THE TRANSITION IS COMPLETE!
WE ARE IN THE PAST!
WELL DONE. NOW TAKE US BACK.
MY DEAR BRIGADIER, WITH TWO TIME LORDS HERE, YOU HARDLY NEED--!
WAIT!
"TIME LORDS!" "TIME LORDS!" THAT IS ALL I HEAR--!

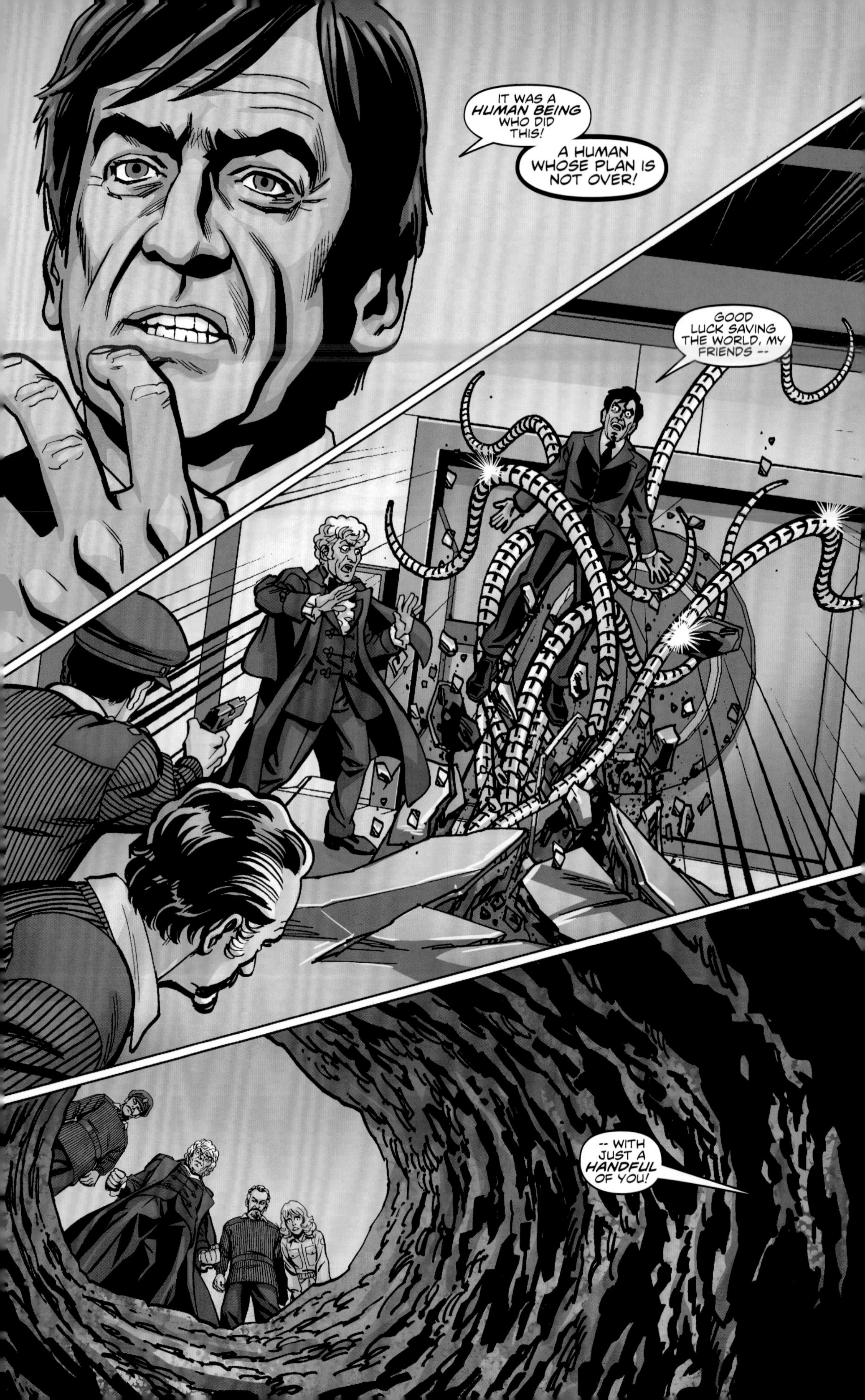
IT WAS A HUMAN BEING WHO DID THIS!
A HUMAN WHOSE PLAN IS NOT OVER!
GOOD LUCK SAVING THE WORLD, MY FRIENDS --
-- WITH JUST A HANDFUL OF YOU!

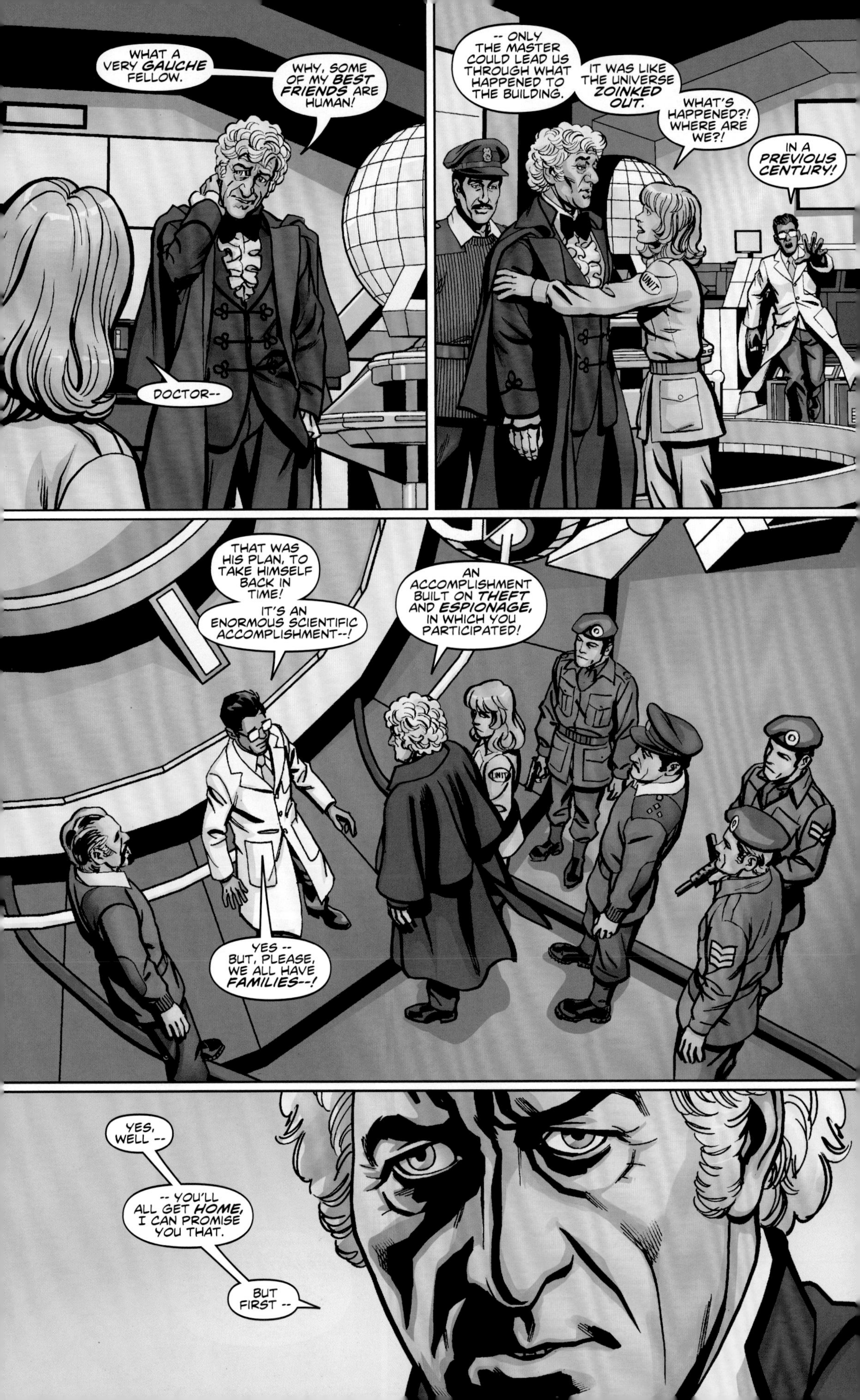
WHAT A VERY GAUCHE FELLOW.
WHY, SOME OF MY BEST FRIENDS ARE HUMAN!
DOCTOR--
-- ONLY THE MASTER COULD LEAD US THROUGH WHAT HAPPENED TO THE BUILDING.
IT WAS LIKE THE UNIVERSE ZOINKED OUT.
WHAT'S HAPPENED?! WHERE ARE WE?!
IN A PREVIOUS CENTURY!
THAT WAS HIS PLAN, TO TAKE HIMSELF BACK IN TIME!
IT'S AN ENORMOUS SCIENTIFIC ACCOMPLISHMENT--!
AN ACCOMPLISHMENT BUILT ON THEFT AND ESPIONAGE, IN WHICH YOU PARTICIPATED!
YES -- BUT, PLEASE, WE ALL HAVE FAMILIES--!
YES, WELL --
-- YOU'LL ALL GET HOME, I CAN PROMISE YOU THAT.
BUT FIRST --

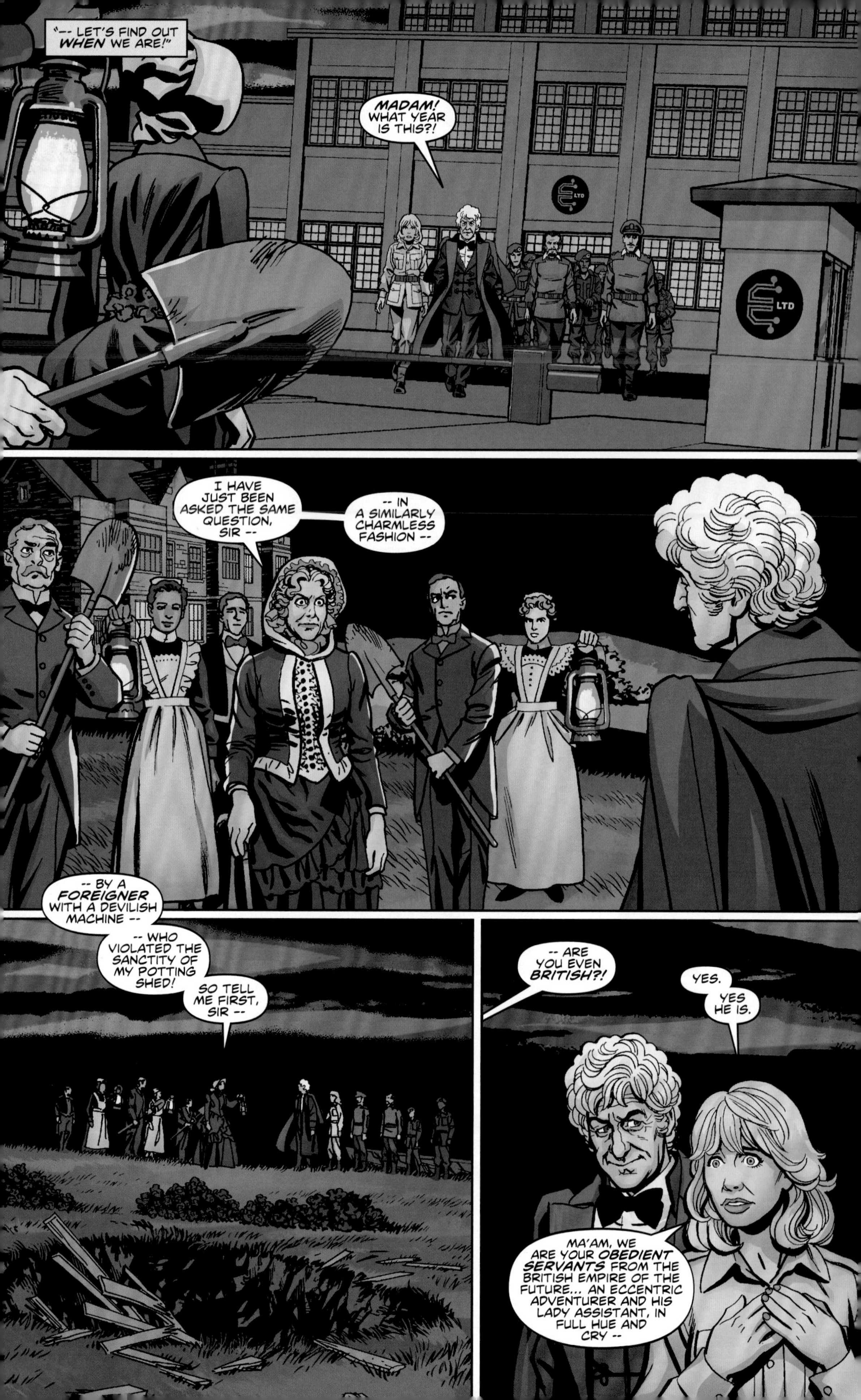
"-- LET'S FIND OUT WHEN WE ARE!"
MADAM! WHAT YEAR IS THIS?!
I HAVE JUST BEEN ASKED THE SAME QUESTION, SIR --
-- IN A SIMILARLY CHARMLESS FASHION --
-- BY A FOREIGNER WITH A DEVILISH MACHINE --
-- WHO VIOLATED THE SANCTITY OF MY POTTING SHED!
SO TELL ME FIRST, SIR --
-- ARE YOU EVEN BRITISH?!
YES.
YES HE IS.
MA'AM, WE ARE YOUR OBEDIENT SERVANTS FROM THE BRITISH EMPIRE OF THE FUTURE... AN ECCENTRIC ADVENTURER AND HIS LADY ASSISTANT, IN FULL HUE AND CRY --

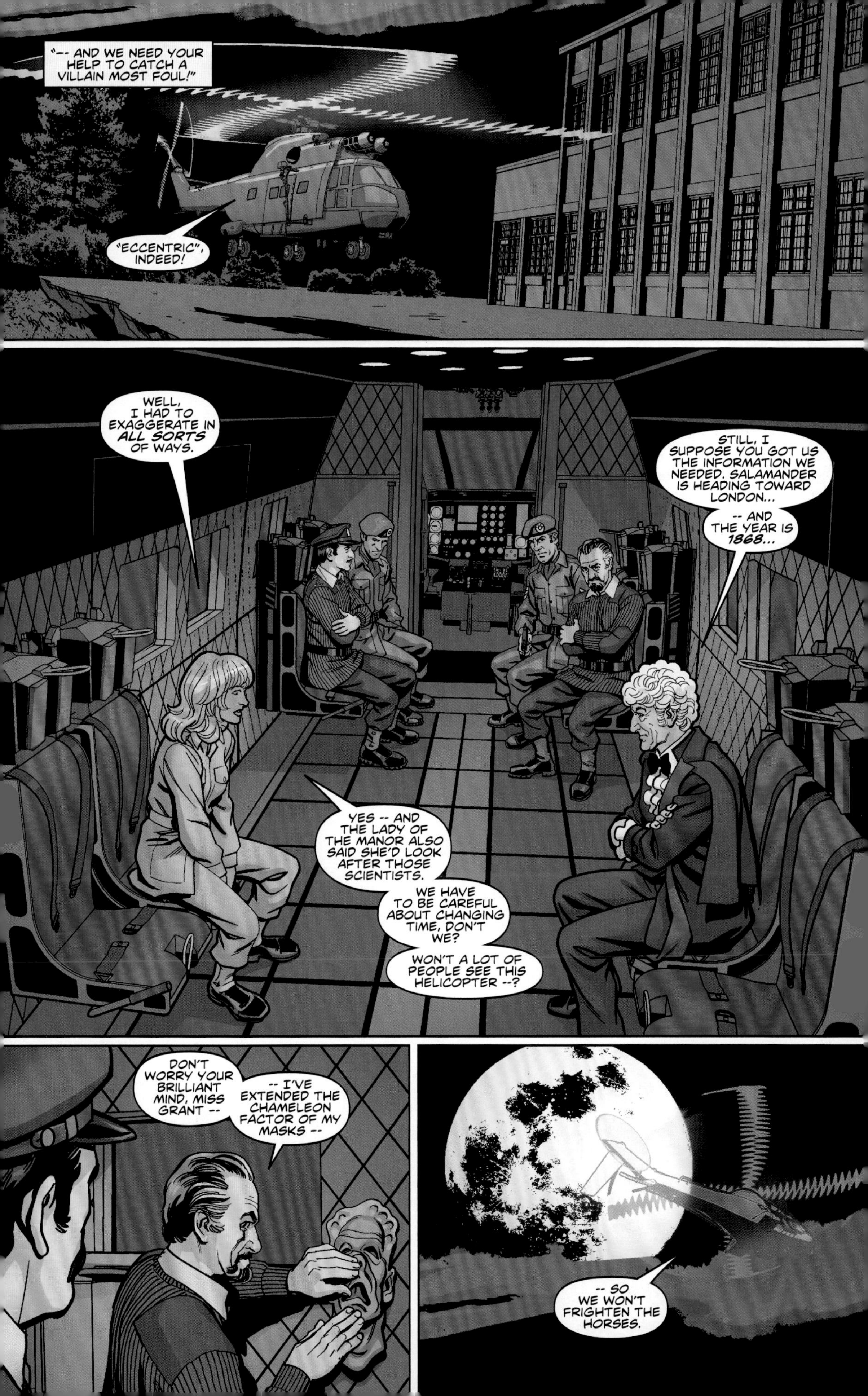
"-- AND WE NEED YOUR HELP TO CATCH A VILLAIN MOST FOUL!"
"ECCENTRIC", INDEED!
WELL, I HAD TO EXAGGERATE IN ALL SORTS OF WAYS.
STILL, I SUPPOSE YOU GOT US THE INFORMATION WE NEEDED. SALAMANDER IS HEADING TOWARD LONDON...
-- AND THE YEAR IS 1868...
YES -- AND THE LADY OF THE MANOR ALSO SAID SHE'D LOOK AFTER THOSE SCIENTISTS.
WE HAVE TO BE CAREFUL ABOUT CHANGING TIME, DON'T WE?
WON'T A LOT OF PEOPLE SEE THIS HELICOPTER --?
DON'T WORRY YOUR BRILLIANT MIND, MISS GRANT --
-- I'VE EXTENDED THE CHAMELEON FACTOR OF MY MASKS --
-- SO WE WON'T FRIGHTEN THE HORSES.

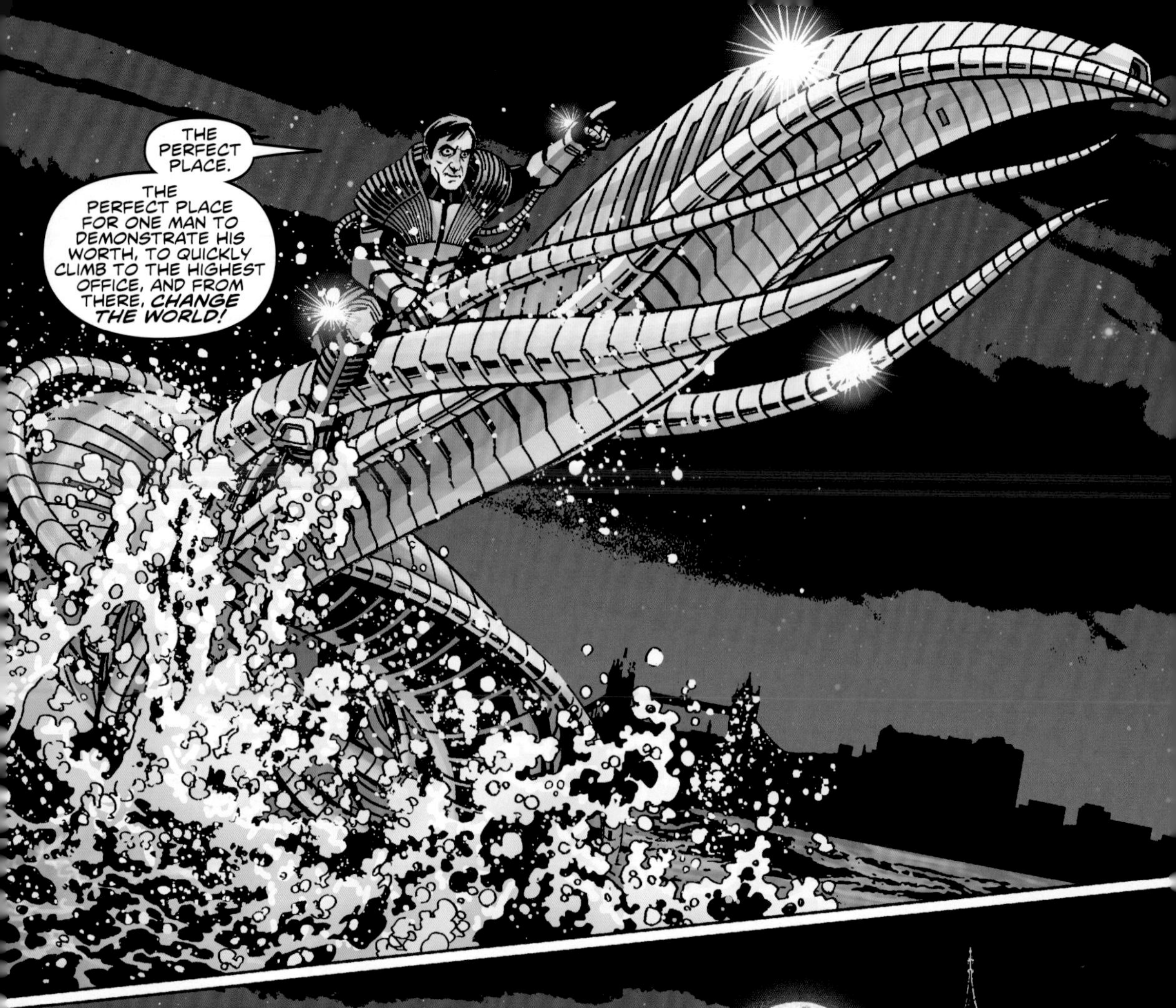
THE PERFECT PLACE.
THE PERFECT PLACE FOR ONE MAN TO DEMONSTRATE HIS WORTH, TO QUICKLY CLIMB TO THE HIGHEST OFFICE, AND FROM THERE, *CHANGE THE WORLD!*

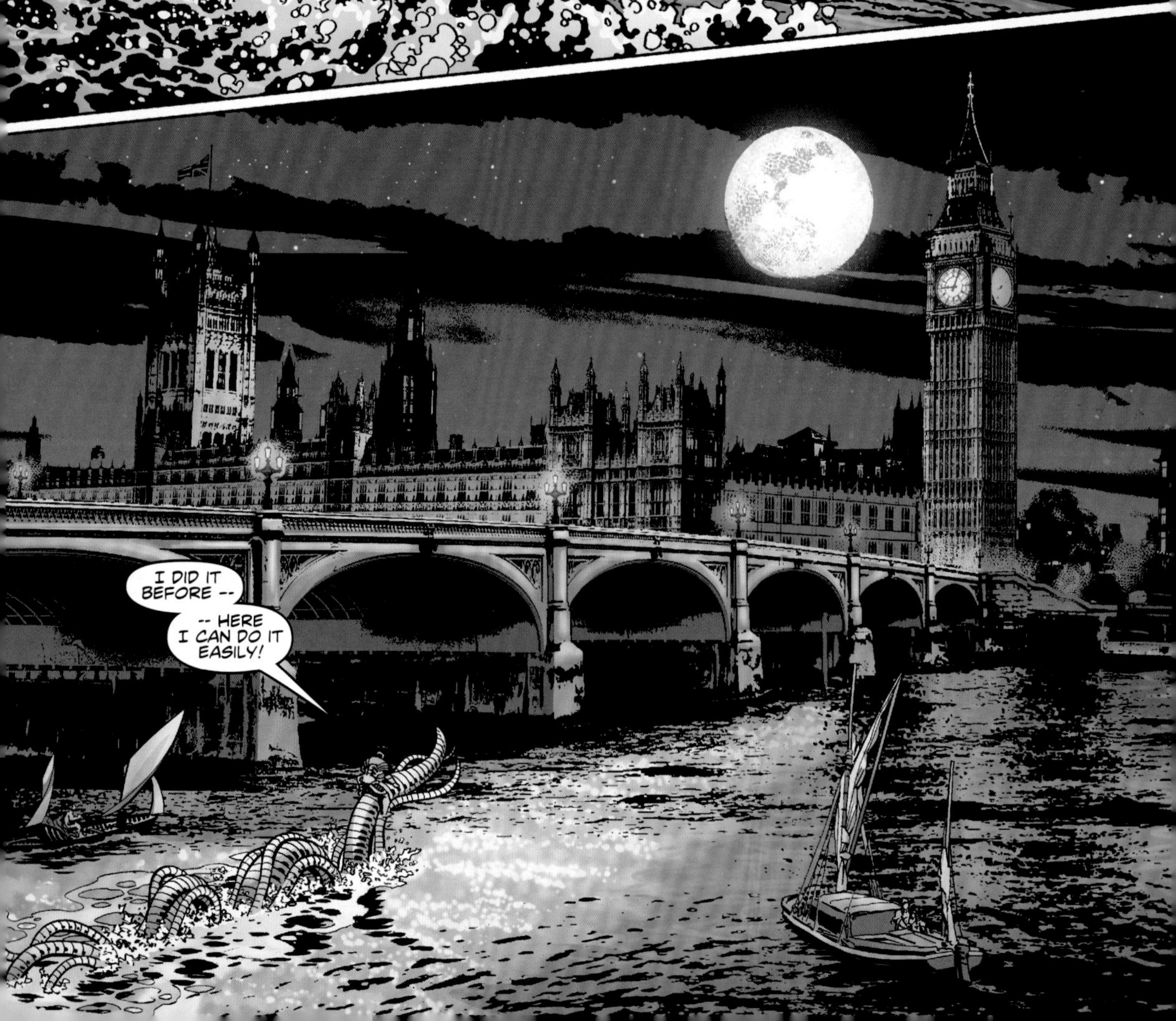
I DID IT BEFORE --
-- HERE I CAN DO IT EASILY!

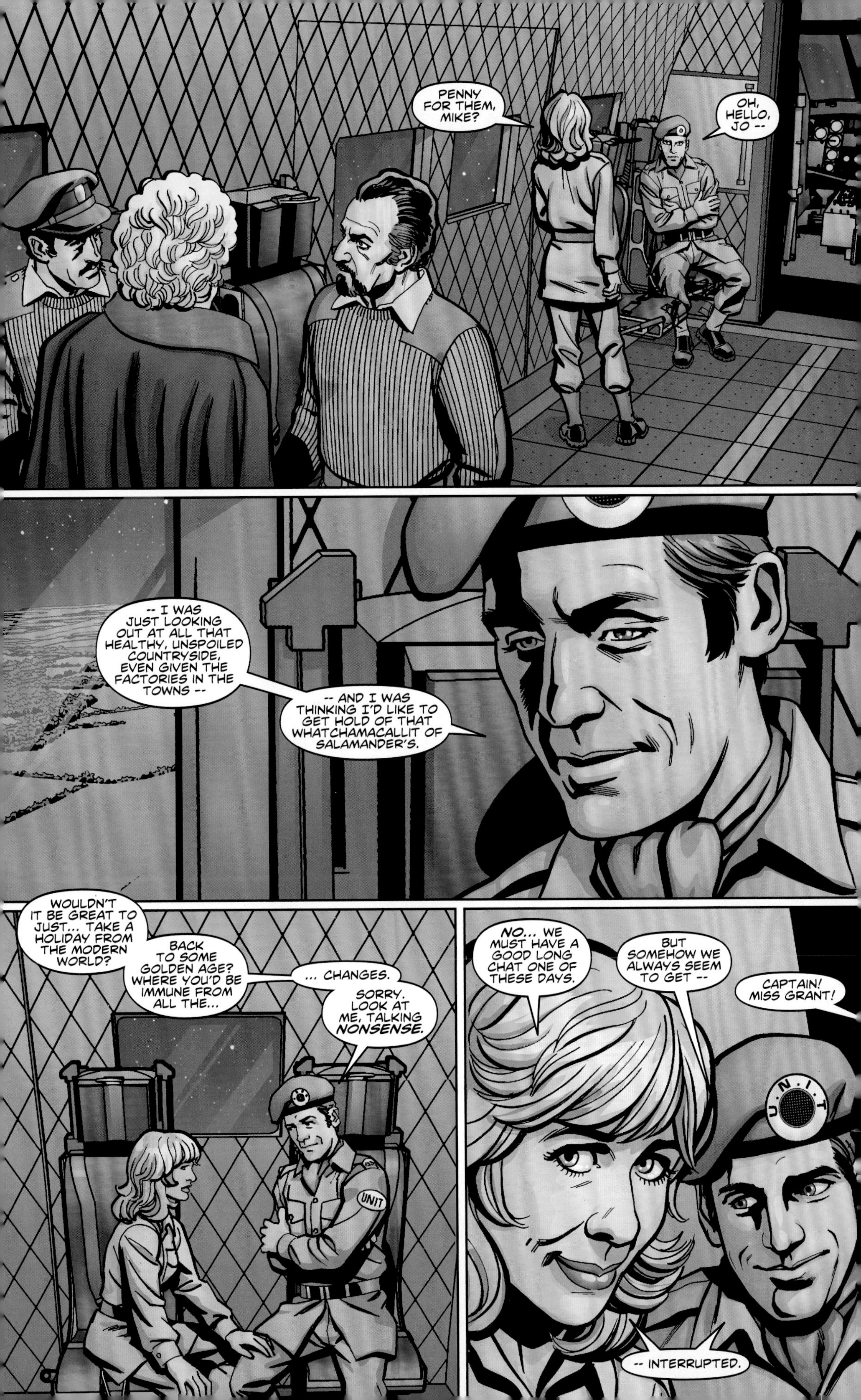
PENNY FOR THEM, MIKE?
OH, HELLO, JO --
-- I WAS JUST LOOKING OUT AT ALL THAT HEALTHY, UNSPOILED COUNTRYSIDE, EVEN GIVEN THE FACTORIES IN THE TOWNS --
-- AND I WAS THINKING I'D LIKE TO GET HOLD OF THAT WHATCHAMACALLIT OF SALAMANDER'S.
WOULDN'T IT BE GREAT TO JUST... TAKE A HOLIDAY FROM THE MODERN WORLD?
BACK TO SOME GOLDEN AGE? WHERE YOU'D BE IMMUNE FROM ALL THE...
... CHANGES.
SORRY. LOOK AT ME, TALKING *NONSENSE*.
UNIT
NO... WE MUST HAVE A GOOD LONG CHAT ONE OF THESE DAYS.
BUT SOMEHOW WE ALWAYS SEEM TO GET --
CAPTAIN! MISS GRANT!
-- INTERRUPTED.
U.N.I.T

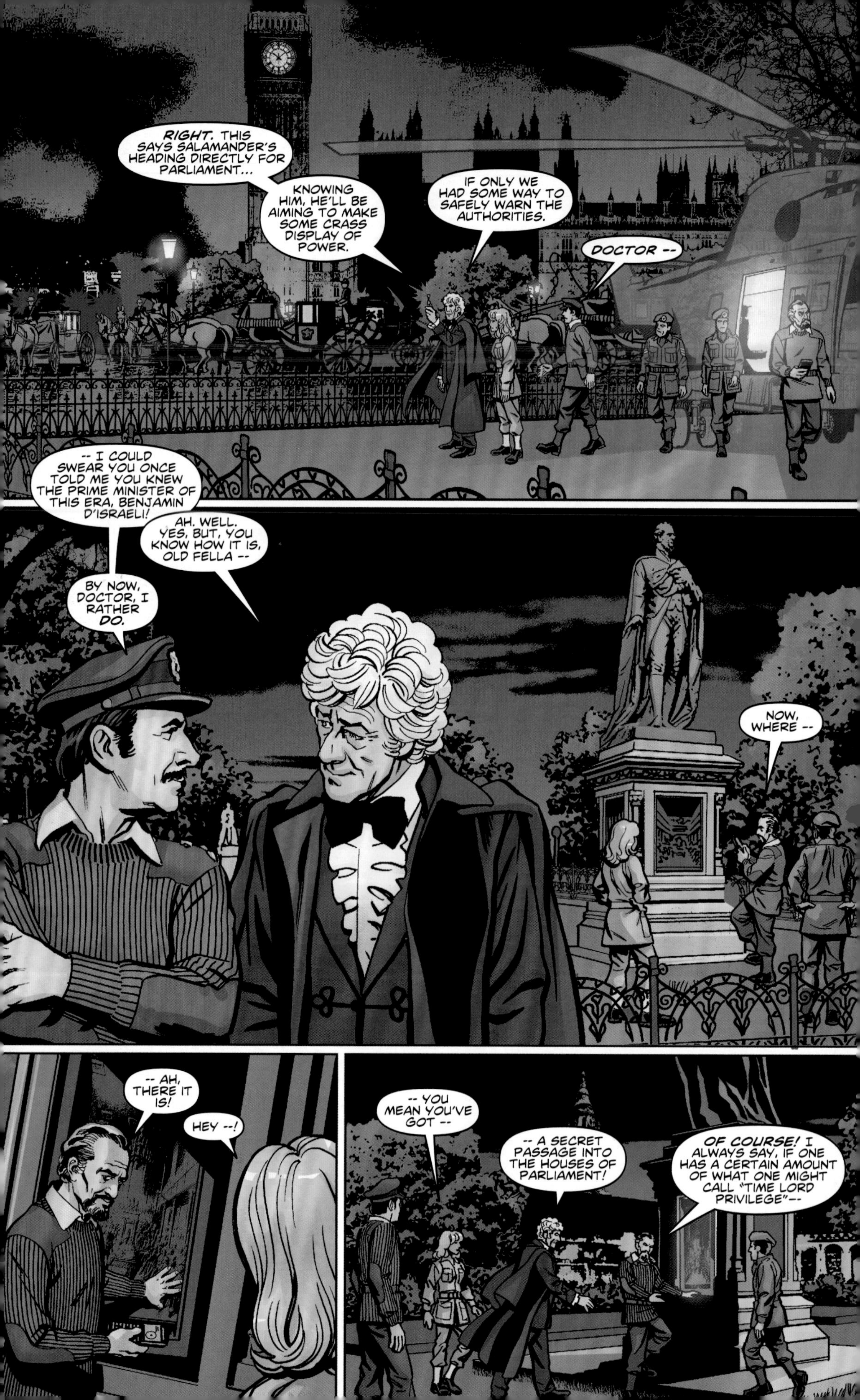
RIGHT. THIS SAYS SALAMANDER'S HEADING DIRECTLY FOR PARLIAMENT...
KNOWING HIM, HE'LL BE AIMING TO MAKE SOME CRASS DISPLAY OF POWER.
IF ONLY WE HAD SOME WAY TO SAFELY WARN THE AUTHORITIES.
DOCTOR --
-- I COULD SWEAR YOU ONCE TOLD ME YOU KNEW THE PRIME MINISTER OF THIS ERA, BENJAMIN D'ISRAELI!
AH. WELL. YES, BUT, YOU KNOW HOW IT IS, OLD FELLA --
BY NOW, DOCTOR, I RATHER DO.
NOW, WHERE --
-- AH, THERE IT IS!
HEY --!
-- YOU MEAN YOU'VE GOT --
-- A SECRET PASSAGE INTO THE HOUSES OF PARLIAMENT!
OF COURSE! I ALWAYS SAY, IF ONE HAS A CERTAIN AMOUNT OF WHAT ONE MIGHT CALL "TIME LORD PRIVILEGE"--

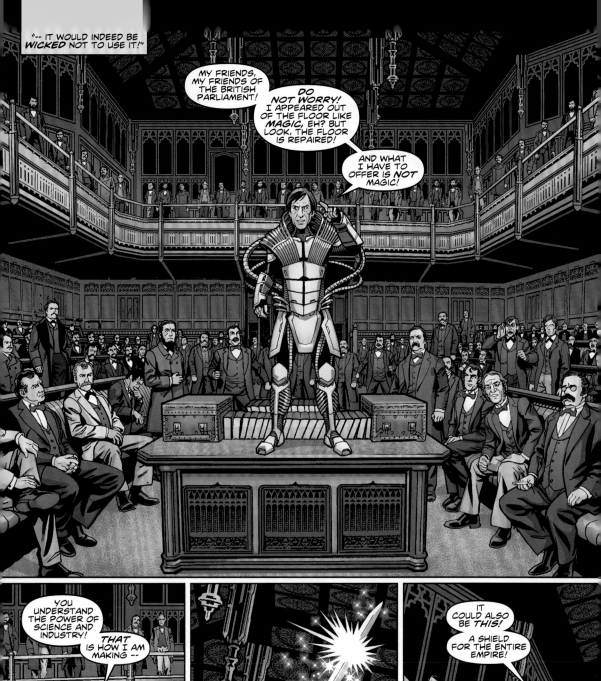

"-- IT WOULD INDEED BE *WICKED* NOT TO USE IT!"

MY FRIENDS, MY FRIENDS OF THE BRITISH PARLIAMENT!

DO NOT WORRY! I APPEARED OUT OF THE FLOOR LIKE *MAGIC*, EH? BUT LOOK, THE FLOOR IS REPAIRED!

AND WHAT I HAVE TO OFFER IS *NOT* MAGIC!

YOU UNDERSTAND THE POWER OF SCIENCE AND INDUSTRY! *THAT* IS HOW I AM MAKING --

-- *THIS!* BUT HAVE NO FEAR!

IT COULD ALSO BE *THIS!* A SHIELD FOR THE ENTIRE EMPIRE!

AN EMPIRE WHICH WOULD SWIFTLY *GROW!*

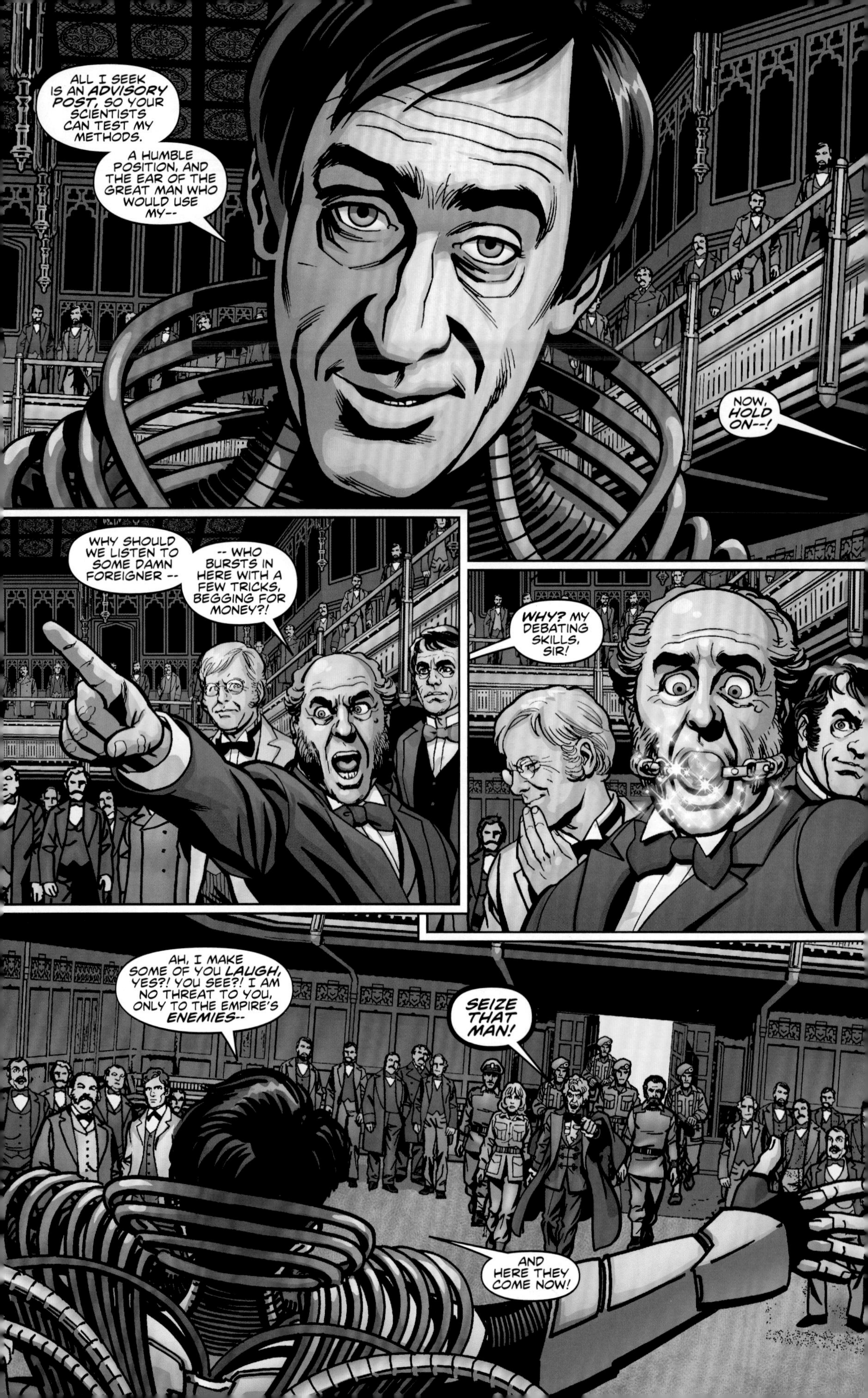

ALL I SEEK IS AN ADVISORY POST, SO YOUR SCIENTISTS CAN TEST MY METHODS.
A HUMBLE POSITION, AND THE EAR OF THE GREAT MAN WHO WOULD USE MY--
NOW, HOLD ON--!
WHY SHOULD WE LISTEN TO SOME DAMN FOREIGNER --
-- WHO BURSTS IN HERE WITH A FEW TRICKS, BEGGING FOR MONEY?!
WHY? MY DEBATING SKILLS, SIR!
AH, I MAKE SOME OF YOU LAUGH, YES?! YOU SEE?! I AM NO THREAT TO YOU, ONLY TO THE EMPIRE'S ENEMIES--
SEIZE THAT MAN!
AND HERE THEY COME NOW!

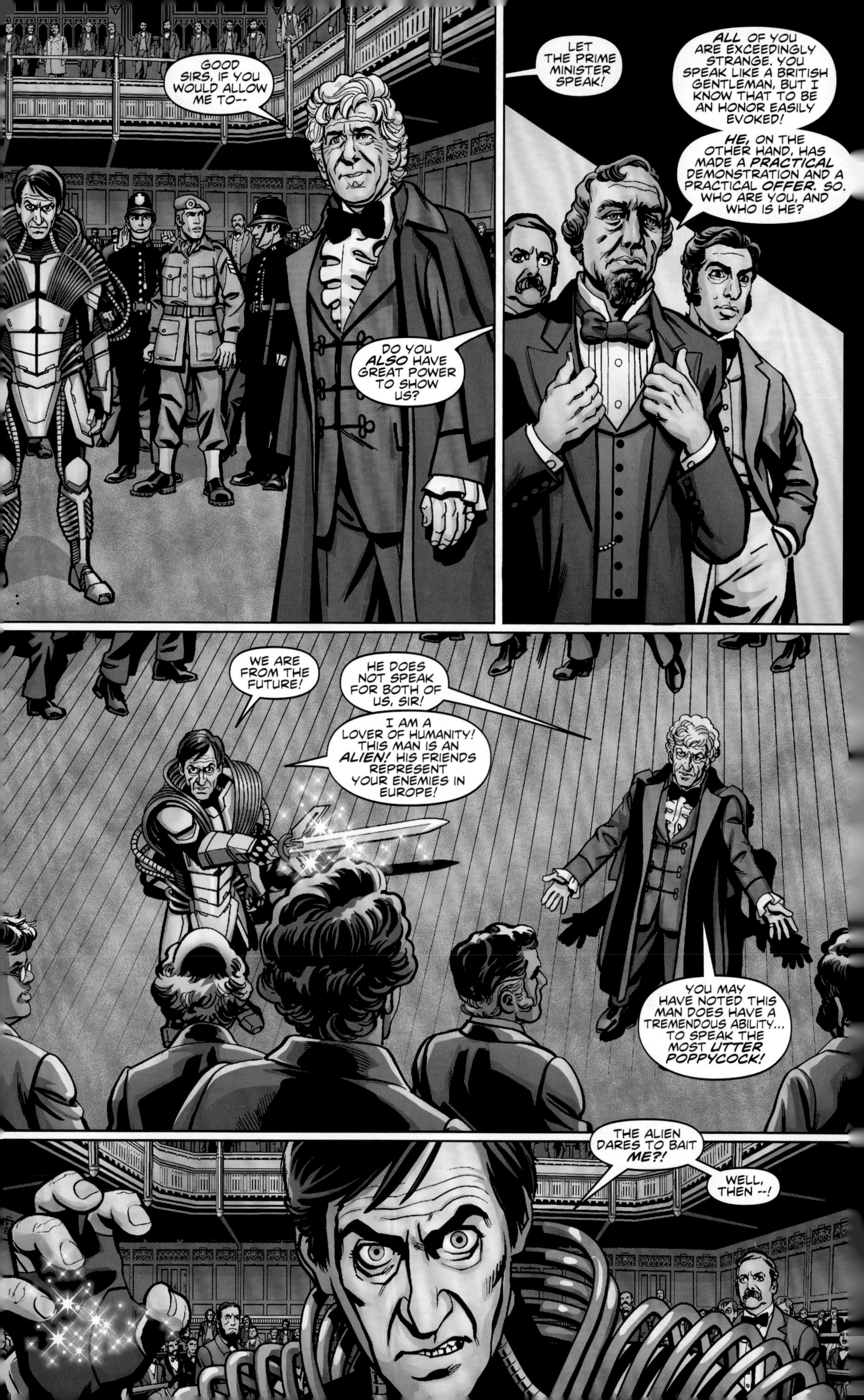
GOOD SIRS, IF YOU WOULD ALLOW ME TO--
DO YOU ALSO HAVE GREAT POWER TO SHOW US?
LET THE PRIME MINISTER SPEAK!
ALL OF YOU ARE EXCEEDINGLY STRANGE. YOU SPEAK LIKE A BRITISH GENTLEMAN, BUT I KNOW THAT TO BE AN HONOR EASILY EVOKED!
HE, ON THE OTHER HAND, HAS MADE A PRACTICAL DEMONSTRATION AND A PRACTICAL OFFER. SO. WHO ARE YOU, AND WHO IS HE?
WE ARE FROM THE FUTURE!
HE DOES NOT SPEAK FOR BOTH OF US, SIR!
I AM A LOVER OF HUMANITY! THIS MAN IS AN ALIEN! HIS FRIENDS REPRESENT YOUR ENEMIES IN EUROPE!
YOU MAY HAVE NOTED THIS MAN DOES HAVE A TREMENDOUS ABILITY... TO SPEAK THE MOST UTTER POPPYCOCK!
THE ALIEN DARES TO BAIT ME?!
WELL, THEN --!

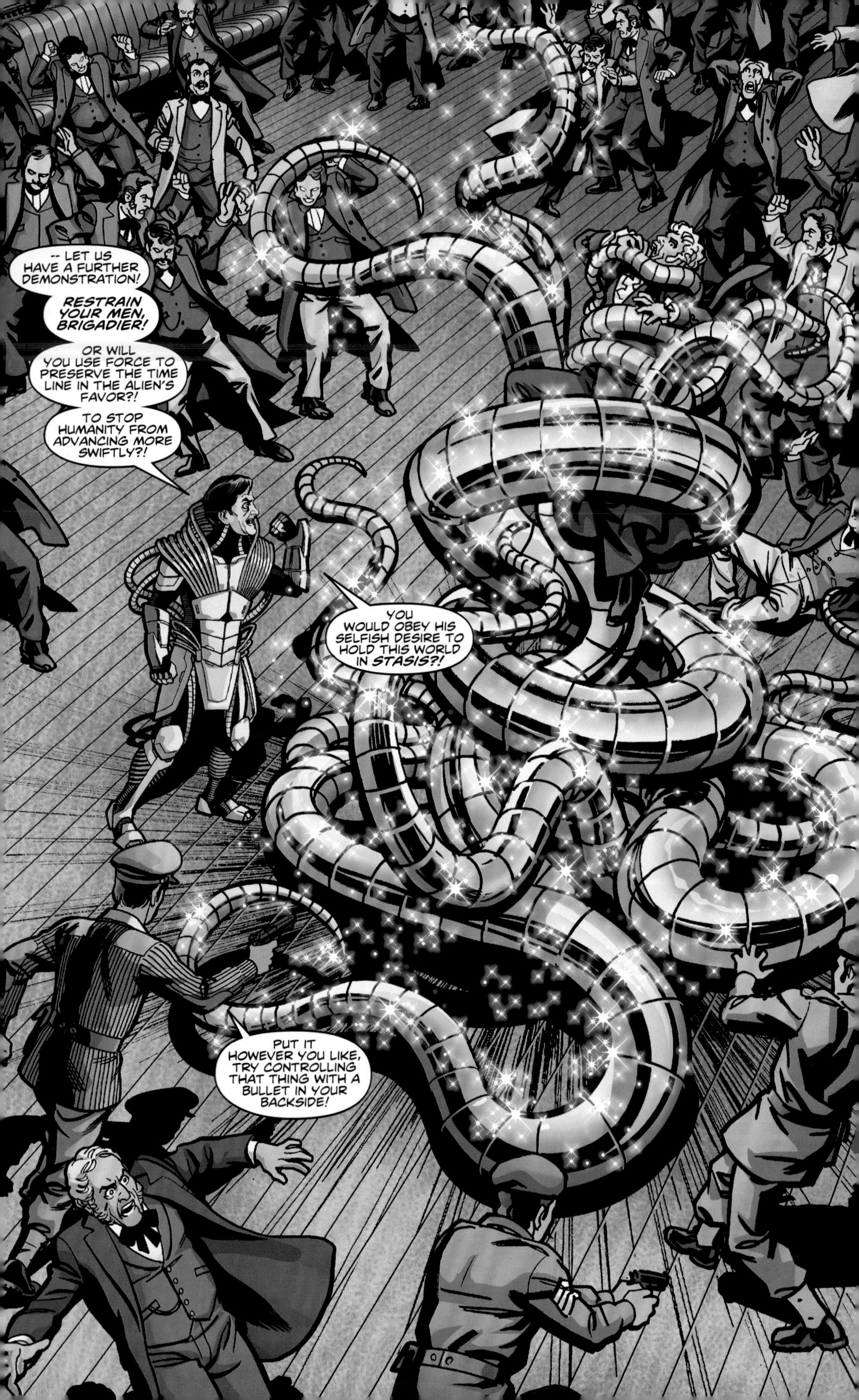
-- LET US HAVE A FURTHER DEMONSTRATION!
RESTRAIN YOUR MEN, BRIGADIER!
OR WILL YOU USE FORCE TO PRESERVE THE TIME LINE IN THE ALIEN'S FAVOR?!
TO STOP HUMANITY FROM ADVANCING MORE SWIFTLY?!
YOU WOULD OBEY HIS SELFISH DESIRE TO HOLD THIS WORLD IN STASIS?!
PUT IT HOWEVER YOU LIKE. TRY CONTROLLING THAT THING WITH A BULLET IN YOUR BACKSIDE!

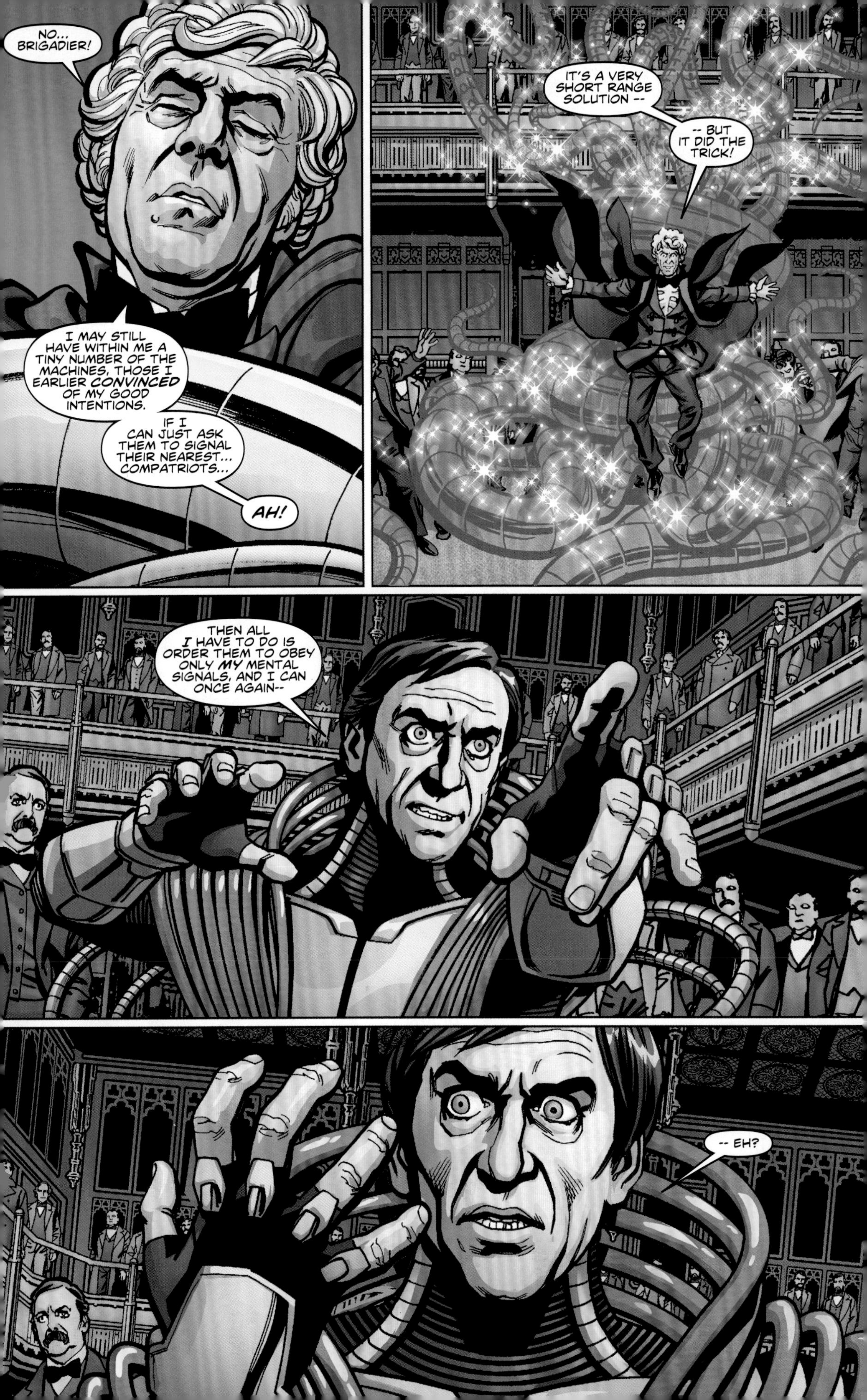
NO... BRIGADIER!
I MAY STILL HAVE WITHIN ME A TINY NUMBER OF THE MACHINES, THOSE I EARLIER CONVINCED OF MY GOOD INTENTIONS.
IF I CAN JUST ASK THEM TO SIGNAL THEIR NEAREST... COMPATRIOTS...
AH!
IT'S A VERY SHORT RANGE SOLUTION --
-- BUT IT DID THE TRICK!
THEN ALL I HAVE TO DO IS ORDER THEM TO OBEY ONLY MY MENTAL SIGNALS, AND I CAN ONCE AGAIN--
-- EH?

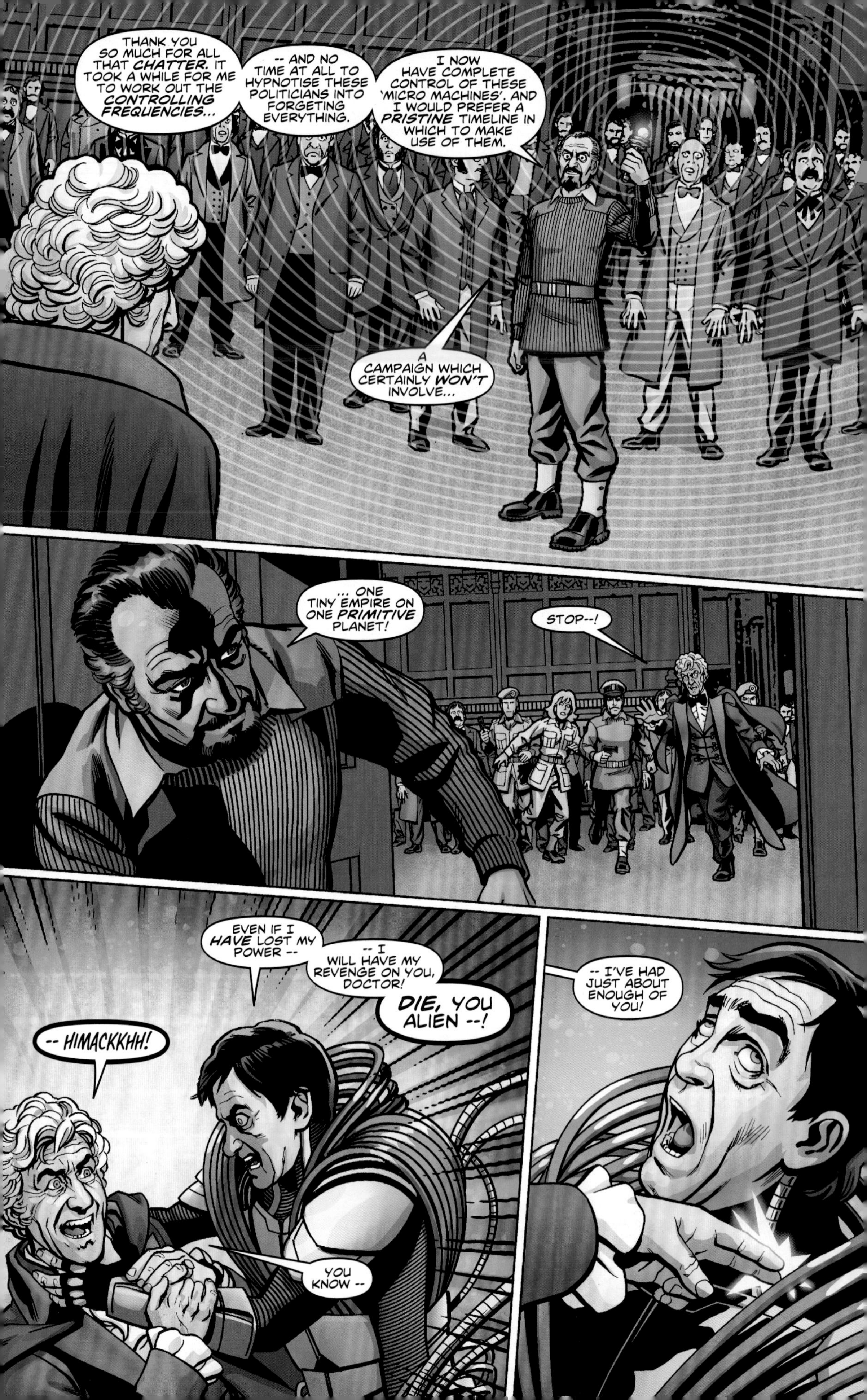
THANK YOU SO MUCH FOR ALL THAT CHATTER. IT TOOK A WHILE FOR ME TO WORK OUT THE CONTROLLING FREQUENCIES...
-- AND NO TIME AT ALL TO HYPNOTISE THESE POLITICIANS INTO FORGETING EVERYTHING.
I NOW HAVE COMPLETE CONTROL OF THESE 'MICRO MACHINES'. AND I WOULD PREFER A PRISTINE TIMELINE IN WHICH TO MAKE USE OF THEM.
A CAMPAIGN WHICH CERTAINLY WON'T INVOLVE...
... ONE TINY EMPIRE ON ONE PRIMITIVE PLANET!
STOP--!
EVEN IF I HAVE LOST MY POWER --
-- I WILL HAVE MY REVENGE ON YOU, DOCTOR!
DIE, YOU ALIEN --!
-- HIMACKKHH!
YOU KNOW --
-- I'VE HAD JUST ABOUT ENOUGH OF YOU!

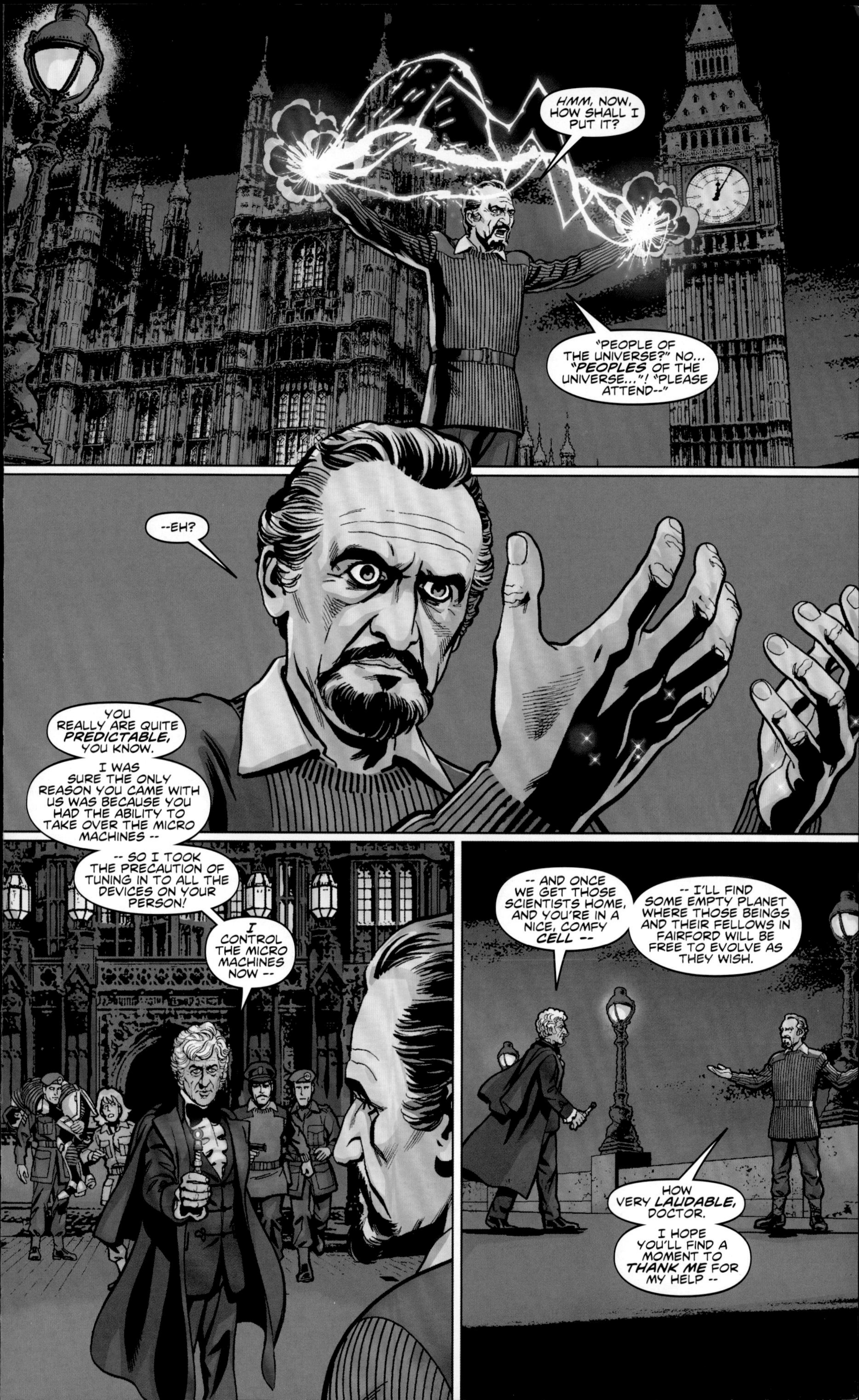
HMM, NOW, HOW SHALL I PUT IT?
"PEOPLE OF THE UNIVERSE?" NO... "PEOPLES OF THE UNIVERSE..."! "PLEASE ATTEND--"
--EH?
YOU REALLY ARE QUITE PREDICTABLE, YOU KNOW.
I WAS SURE THE ONLY REASON YOU CAME WITH US WAS BECAUSE YOU HAD THE ABILITY TO TAKE OVER THE MICRO MACHINES --
-- SO I TOOK THE PRECAUTION OF TUNING IN TO ALL THE DEVICES ON YOUR PERSON!
I CONTROL THE MICRO MACHINES NOW --
-- AND ONCE WE GET THOSE SCIENTISTS HOME, AND YOU'RE IN A NICE, COMFY CELL --
-- I'LL FIND SOME EMPTY PLANET WHERE THOSE BEINGS AND THEIR FELLOWS IN FAIRFORD WILL BE FREE TO EVOLVE AS THEY WISH.
HOW VERY LAUDABLE, DOCTOR.
I HOPE YOU'LL FIND A MOMENT TO THANK ME FOR MY HELP --

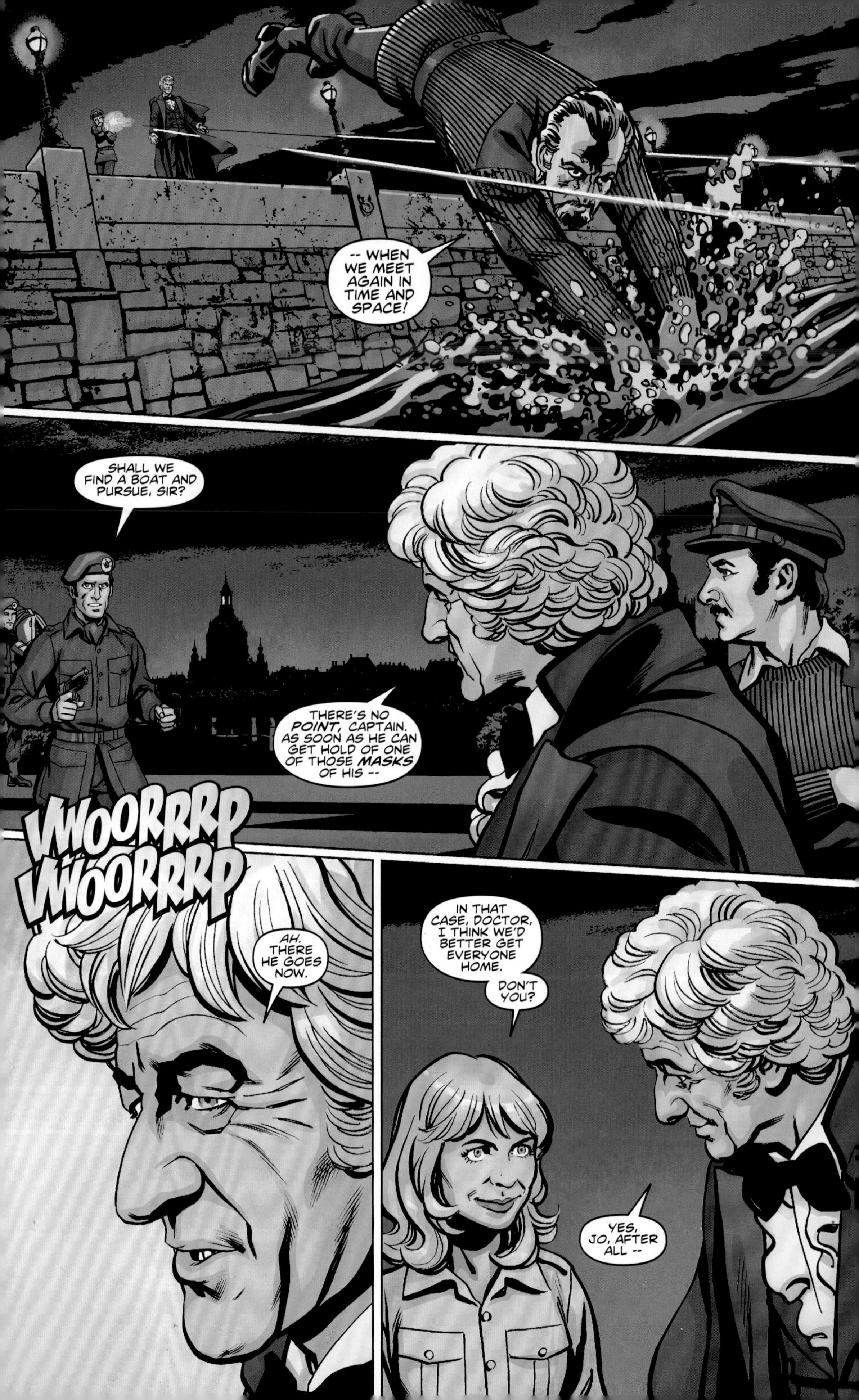
-- WHEN WE MEET AGAIN IN TIME AND SPACE!
SHALL WE FIND A BOAT AND PURSUE, SIR?
THERE'S NO POINT, CAPTAIN. AS SOON AS HE CAN GET HOLD OF ONE OF THOSE MASKS OF HIS --
VWOORRRP VWOORRRP
AH. THERE HE GOES NOW.
IN THAT CASE, DOCTOR, I THINK WE'D BETTER GET EVERYONE HOME.
DON'T YOU?
YES, JO, AFTER ALL --

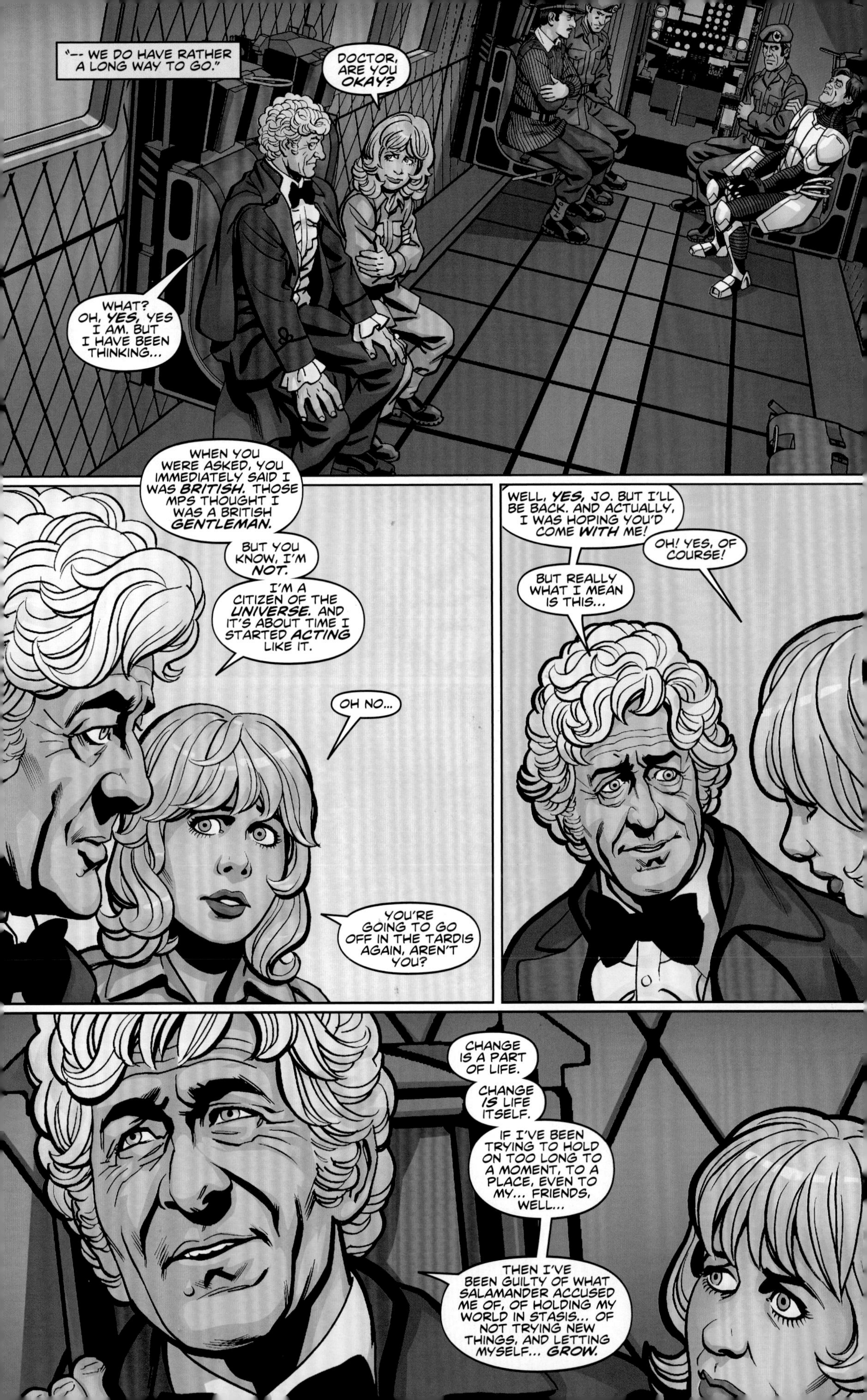
"-- WE DO HAVE RATHER A LONG WAY TO GO."
DOCTOR, ARE YOU OKAY?
WHAT? OH, YES, YES I AM. BUT I HAVE BEEN THINKING...
WHEN YOU WERE ASKED, YOU IMMEDIATELY SAID I WAS BRITISH. THOSE MPS THOUGHT I WAS A BRITISH GENTLEMAN.
BUT YOU KNOW, I'M NOT.
I'M A CITIZEN OF THE UNIVERSE. AND IT'S ABOUT TIME I STARTED ACTING LIKE IT.
OH NO...
YOU'RE GOING TO GO OFF IN THE TARDIS AGAIN, AREN'T YOU?
WELL, YES, JO. BUT I'LL BE BACK. AND ACTUALLY, I WAS HOPING YOU'D COME WITH ME!
OH! YES, OF COURSE!
BUT REALLY WHAT I MEAN IS THIS...
CHANGE IS A PART OF LIFE.
CHANGE IS LIFE ITSELF.
IF I'VE BEEN TRYING TO HOLD ON TOO LONG TO A MOMENT, TO A PLACE, EVEN TO MY... FRIENDS, WELL...
THEN I'VE BEEN GUILTY OF WHAT SALAMANDER ACCUSED ME OF, OF HOLDING MY WORLD IN STASIS... OF NOT TRYING NEW THINGS, AND LETTING MYSELF... GROW.

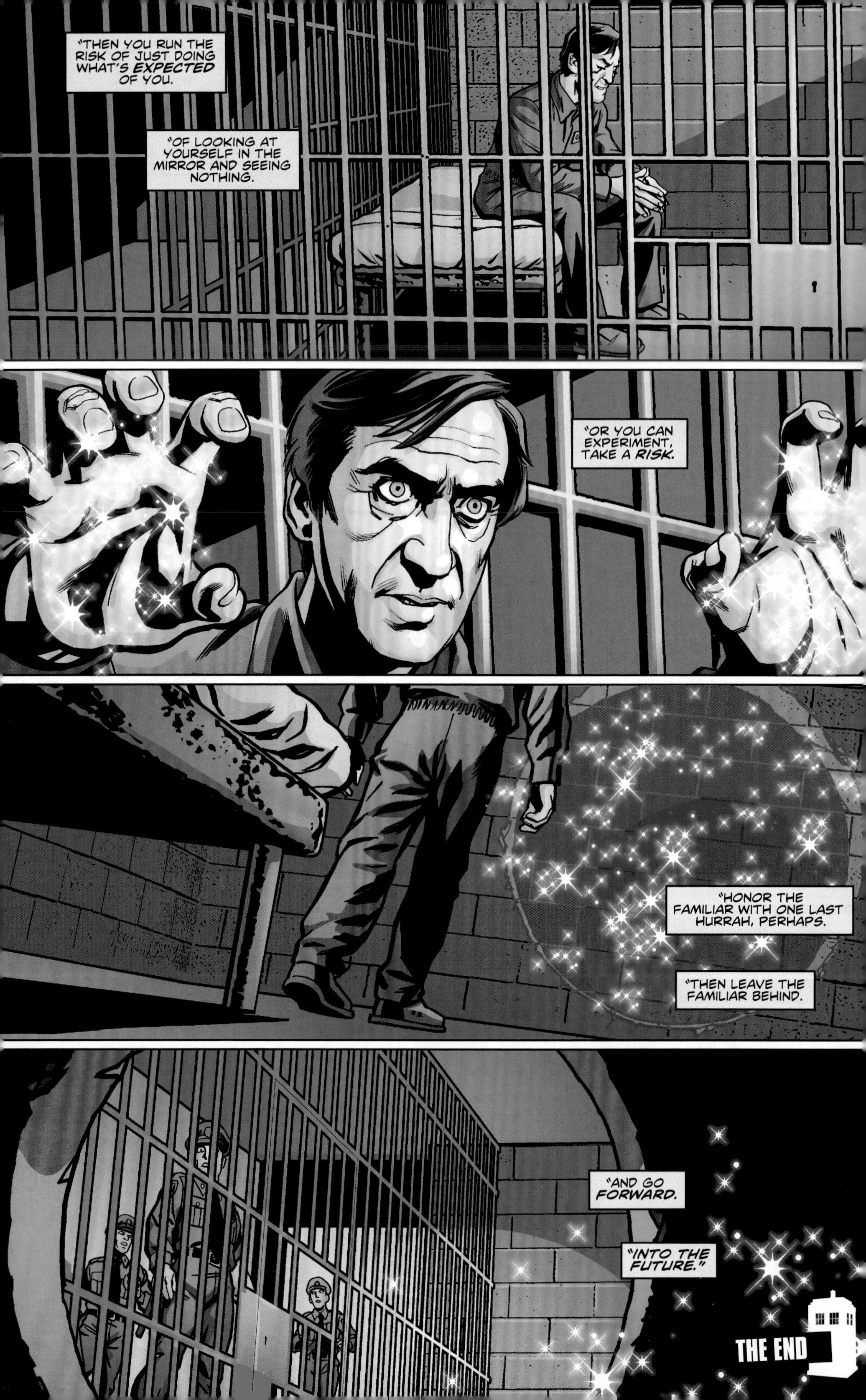
"THEN YOU RUN THE RISK OF JUST DOING WHAT'S *EXPECTED* OF YOU.
"OF LOOKING AT YOURSELF IN THE MIRROR AND SEEING NOTHING.
"OR YOU CAN EXPERIMENT, TAKE A *RISK*.
"HONOR THE FAMILIAR WITH ONE LAST HURRAH, PERHAPS.
"THEN LEAVE THE FAMILIAR BEHIND.
"AND GO *FORWARD*.
"*INTO THE FUTURE.*"
THE END

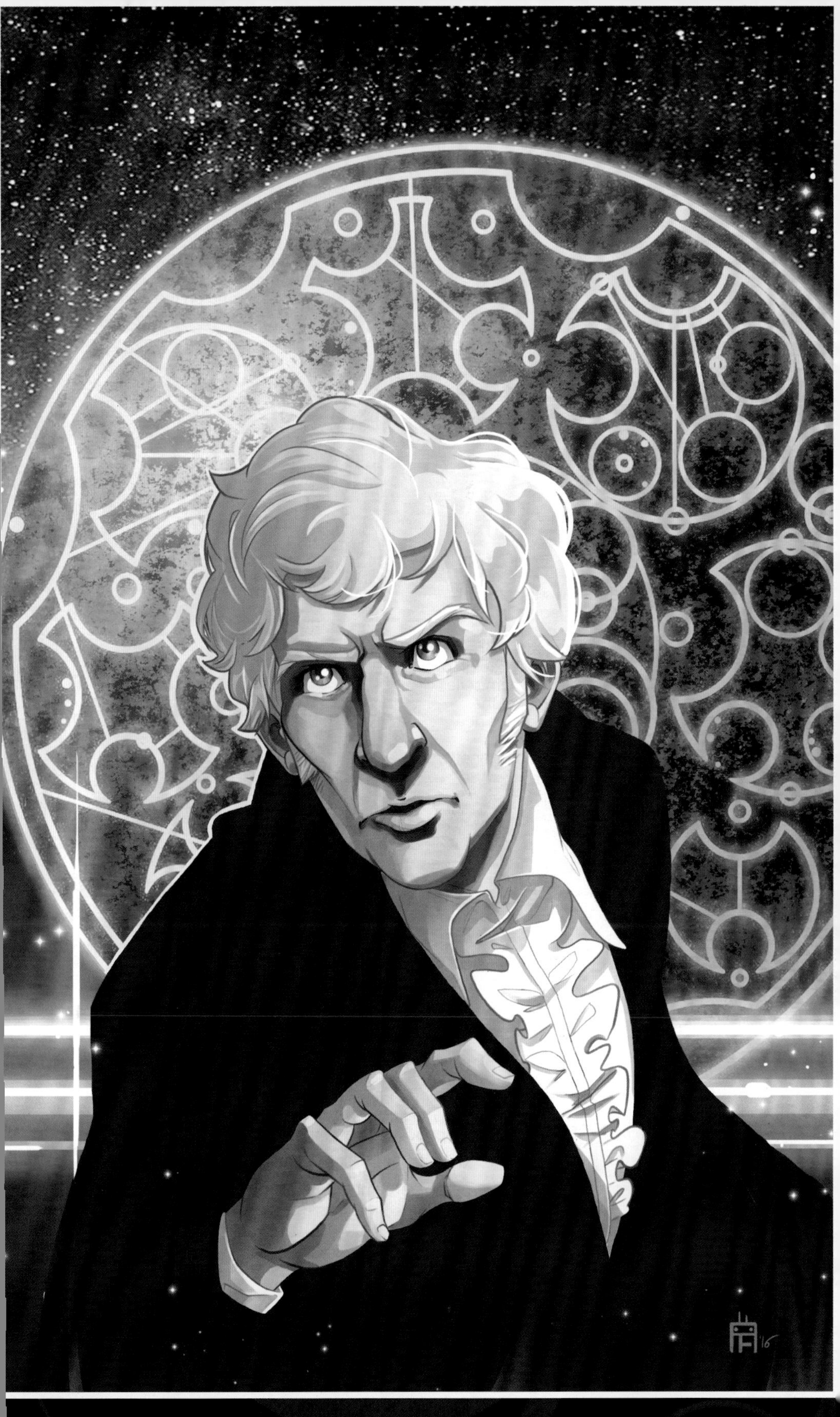

HERALDS OF DESTRUCTION: ISSUE #3

Cover A: ARIANNA FLOREAN

BBC DOCTOR WHO

PAUL CORNELL'S WRITER'S COMMENTARY

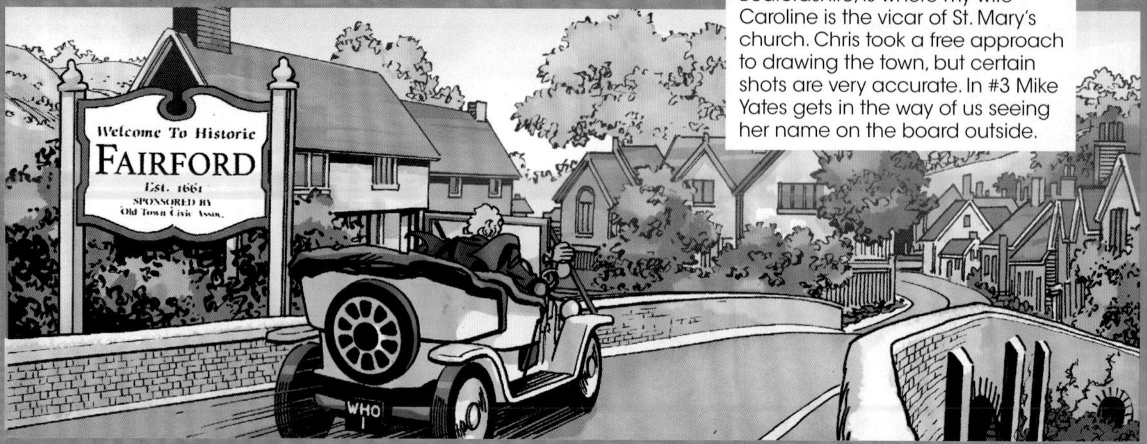
Welcome To Historic
FAIRFORD
Est. 1661
SPONSORED BY
Old Town Civic Assoc.
WHO 1

1 Fairford, though it's not in Bedfordshire, is where my wife Caroline is the vicar of St. Mary's church. Chris took a free approach to drawing the town, but certain shots are very accurate. In #3 Mike Yates gets in the way of us seeing her name on the board outside.

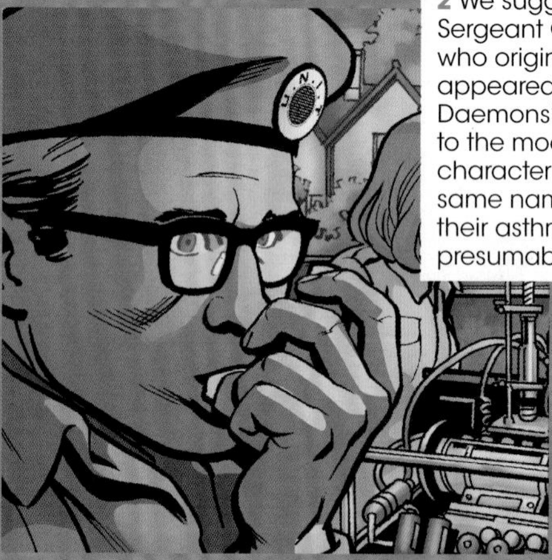

2 We suggest that Sergeant Osgood, who originally appeared in 'The Daemons', is related to the modern series character of the same name, since their asthma is presumably genetic.

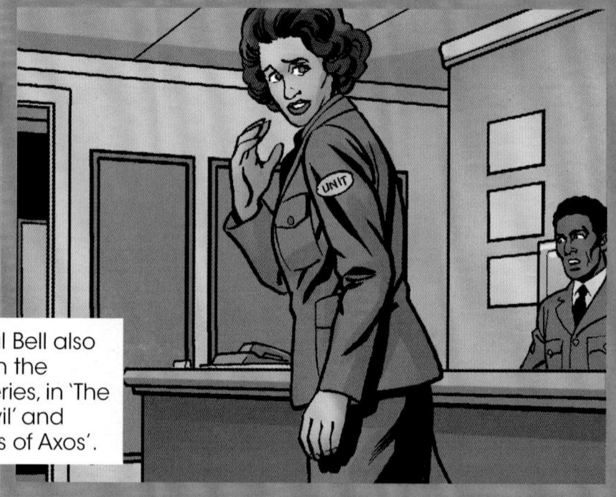
UNIT

3 Corporal Bell also appears in the original series, in 'The Mind of Evil' and 'The Claws of Axos'.

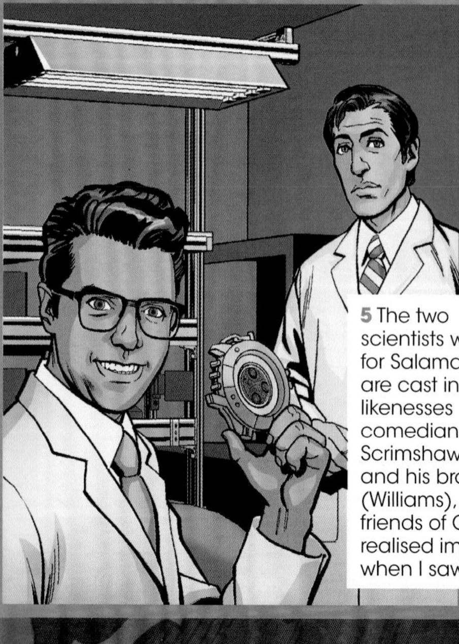

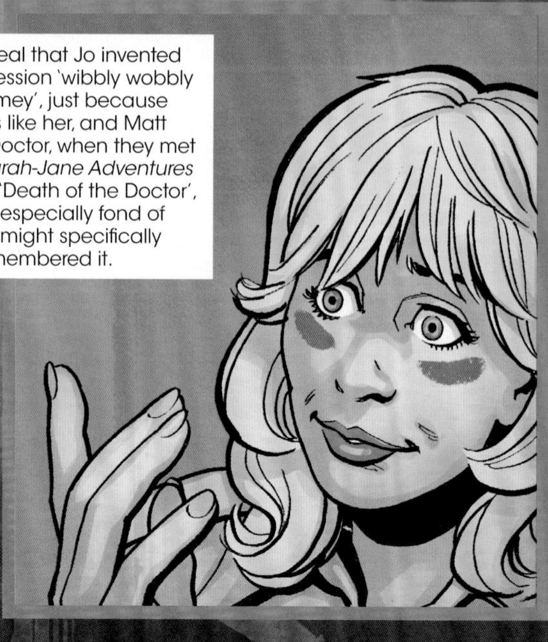

4 We reveal that Jo invented the expression 'wibbly wobbly timey-wimey', just because it sounds like her, and Matt Smith's Doctor, when they met in *The Sarah-Jane Adventures* episode 'Death of the Doctor', seemed especially fond of her, and might specifically have remembered it.

5 The two scientists working for Salamander are cast in the likenesses of geek comedian Joseph Scrimshaw (Draper) and his brother (Williams), who are friends of Chris. As I realised immediately when I saw the art!

TEN THINGS YOU MAY HAVE MISSED...

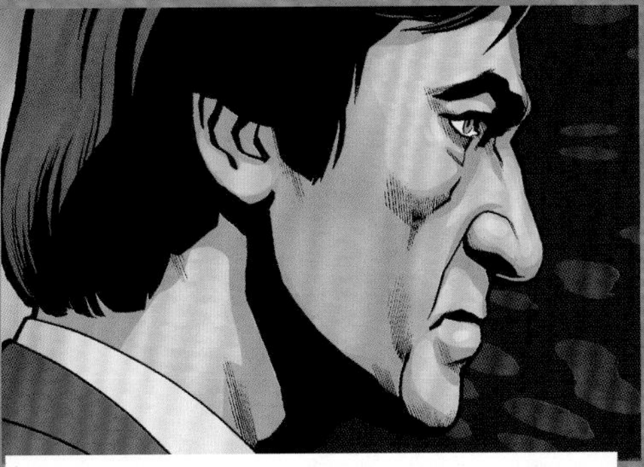

6 Critic Phil Sandifer has made much of David Whitaker's insertion of alchemical motifs into his stories, and so I took great delight in Whitaker's character, Salamander, speaking of 'living in the fire', as alchemical Salamanders do, in #4. 'Ingram's work at the Newton' is seen in the TV serial 'The Time Monster'.

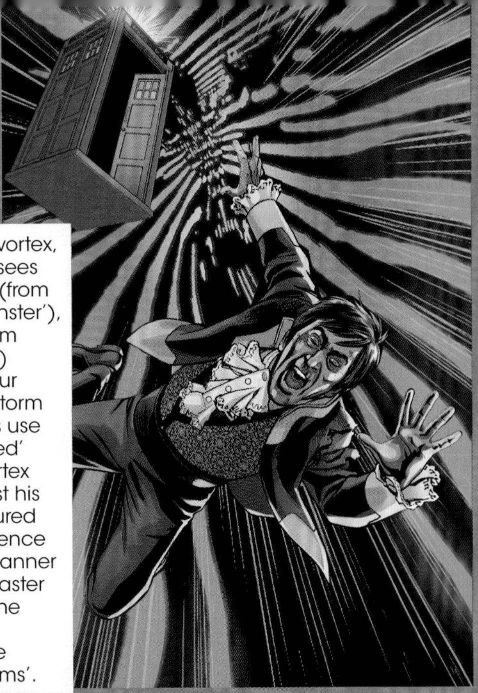

7 In the time vortex, Salamander sees Chronovores (from 'The Time Monster'), a Reaper (from 'Father's Day') and a Vortisaur (Big Finish's 'Storm Warning'). His use of 'untempered' about the vortex might suggest his brain was injured by the experience in a similar manner to how the Master was hurt by The Untempered Schism in 'The Sound of Drums'.

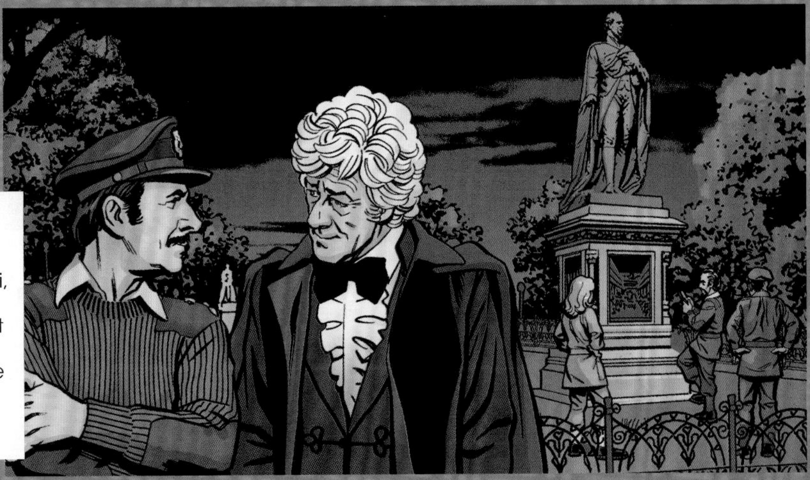

8 The start of issue #5 is also the (slightly modified) opening of 'Ballroom Blitz', a 1973 glam rock hit by The Sweet.

9 The Earl of Derby's statue, as seen in #5, is real, and Chris gives us a good likeness of Prime Minister Benjamin Disraeli, in my attempt at a pastiche of the Third Doctor era's penchant for budget-busting changes of location in the last episode. The Master finally works out what he'd like to say to the universe by the time of 'Logopolis'.

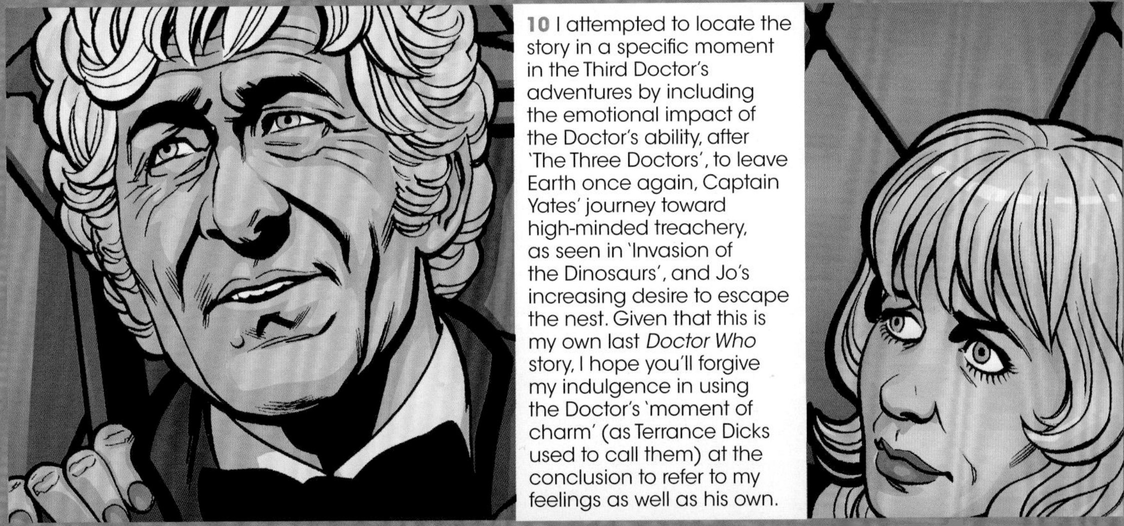

10 I attempted to locate the story in a specific moment in the Third Doctor's adventures by including the emotional impact of the Doctor's ability, after 'The Three Doctors', to leave Earth once again, Captain Yates' journey toward high-minded treachery, as seen in 'Invasion of the Dinosaurs', and Jo's increasing desire to escape the nest. Given that this is my own last *Doctor Who* story, I hope you'll forgive my indulgence in using the Doctor's 'moment of charm' (as Terrance Dicks used to call them) at the conclusion to refer to my feelings as well as his own.

BBC
DOCTOR WHO
THE THIRD DOCTOR

COVER GALLERY

A

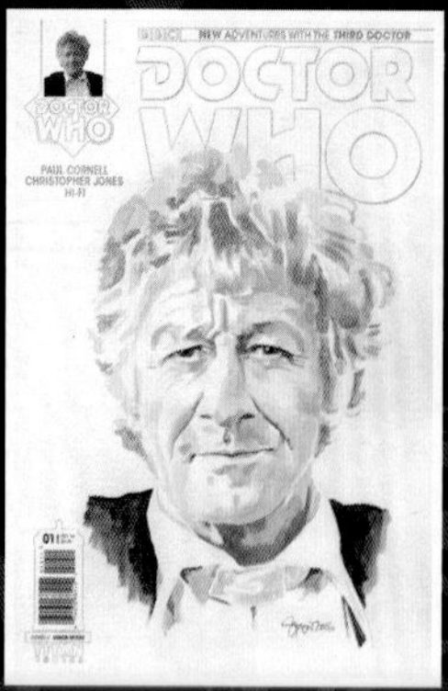

C

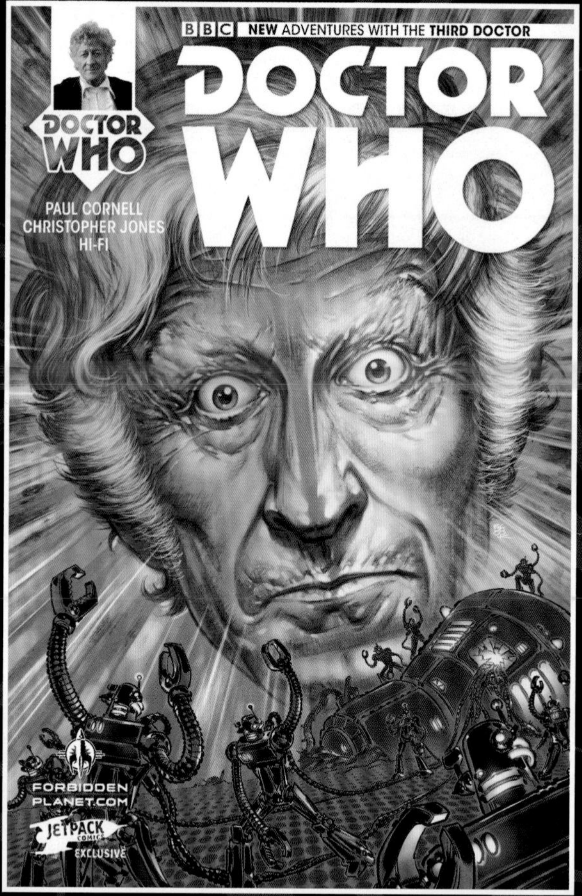
BBC NEW ADVENTURES WITH THE THIRD DOCTOR
DOCTOR WHO
DOCTOR WHO
PAUL CORNELL
CHRISTOPHER JONES
HI-FI
FORBIDDEN PLANET.COM
JETPACK COMICS
EXCLUSIVE

B

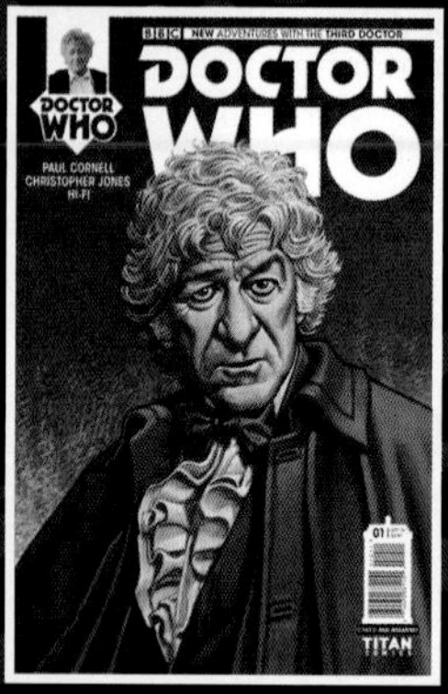
BBC NEW ADVENTURES WITH THE THIRD DOCTOR
DOCTOR WHO
DOCTOR WHO
PAUL CORNELL
CHRISTOPHER JONES
HI-FI
TITAN

D

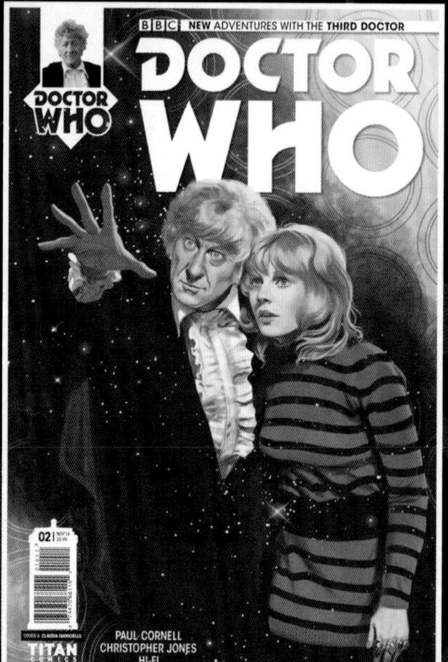
BBC NEW ADVENTURES WITH THE THIRD DOCTOR
DOCTOR WHO
DOCTOR WHO
PAUL CORNELL
CHRISTOPHER JONES
HI-FI
TITAN COMICS

E

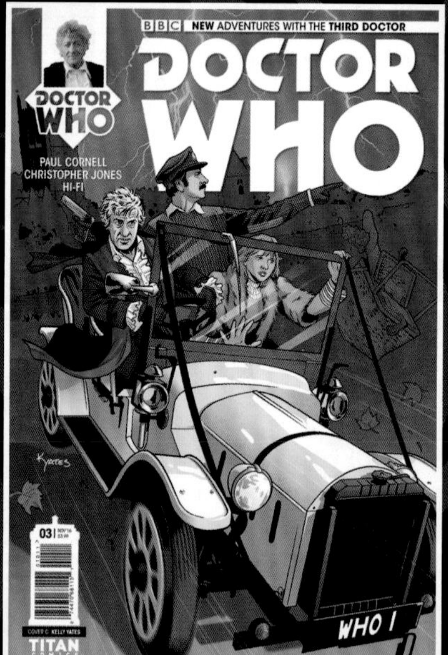
BBC NEW ADVENTURES WITH THE THIRD DOCTOR
DOCTOR WHO
DOCTOR WHO
PAUL CORNELL
CHRISTOPHER JONES
HI-FI
WHO 1
TITAN COMICS

ISSUES #1-3

A. #1C - SIMON MYERS
B. #1D - PAUL MCCAFFREY
C. #1 FORBIDDEN PLANET / JETPACK EXCLUSIVE - BOO COOK
D. #2A - CLAUDIA IANNICIELLO
E. #3C - KELLY YATES

A

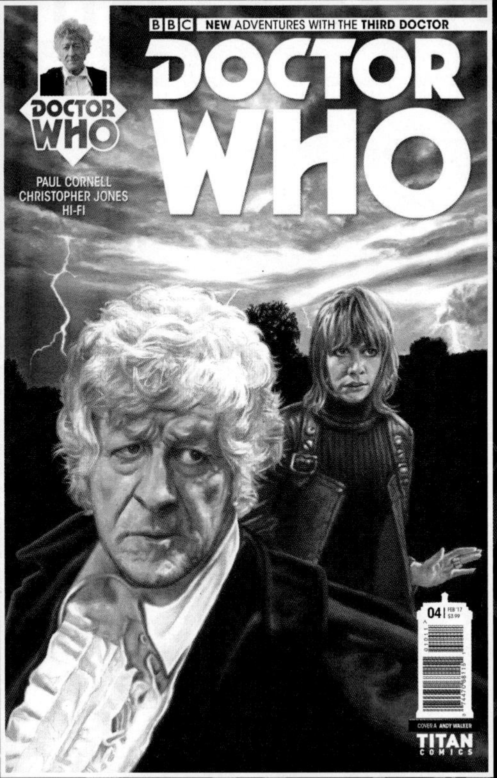
BBC
NEW ADVENTURES WITH THE THIRD DOCTOR
DOCTOR WHO
DOCTOR WHO
PAUL CORNELL
CHRISTOPHER JONES
HI-FI
04 FEB '17 $3.99
COVER A ANDY WALKER
TITAN COMICS

B

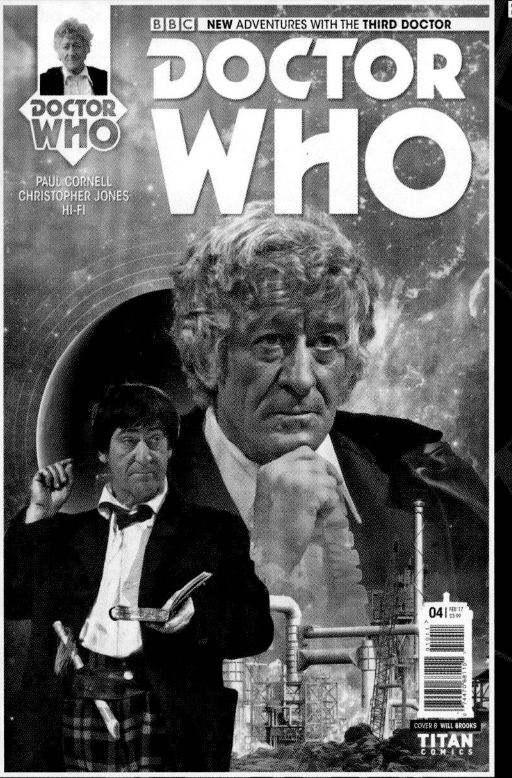
BBC
NEW ADVENTURES WITH THE THIRD DOCTOR
DOCTOR WHO
DOCTOR WHO
PAUL CORNELL
CHRISTOPHER JONES
HI-FI
04 FEB '17 $3.99
COVER B WILL BROOKS
TITAN COMICS

C

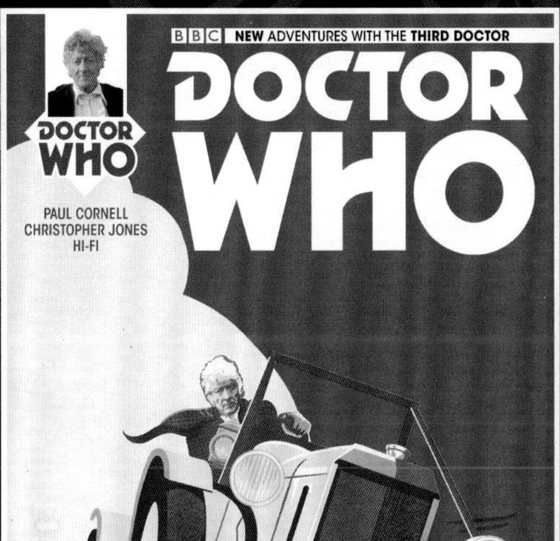
BBC
NEW ADVENTURES WITH THE THIRD DOCTOR
DOCTOR WHO
DOCTOR WHO
PAUL CORNELL
CHRISTOPHER JONES
HI-FI
WHO I
05 MAR '17 $3.99
TITAN COMICS

D

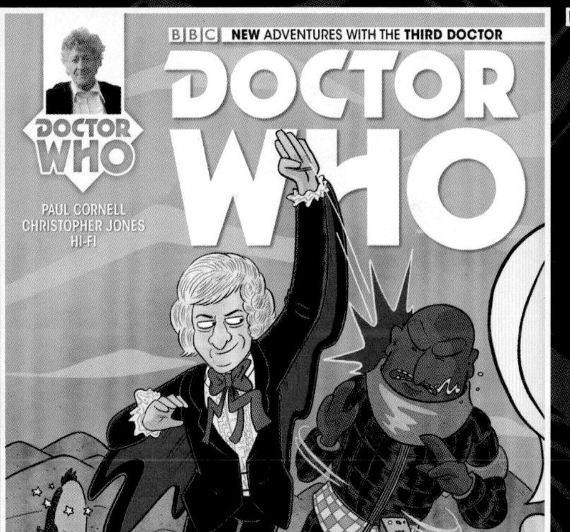
BBC
NEW ADVENTURES WITH THE THIRD DOCTOR
DOCTOR WHO
DOCTOR WHO
PAUL CORNELL
CHRISTOPHER JONES
HI-FI
05 MAR '17 $3.99
TITAN

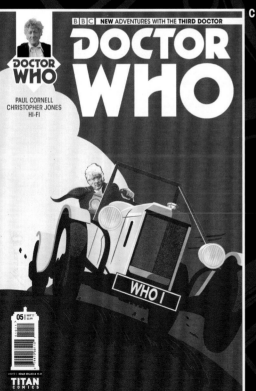

ISSUES #4-5

A. #4A - ANDY WALKER
B. #4B - **PHOTO** – WILL BROOKS

BBC DOCTOR WHO

READER'S GUIDE

With so many amazing *Doctor Who* comics collections, it can be difficult to know where to start! That's where this handy guide comes in.

THE TWELFTH DOCTOR – ONGOING

DOCTOR WHO
TERRORFORMER
DOCTOR WHO
FRACTURES
DOCTOR WHO
HYPERION
DOCTOR WHO
THE SCHOOL OF DEATH
DOCTOR WHO
THE TWIST

VOL. 1: TERRORFORMER

VOL. 2: FRACTURES

VOL. 3: HYPERION

YEAR TWO BEGINS! VOL. 4: SCHOOL OF DEATH

VOL. 5: THE TWIST

THE ELEVENTH DOCTOR – ONGOING

DOCTOR WHO
AFTER LIFE
DOCTOR WHO
SERVE YOU
DOCTOR WHO
CONVERSION
DOCTOR WHO
THE THEN AND THE NOW
DOCTOR WHO
THE ONE

VOL. 1: AFTER LIFE

VOL. 2: SERVE YOU

VOL. 3: CONVERSION

YEAR TWO BEGINS! VOL. 4: THE THEN AND THE NOW

VOL. 5: THE ONE

THE TENTH DOCTOR – ONGOING

DOCTOR WHO
REVOLUTIONS OF TERROR
DOCTOR WHO
THE WEEPING ANGELS OF MONS
DOCTOR WHO
THE FOUNTAINS OF FOREVER
DOCTOR WHO
THE ENDLESS SONG
DOCTOR WHO
ARENA OF FEAR

VOL. 1: REVOLUTIONS OF TERROR

VOL. 2: THE WEEPING ANGELS OF MONS

VOL. 3: THE FOUNTAINS OF FOREVER

YEAR TWO BEGINS! VOL. 4: THE ENDLESS SONG

VOL. 5: ARENA OF FEAR

THE NINTH DOCTOR – ONGOING

DOCTOR WHO
WEAPONS OF PAST DESTRUCTION
DOCTOR WHO
DOCTORMANIA
DOCTOR WHO
OFFICIAL SECRETS
DOCTOR WHO
SIN EATERS

VOL. 1: WEAPONS OF PAST DESTRUCTION

VOL. 2: DOCTORMANIA

VOL. 3: OFFICIAL SECRETS

VOL. 4: SIN EATERS

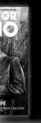

There are currently four ongoing *Doctor Who* series, each following a different Doctor.
Each ongoing series is **entirely self-contained**, so you can follow one, two, or all of your favorite Doctors, as you wish! The ongoings are arranged in season-like **Years**, collected into roughly three books per Year. Feel free to start at Volume 1 of any series, or jump straight to Volume 4, for an equally-accessible new season premiere!
Each book, and every comic, features a **catch-up and character guide** at the beginning, making it easy to jump on board – and each ongoing has a very different flavor, representative of that Doctor's era on screen.

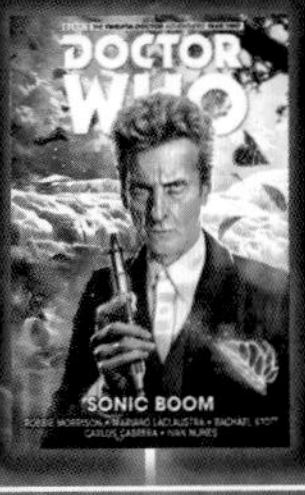
DOCTOR WHO
SONIC BOOM

VOL. 6:
SONIC BOOM

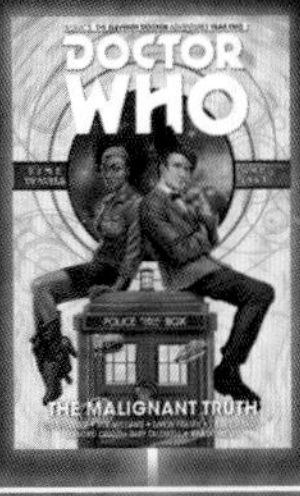
DOCTOR WHO
THE MALIGNANT TRUTH

VOL. 6:
THE MALIGNANT TRUTH

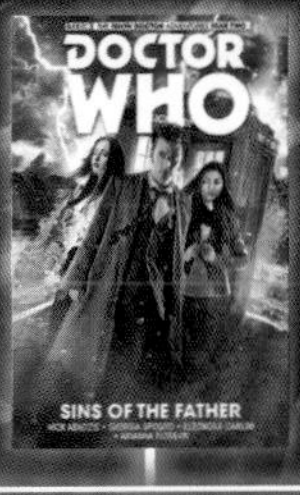
DOCTOR WHO
SINS OF THE FATHER

VOL. 6:
SINS OF THE FATHER

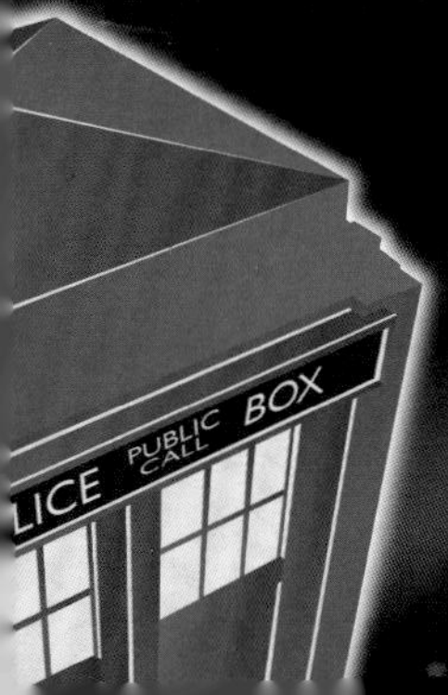
POLICE PUBLIC CALL BOX

THIRD DOCTOR

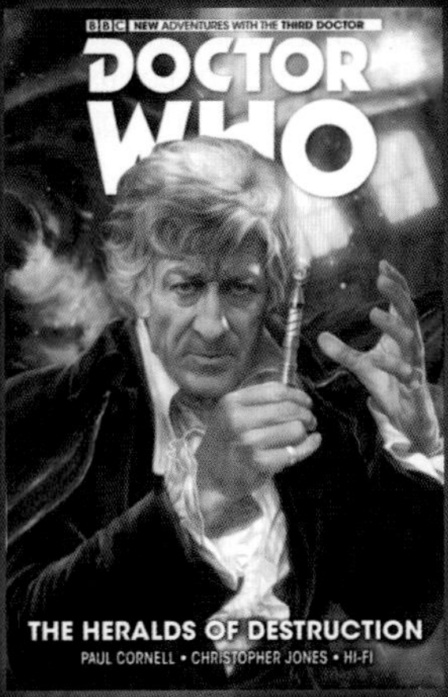
BBC NEW ADVENTURES WITH THE THIRD DOCTOR
DOCTOR WHO
THE HERALDS OF DESTRUCTION
PAUL CORNELL • CHRISTOPHER JONES • HI-FI

As well as the four ongoing series, we have published three major **past Doctor miniseries**, for the Third, Fourth, and Eighth Doctors. These volumes are each a **complete** and **self-contained** story.

There are also two fantastic **crossover event** volumes, starring the Ninth, Tenth, Eleventh, and Twelfth Doctors – the first, *Four Doctors*, sees an impossible team-up, and the second, *Supremacy of the Cybermen*, sees the monstrous cyborgs rule victorious over the universe... unless the Doctors can stop them!

FOURTH DOCTOR

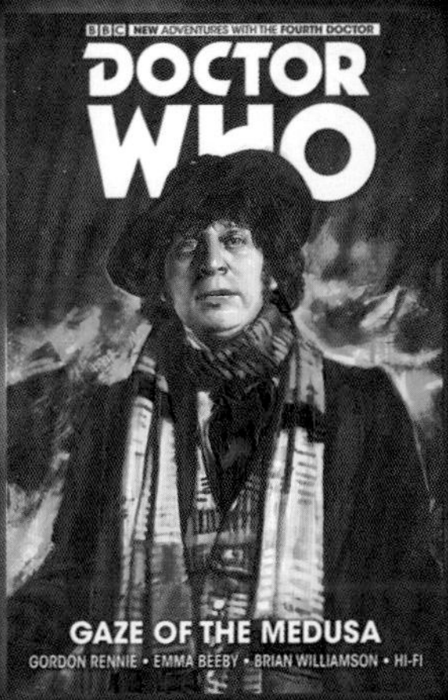
BBC NEW ADVENTURES WITH THE FOURTH DOCTOR
DOCTOR WHO
GAZE OF THE MEDUSA
GORDON RENNIE • EMMA BEEBY • BRIAN WILLIAMSON • HI-FI

FOUR DOCTORS

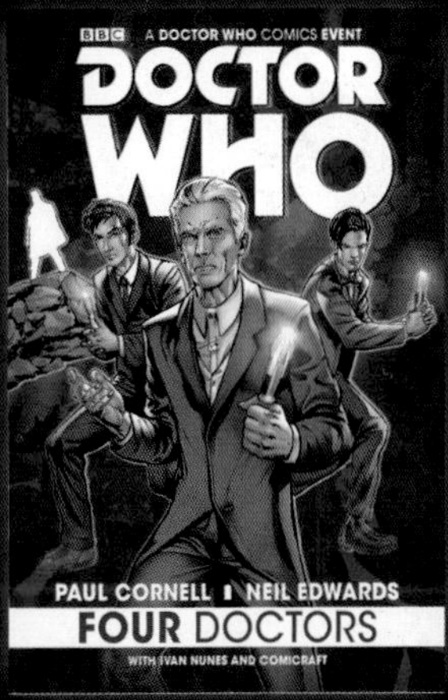
BBC A DOCTOR WHO COMICS EVENT
DOCTOR WHO
PAUL CORNELL | NEIL EDWARDS
FOUR DOCTORS
WITH IVAN NUNES AND COMICRAFT

EIGHTH DOCTOR

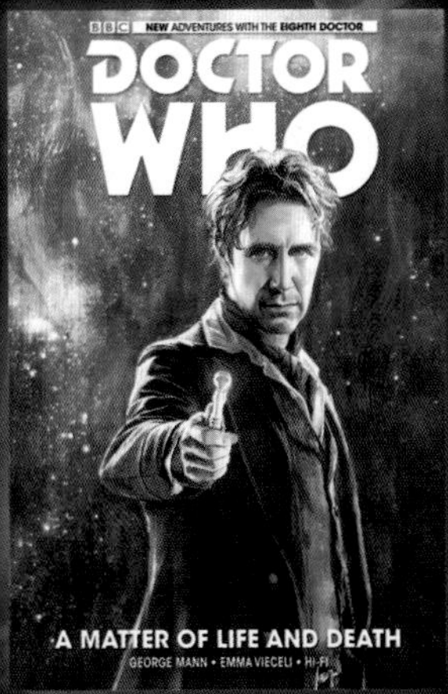
BBC NEW ADVENTURES WITH THE EIGHTH DOCTOR
DOCTOR WHO
A MATTER OF LIFE AND DEATH
GEORGE MANN • EMMA VIECELI • HI-FI

SUPREMACY OF THE CYBERMEN

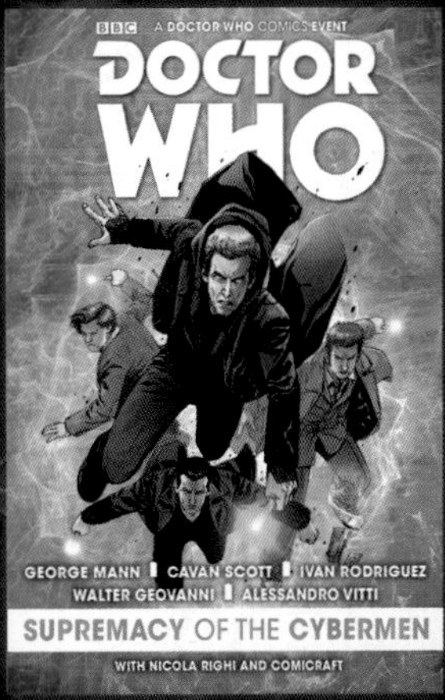
BBC A DOCTOR WHO COMICS EVENT
DOCTOR WHO
GEORGE MANN | CAVAN SCOTT | IVAN RODRIGUEZ
WALTER GEOVANNI | ALESSANDRO VITTI
SUPREMACY OF THE CYBERMEN
WITH NICOLA RIGHI AND COMICRAFT

VISIT **TITAN-COMIC.COM**

BIOGRAPHIES

Paul Cornell is a writer of science fiction and fantasy in prose, comics, and TV, one of only two people to be Hugo Award-nominated for all three media. He has written *Doctor Who* for the BBC (*Father's Day*, *Human Nature*, *Family of Blood*), *Action Comics* for DC, and *Wolverine* and *Captain Britain* for Marvel. He has won the BSFA Award for his short fiction, an Eagle Award for his comics, and shares in a Writer's Guild Award for his television writing. His urban fantasy novel series, from Tor, begins with *The Severed Streets*. He lives in Buckinghamshire with his wife and son.

Christopher Jones has worked for numerous comic book publishers including DC, Marvel, Titan, Slave Labor Graphics, Image, Malibu, Caliber, and more. He was the regular artist on DC Comics *Young Justice*, based on the popular Cartoon Network animated TV series. His other credits include work on DC's popular *Batman '66* title, based on the 1960s *Batman* TV Series with Adam West, written by Jeff Parker, *Batman & Robin*, *Day of Judgment* and the cult series *Young Heroes in Love*; and the sci-fi/fantasy graphic novel *Also Known As*, written by Tony Lee and Andrew Nicholaou, with color by Charlie Kirchoff. He lives in Minnesota.

Hi-Fi Colour Design was founded in 1998 by Brian and Kristy Miller and provides digital color for comic books, toys, video games, and animation, and tutorials on color through masterdigitalcolor.com.

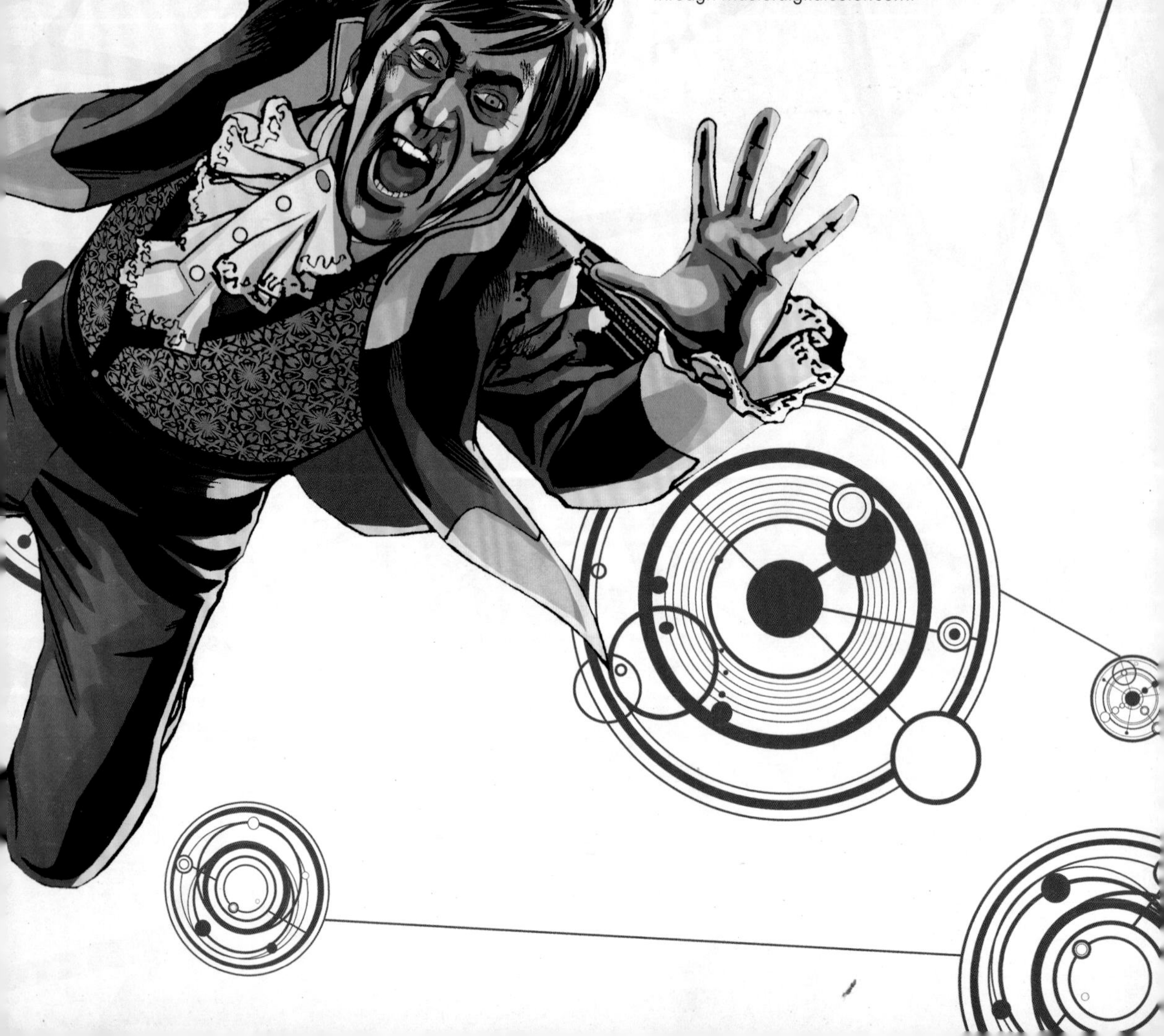